P9-ARU-925

5.95

C. G. JUNG:

PSYCHOLOGICAL

REFLECTIONS

A New Anthology of His Writings
1905-1961

James Washburn
Scarbo 6 e buy 1989

John Dewey Library

C. G. JUNG:

PSYCHOLOGICAL REFLECTIONS

A New Anthology of His Writings

1905-1961

SELECTED AND EDITED BY

JOLANDE JACOBI

IN COLLABORATION WITH R. F. C. HULL

BOLLINGEN SERIES XXXI

PRINCETON UNIVERSITY PRESS

150.1954
J 954
8915c

JY 20 '00

Copyright 1953 by Bollingen Foundation Inc., New York, N.Y.
New edition copyright © 1970 by Princeton University Press
Published by Princeton University Press, Princeton, New Jersey

First Princeton/Bollingen Paperback Printing, 1973

Fourth printing, 1978

THIS IS THE THIRTY-FIRST IN A SERIES
OF BOOKS SPONSORED BY BOLLINGEN FOUNDATION

The present edition is based on the 1953 publication by Bollingen
Foundation but constitutes a complete revision of the original.
In particular, all quotations from Jung's works are taken from
the definitive edition of the Collected Works, with the exception of
a few papers not available there (see Key to Sources, p. xv)..

Originally published in German as *Psychologische Betrachtungen:
Eine Auslese aus den Schriften von C. G. Jung*
by Rascher Verlag, Zurich, 1945.

Revised as *C. G. Jung: Mensch und Seele,*
Walter-Verlag, Olten and Freiburg im B., 1971.

Library of Congress Catalogue Card No. 71-120756
ISBN 0-691-01786-7 (paperback edn.)
ISBN 0-691-09862-X (hardcover edn.)
Manufactured in the United States of America
by Princeton University Press at Princeton, N.J.

Table of Contents

Preface to the First Edition

Western man today, engaged in a mighty outward and inward struggle for a new and universally binding order of life, stands at a point where two worlds meet, amid an almost inconceivable devastation of traditional values. No clear orientation is possible, nothing can yet show us the way ahead, all bearings have been lost in this whirlwind of elemental forces striving for form. Human existence itself, in all its dubiousness and uncertainty, must submit to a thorough re-examination. The colossal material destruction wrought by the war directs our gaze more imperatively than ever to the realm of spiritual and psychic realities. Everywhere people are at last turning in this direction with deepened interest. Perhaps psychology, they think—this youngest and still neglected stepchild of the natural sciences—may help them to understand some of those incomprehensible things man has been relentlessly confronted with ever since the turn of the century, and may guide his pathless present towards a more meaningful future. It is beginning to dawn on him that the root of all good and evil lies in his own psyche and that the world around him is as he himself has shaped it; perhaps he dimly senses, too, that the fate of the world grows out of what happens in the psyches of human beings. But how can there be law and order in the great edifice of the world when he cannot even find his way about in the inner chambers of his own psyche?

Thus, after the countless endeavours that have been made from various sides to say something of substance about man and the universe, it would seem to be high time, indeed urgently necessary, to attempt to extract a more comprehensive meaning from the psychological side as well. Modern depth psychology has the advantage of occupying a position midway between the natural and the humane sciences, bridging the two and at the same time committed to both, and affording besides the possibility, as no other science can, of learning by direct experience the reality of everything the psychic realm has created and brought to birth. That the far-ranging and massive lifework of the Swiss psychologist C. G. Jung, which probes to the remotest depths of the psyche, should be taken as a basis for this purpose hardly needs further justification. Moreover, his seventieth birthday this year provides a fitting and welcome occasion; for such an anniversary represents in the life of a man a milestone from which to look round and look back, a pause in which to meditate and take stock, and this is all the more permissible when, as with Jung, the stream of creative energy is still in full flood. Thus the general purpose of the book became associated quite naturally with a personal one.

This book does not set out to assess Jung and his work in any comprehensive way. Nevertheless, the essence and value of the work as directly presented in the following selection of quotations will reveal at the same time the essence and value of its author. Jung is first and foremost an empiricist and practising psychologist; his personal experiences form the foundation of his theories. Whatever he says is always in closest proximity to the living processes of the psyche; they are the mainspring of the man himself and his whole personality. He is no friend of the aphoristic, the sententious, the speculative, of any borrowings from the crystalline realm of abstract thought. Even though his words may sometimes give the contrary impression, they are always the outcome of some deeply felt experience—the precipitate, so to speak, of his empirical work on the psyche. But because Jung is not only a scientific empiricist but also a true artist, who is fascinated by the shimmering, mysterious, boundless world of primordial images, his words have that unique, compelling power which leaves no one unmoved. Everything experienced in daily life or in the consulting room is permeated with his inner vision and turns into a highly personal and original panoramic view encompassing almost all the facets of human existence. No one who does not stand aside from life will be able to avoid coming to grips with Jung, whether in agreement or disagreement. Himself gripped by the mystery of the psyche, Jung is able to grip others as few men can.

Since the purpose of this selection is not to present Jung's theories in their purely scientific aspect but rather to show, as in a cross-section, some of the most important areas of ordinary human existence in the light of psychology, everything "technical" in the narrower sense of the word has been excluded from the start. It was also necessary to disregard the foundations of his theories, the basic features of his analytical psychology with its numerous definitions and network of concepts, together with all case material and amplificatory evidence drawn from the auxiliary sciences, and much else besides. Anyone who is particularly interested in this side or is seeking precise information in the domain of analytical psychology should turn to the long series of Jung's specialist studies. The present selection is limited to particularly characteristic, self-contained statements of a more general nature, such as are fitted to provide a "look-out" from the psychological observatory. To try to see them as moralizing precepts, recipes for living, or admonitions would be a complete mistake; it would be a crucial misunderstanding of Jung's views and a fundamental contradiction of the aims of his psychology. Because of his daily encounter with the disastrous results of an unthinking acceptance of rules, and of engrafted opinions sometimes hammered in during early childhood, never properly assimilated and mostly misunderstood or totally uncomprehended, his urgent endeavour is to lead people to a responsible attitude and way of living suited to the individual peculiarities of each man; to an inner and outer mode of behaviour when it is not the collective norm "Man" that exercises sole power, but when the inborn, most personal law of each individual allows him sufficient room for self-development.

Many of the selected passages may therefore seem at first sight unusual, controversial, or even weird when contrasted with the views now current in society. But people have so often entirely ignored the psychological aspect of things in their evaluations and judgments that it is no wonder if a great deal appears in a new and peculiar light when seen from this standpoint. Besides, it should not be overlooked that as soon as one enters the realm of the psyche everything has to be judged in accordance with the psyche's own structural polarity. Every pronouncement in psychology has to take this fact into account and every psychological statement bears witness to it. The apparent contradictions that may be found in the following selection are due to this structural antinomy which is inherent in the psyche because of the fundamental tension of opposites between consciousness and the unconscious. The recognition of this polarity forces itself irresistibly on everyone today; on it depends whether man in the future will be able to find his way out of the entanglements of fate back to some kind of order, or whether, in ignorance of his own psychic foundations and those of his fellow men, he will remain at the mercy of the powers of darkness which we have already experienced with horror in this present age, so puffed up with pride at its cultural and technological progress.

The selected passages are not arranged in the chronological order of Jung's writings nor in the sequence in which they appear within each work. The aim of the arrangement is to relate them to various themes, and they were chosen with regard only to their content, in order to do justice to the richness of Jung's psychological outlook as well as to the variety of themes this encompasses. Nevertheless, care was always taken to give each theme the widest possible scope; consequently, a number of ideas not in the mainstream of

Jung's thought had to be sacrificed in order to devote whole sections to more significant areas of life. The result is a kind of all-round survey of some of the more important aspects of human existence, a sharper and more extensive light being thrown on some, a dimmer and more restricted light on others. The quotations in each of the sixteen sections are not juxtaposed arbitrarily and loosely; there is always an inner connection of meaning to form when possible a sequence. Thus each quotation is linked with the preceding or following one by a continuity of thought, the theme being either developed or presented under a different aspect, and any apparent obscurity can usually be cleared up by reading the next quotation or the next but one.

Quotations are taken only from works so far published in German. The use of the many still unpublished manuscripts and of works existing only in multigraphed form for private circulation, such as the seminar reports, would have enlarged this volume to at least twice its present size, and in these cases comparison with the original texts would have been impossible.*

Considering the rich diversity of Jung's work, it would have been hopeless to attempt a complete and exhaustive representation of it, and this was not the aim of the present selection. It had to be limited to a survey of the common human aspect of Jung's psychological insights, singling them out by design and freeing them from the narrow confines of pure science. The book is not meant for the expert but for all who seek knowledge and understanding of the inner forces by which they and the whole world are moved; for all in search of a beacon to guide them through this life, oscillating between light and darkness; and finally

---

* [An exception was made of the so-called "Basel Seminar" (1934), since this is the only one of the multigraphed works to have been published in part, though only in French (see Roland Cahen, *L'Homme à la découverte de son âme*, Geneva, 1944).]

for all men of good will who are ready to acknowledge the reality of the psyche, to restore to it its true dignity, and to work together for a better understanding of a regenerated humanity.

JOLANDE JACOBI

Zurich, Spring 1945

Preface to the Second Edition

A quarter of a century has passed since this book was first published, in German, in 1945; the English edition appeared in 1953. The world has changed its face in many respects, but the truths of man's innermost soul, his sorrows and cares, his joys and longings have remained the same. Perhaps they have multiplied a little, perhaps they have deepened, become more pervasive, and been brought nearer to consciousness, yet their interpretation continues to be an object of research. Psychology, particularly that branch of it named depth psychology, has made great headway; increasingly it is called upon for an understanding of life, of man, and of why he is as he is. Thus the deep-probing writings of C. G. Jung have become more and more topical and sought after. This seemed a justification for presenting a selection of quotations to the public in a new and expanded edition containing statements from the last years of his life.

When the first edition of this selection appeared, the quotations were drawn from Jung's key works, collections of essays, individual papers, and shorter pieces, making use of sixty sources,* though these were far from representing his total output at the time. Jung's productivity during his lifespan was immense: so far as can be estimated at present, it amounted to nearly four hundred original publications in German, English, and French—quite apart from some fifty-five mimeographed volumes of seminar notes for private circulation. In the years following 1946, up to his death in 1961, he produced six books of major importance—among them his magnum opus, *Mysterium Coniunctionis*, and an equal number of important essays, besides numerous minor

---

* In the first edition, a volume of essays was listed as a single source; in the present edition, each essay in such a volume is given a separate number in the List of Sources at the end of the book.

writings. From this late flowering, the present edition has made use of over thirty additional sources, including interviews and posthumously published works. The aim has been to make room for new and significant statements, with particular emphasis on religious and social problems, and for quotations showing the continuous development of Jung's central ideas. Old quotations of limited interest have been deleted, others have been replaced by clearer or more pungent formulations of the same theme. The expanded selection offers a comprehensive view of Jung's non-technical work, as well as a deep insight into the treasure-house of experience and the far-ranging thoughts of this great student of the psyche and of mankind.

For enabling me to bring out this new and expanded edition I am indebted to the Bollingen Foundation, which supported the preparatory work, and to Princeton University Press; also to William McGuire, managing editor of Bollingen Series, who fostered the project and supervised the compilation.

The arrangement of the book remains essentially the same as in the first edition, and the same principles govern the selection or exclusion of new material. In selecting passages from the post-1945 writings, I was assisted by the sure eye and friendly exertions of R.F.C. Hull, translator of Jung's Collected Works. He was also responsible for reorganizing the individual sections of the book and fitting the new quotations among the old. His knowledge of Jung's writings and his constant helpfulness made him an irreplaceable collaborator in the preparation of this new edition. May it meet with as widespread interest and response as did the first; may it lead men to greater thoughtfulness and meditation upon themselves.

JOLANDE JACOBI

Zurich, Autumn 1969

Key to Sources

In this new edition, all but relatively few of the quotations are taken from the Collected Works of C. G. Jung, published by Princeton University Press under the sponsorship of Bollingen Foundation,† and by Routledge & Kegan Paul, Ltd., London. Each quotation is followed by a double reference number. The first part of the number indicates the book or essay given in the numbered List of Sources (pages 369 ff.); the second indicates the paragraph of the relevant volume in the Collected Works. Thus the first quotation on page 3 is numbered 67:187, 67 referring to "Psychological Aspects of the Mother Archetype," and 187 to the paragraph in Volume 9, Part I: *The Archetypes and the Collective Unconscious.*

Exceptions to the foregoing system are quotations from sources which were later included in Volume 18, *The Symbolic Life* (1976); quotations which are omitted from the Collected Works because of Jung's own revisions; and a few quotations from the Collected Works which appear (usually in a preface) on pages without paragraph numbers. In order to reference these quotations, original sources are cited, and the second part of the reference number, with asterisk, indicates the page. Thus the quotation at the bottom of page 3 is numbered 8:64*, 8 referring to Jung's essay "Approaching the Unconscious" in the symposium *Man and His Symbols*, and 64* to the page. For certain short writings, no page citation is given. The sources for quotations

---

† The American edition was published 1953-1960 by Pantheon Books, Inc., New York, for Bollingen Foundation; 1961-1967, by Bollingen Foundation and distributed by Pantheon Books, a division of Random House, Inc.; from 1967, by Princeton University Press, Princeton, New Jersey, under the sponsorship of Bollingen Foundation.

omitted from the Collected Works are 4A, 10A, 11, 39A-H,*
97A, and 100A in the List of Sources. Reference is occasionally made to the Gesammelte Werke, being published
by Rascher Verlag, Zurich, in general according to the plan
of the Collected Works.

* Published in *C. G. Jung Speaking: Interviews and Encounters*,
edited by William McGuire and R.F.C. Hull (1977).

Futile the talk that is bandied about, when many
Join in, each listening only to his own words or hearing
Only himself speaking in the words of his neighbour.
It is the same with books; for everyone will
Read out of the book only himself or will forcibly
Read himself into it, making the strangest amalgam.
Utterly futile, therefore, to endeavour by writing
To change a man's fixed inclination, the bent of his mind.
You will only succeed in confirming him in his opinions
Or, if he has none, drenching him with your own.

GOETHE, "First Epistle"

THE NATURE AND ACTIVITY

OF THE PSYCHE

Recognition of the Psyche

"All that is outside, also is inside," we could say with Goethe. But this "inside," which modern rationalism is so eager to derive from "outside," has an *a priori* structure of its own that antedates all conscious experience. It is quite impossible to conceive how "experience" in the widest sense, or, for that matter, anything psychic, could originate exclusively in the outside world. The psyche is part of the inmost mystery of life, and it has its own peculiar structure and form like every other organism. Whether this psychic structure and its elements, the archetypes, ever "originated" at all is a metaphysical question and therefore unanswerable. The structure is something given, the precondition that is found to be present in every case. And this is the mother, the matrix—the form into which all experience is poured.   67:187

A wrong functioning of the psyche can do much to injure the body, just as conversely a bodily illness can affect the psyche; for psyche and body are not separate entities, but one and the same life.   104A:194

The psyche consists essentially of images. It is a series of images in the truest sense, not an accidental juxtaposition or sequence, but a structure that is throughout full of meaning and purpose; it is a "picturing" of vital activities. And just as the material of the body that is ready for life has need of the psyche in order to be capable of life, so the psyche presupposes the living body in order that its images may live.   91:618

There is no difference in principle between organic and psychic formations. As a plant produces its flowers, so the psyche creates its symbols.   8:64*

Despite the materialistic tendency to understand the psyche as a mere reflection or imprint of physical and chemical processes, there is not a single proof of this hypothesis. Quite the contrary, innumerable facts prove that the psyche translates physical processes into sequences of images which have hardly any recognizable connection with the objective process. The materialistic hypothesis is much too bold and flies in the face of experience with almost metaphysical presumption. The only thing that can be established with certainty, in the present state of our knowledge, is our ignorance of the nature of the psyche. There is thus no ground at all for regarding the psyche as something secondary or as an epiphenomenon; on the contrary, there is every reason to regard it, at least hypothetically, as a factor *sui generis*, and to go on doing so until it has been sufficiently proved that psychic processes can be fabricated in a retort.   16: 117

A psychology that treats the psyche as an epiphenomenon would better call itself brain-psychology, and remain satisfied with the meagre results that such a psycho-physiology can yield. The psyche deserves to be taken as a phenomenon in its own right; there are no grounds at all for regarding it as a mere epiphenomenon, dependent though it may be on the functioning of the brain. One would be as little justified in regarding life as an epiphenomenon of the chemistry of carbon compounds.   54: 10

Restriction to material reality carves an exceedingly large chunk out of reality as a whole, but it nevertheless remains a fragment only, and all round it is a dark penumbra which one would have to call unreal or surreal. This narrow perspective is alien to the Eastern view of the world, which therefore has no need of any philosophical conception of super-reality. Our arbitrarily delimited reality is continually menaced by the "supersensual," the "supernatural," the "superhuman," and a whole lot more besides. Eastern reality includes all this as a matter of course. For us the zone of disturbance already begins with the concept of the "psychic." In our reality the psychic cannot be anything except an effect at third hand, produced originally by physical causes; a "secretion of the brain," or something equally savoury. At the same time, this appendage of the material world is credited with the power to pull itself up by its own bootstraps, so to speak; and not only to fathom the secrets of the physical world, but also, in the form of "mind," to know itself. All this, without its being granted anything more than an indirect reality.   81:743

Since psyche and matter are contained in one and the same world, and moreover are in continuous contact with one another and ultimately rest on irrepresentable, transcendental factors, it is not only possible but fairly probable, even, that psyche and matter are two different aspects of one and the same thing.   53:418

Every science is a function of the psyche, and all knowledge is rooted in it. The psyche is the greatest of all cosmic wonders.   53:357

It does not surprise me that psychology debouches into philosophy, for the thinking that underlies philosophy is after all a psychic activity which, as such, is the proper study of psychology. I always think of psychology as encompassing the whole of the psyche, and that includes philosophy and theology and many other things besides. For underlying all philosophies and all religions are the facts of the human soul, which may ultimately be the arbiters of truth and error.   30:525

Every science is descriptive at the point where it can no longer proceed experimentally, without on that account ceas-

ing to be scientific. But an experimental science makes itself impossible when it delimits its field of work in accordance with theoretical concepts. The psyche does not come
to an end where some physiological assumption or other
stops. In other words, in each individual case that we observe scientifically, we have to consider the manifestations
of the psyche in their totality.   16:113

The psychological investigator is always finding himself
obliged to make extensive use of an indirect method of description in order to present the reality he has observed.
Only in so far as elementary facts are communicated which
are amenable to quantitative measurement can there be any
question of a direct presentation. But how much of the
actual psychology of man can be experienced and observed
as quantitatively measurable facts?   69:672

There is no Archimedean point from which to judge,
since the psyche is indistinguishable from its manifestations.
The psyche is the object of psychology, and—fatally
enough—also its subject. There is no getting away from this
fact.   74:87

Every other science has so to speak an outside; not so
psychology, whose object is the inside subject of all science.
                                                            53:429

Far from being a material world, this is a psychic world,
which allows us to make only indirect and hypothetical in-
ferences about the real nature of matter. The psychic
alone has immediate reality, and this includes all forms of
the psychic, even "unreal" ideas and thoughts which refer to
nothing "external." We may call them "imagination" or
"delusion," but that does not detract in any way from their
effectiveness. Indeed, there is no "real" thought that cannot,

at times, be thrust aside by an "unreal" one, thus proving that the latter is stronger and more effective than the former. Greater than all physical dangers are the tremendous effects of delusional ideas, which are yet denied all reality by our world-blinded consciousness. Our much vaunted reason and our boundlessly overestimated will are sometimes utterly powerless in the face of "unreal" thoughts. The world-powers that rule over all mankind, for good or ill, are unconscious psychic factors, and it is they that bring consciousness into being and hence create the *sine qua non* for the existence of any world at all. We are steeped in a world that was created by our own psyche. 81:747

Since we do not know everything, practically every experience, fact, or object contains something unknown. Hence, if we speak of the totality of an experience, the word "totality" can refer only to the conscious part of it. As we cannot assume that our experience covers the totality of the object, it is clear that its absolute totality must necessarily contain the part that has not been experienced. The same holds true, as I have mentioned, of every experience and also of the psyche, whose absolute totality covers a greater area than consciousness. In other words, the psyche is no exception to the general rule that the universe can be established only so far as our psychic organism permits. 74:68

Not only in the psychic man is there something unknown, but also in the physical. We should be able to include this unknown quantity in a total picture of man, but we cannot. Man himself is partly empirical, partly transcendental ... Also, we do not know whether what we on the empirical plane regard as physical may not, in the Unknown beyond our experience, be identical with what on this side of the border we distinguish from the physical as psychic. 48:765

Although common prejudice still believes that the sole essential basis of our knowledge is given exclusively from outside, and that "nihil est in intellectu quod non antea fuerit in sensu," it nevertheless remains true that the thoroughly respectable atomic theory of Leucippus and Democritus was not based on any observations of atomic fission but on a "mythological" conception of smallest particles, which, as the smallest animated parts, the soul-atoms, are known even to the still palaeolithic inhabitants of central Australia. How much "soul" is projected into the unknown in the world of external appearances is, of course, familiar to anyone acquainted with the natural science and natural philosophy of the ancients. It is, in fact, so much that we are absolutely incapable of saying how the world is constituted in itself—and always shall be, since we are obliged to convert physical events into psychic processes as soon as we want to say anything about knowledge. But who can guarantee that this conversion produces anything like an adequate "objective" picture of the world?   16:116

All that *is* is not encompassed by our knowledge, so that we are not in a position to make any statements about its total nature. Microphysics is feeling its way into the unknown side of matter, just as complex psychology is pushing forward into the unknown side of the psyche. Both lines of investigation have yielded findings which can be conceived only by means of antinomies, and both have developed concepts which display remarkable analogies. If this trend should become more pronounced in the future, the hypothesis of the unity of their subject-matters would gain in probability. Of course there is little or no hope that the unitary Being can ever be conceived, since our powers of thought and language permit only of antinomian statements. But this much we do know beyond all doubt, that empirical reality has a transcendental background.

❖   48:768

It is a remarkable fact, which we come across again and again, that absolutely everybody, even the most unqualified layman, thinks he knows all about psychology as though the psyche were something that enjoyed the most universal understanding. But anybody who really knows the human psyche will agree with me when I say that it is one of the darkest and most mysterious regions of our experience. There is no end to what can be learned in this field.   72:2

The ego, ostensibly the thing we know most about, is in fact a highly complex affair full of unfathomable obscurities. Indeed, one could even define it as a relatively constant personification of the unconscious itself, or as the Schopenhauerian mirror in which the unconscious becomes aware of its own face.   48:129

The psyche creates reality every day. The only expression I can use for this activity is *fantasy*. Fantasy is just as much feeling as thinking, as much intuition as sensation. There is no psychic function that, through fantasy, is not inextricably bound up with the other psychic functions. Sometimes it appears in primordial form, sometimes it is the ultimate and boldest product of all our faculties combined. Fantasy, therefore, seems to me the clearest expression of the specific activity of the psyche. It is, pre-eminently, the creative activity from which the answers to all answerable questions come; it is the mother of all possibilities, where, like all psychological opposites, the inner and outer worlds are joined together in living union.   69:78

What we call fantasy is simply spontaneous psychic activity, and it wells up wherever the inhibitive action of the conscious mind abates or, as in sleep, ceases altogether.
                                                    63:125

Psychic existence is the only category of existence of which we have *immediate* knowledge, since nothing can be known unless it first appears as a psychic image. Only psychic existence is immediately verifiable. To the extent that the world does not assume the form of a psychic image, it is virtually nonexistent.   23:769

Every psychic process is an image and an "imagining," otherwise no consciousness could exist and the occurrence would lack phenomenality. Imagination itself is a psychic process, for which reason it is completely irrelevant whether the enlightenment be called "real" or "imaginary." The person who has the enlightenment, or alleges that he has it, thinks at all events that he is enlightened. What others think about it decides nothing whatever for him in regard to his experience. Even if he were lying, his lie would still be a psychic fact.   98:889

What is "illusion"? By what criterion do we judge something to be an illusion? Does anything exist for the psyche that we are entitled to call illusion? What we are pleased to call illusion may be for the psyche an extremely important life-factor, something as indispensable as oxygen for the body—a psychic actuality of overwhelming significance. Presumably the psyche does not trouble itself about our categories of reality; for it, everything that *works* is real. The investigator of the psyche must not confuse it with his consciousness, else he veils from his sight the object of his investigation. On the contrary, to recognize it at all, he must learn to see how different it is from consciousness. Nothing is more probable than that what we call illusion is very real for the psyche—for which reason we cannot take psychic reality to be commensurable with conscious reality.   2:111

"Physical" is not the only criterion of truth: there are also *psychic* truths which can neither be explained nor proved nor contested in any physical way. If, for instance, a general belief existed that the river Rhine had at one time flowed backwards from its mouth to its source, then this belief would in itself be a fact even though such an assertion, physically understood, would be deemed utterly incredible. Beliefs of this kind are psychic facts which cannot be contested and need no proof.   7:553

All psychological facts which cannot be verified with the help of scientific apparatus and exact measurement are assertions and opinions, and, as such, are psychic realities.

71:839

The protean life of the psyche is a greater, if more inconvenient, truth than the rigid certainty of the one-eyed point of view. It certainly does not make the problems of psychology any easier. But it does free us from the incubus of "nothing but,"* which is the insistent leitmotiv of all one-sidedness.   4:156

Natural man is not a "self"—he is the mass and a particle in the mass, collective to such a degree that he is not even sure of his own ego. That is why since time immemorial he has needed the transformation mysteries to turn him into something, and to rescue him from the animal collective psyche, which is nothing but an assortment, a "variety performance."   72:104

* The term "nothing but" (*nichts als*) occurs frequently in Jung and is borrowed from William James, *Pragmatism* (1907), p. 16: "What is higher is explained by what is lower and treated forever as a case of 'nothing but'—nothing but something else of a quite inferior sort."

So long as one knows nothing of psychic actuality, it will be projected, if it appears at all. Thus the first knowledge of psychic law and order was found in the stars, and was later extended by projections into unknown matter. These two realms of experience branched off into sciences: astrology became astronomy, and alchemy chemistry. On the other hand, the peculiar connection between character and the astronomical determination of time has only very recently begun to turn into something approaching an empirical science. The really important psychic facts can neither be measured, weighed, nor seen in a test tube or under a microscope. They are therefore supposedly indeterminable, in other words they must be left to people who have an inner sense for them, just as colours must be shown to the seeing and not to the blind.   92:285

So far mythologists have always helped themselves out with solar, lunar, meteorological, vegetal, and other ideas of the kind. The fact that myths are first and foremost psychic phenomena that reveal the nature of the soul is something they have absolutely refused to see until now. Primitive man is not much interested in objective explanations of the obvious, but he has an imperative need—or rather, his unconscious psyche has an irresistible urge—to assimilate all outer sense experiences to inner, psychic events. It is not enough for the primitive to see the sun rise and set; this external observation must at the same time be a psychic happening: the sun in its course must represent the fate of a god or hero who, in the last analysis, dwells nowhere except in the soul of man. All the mythologized processes of nature, such as summer and winter, the phases of the moon, the rainy seasons, and so forth, are in no sense allegories of these objective occurrences; rather they are symbolic expressions of the inner, unconscious drama of the psyche which becomes accessible to man's consciousness by way of projection—that is, mirrored in the events of nature.

10:7

It is not storms, not thunder and lightning, not rain and cloud that remain as images in the psyche, but the fantasies caused by the affects they arouse. I once experienced a violent earthquake, and my first, immediate feeling was that I no longer stood on the solid and familiar earth, but on the skin of a gigantic animal that was heaving under my feet. It was this image that impressed itself on me, not the physical fact. Man's curses against devastating thunderstorms, his terror of the unchained elements—these affects anthropomorphize the passion of nature, and the purely physical element becomes an angry god.   96:331

It remained for modern science to despiritualize nature through its so-called objective knowledge of matter. All anthropomorphic projections were withdrawn from the object one after another, with a twofold result: firstly man's mystical identity with nature was curtailed as never before, and secondly the projections falling back into the human soul caused such a terrific activation of the unconscious that in modern times man was compelled to postulate the existence of an unconscious psyche. Instead of the lost Olympian gods, there was disclosed the inner wealth of the soul which lies in every man's heart.   103:375

The old alchemists were nearer to the central truth of the psyche than Faust when they strove to deliver the fiery spirit from the chemical elements, and treated the mystery as though it lay in the dark and silent womb of nature. It was still outside them. The upward thrust of evolving consciousness was bound sooner or later to put an end to the projection, and to restore to the psyche what had been psychic from the beginning. Yet, ever since the Age of Enlightenment and in the era of scientific rationalism, what indeed was the psyche: It had become synonymous with consciousness. The psyche was "what I know."

There was no psyche outside the ego. Inevitably, then, the ego identified with the contents accruing from the withdrawal of projections. Gone were the days when the psyche was still for the most part "outside the body" and imagined "those greater things" which the body could not grasp. The contents that were formerly projected were now bound to appear as personal possessions, as chimerical phantasms of the ego-consciousness. The fire chilled to air, and the air became the great wind of Zarathustra and caused an inflation of consciousness which, it seems, can be damped down only by the most terrible catastrophe to civilization, another deluge let loose by the gods upon inhospitable humanity.

72:562

It is my conviction that the investigation of the psyche is the science of the future. Psychology is the youngest of the sciences and is only at the beginning of its development. It is, however, the science we need most. Indeed, it is becoming ever more obvious that it is not famine, not earthquakes, not microbes, not cancer but man himself who is man's greatest danger to man, for the simple reason that there is no adequate protection against psychic epidemics, which are infinitely more devastating than the worst of natural catastrophes. The supreme danger which threatens individuals as well as whole nations is a *psychic danger*.

15:339*f**

The world today hangs by a thin thread, and that thread is the psyche of man.   39E:17*

It is not only primitive man whose psychology is archaic. It is the psychology also of modern, civilized man, and not merely of individual "throw-backs" in modern society.

On the contrary, every civilized human being, however high his conscious development, is still an archaic man at the deeper levels of his psyche. Just as the human body connects us with the mammals and displays numerous vestiges of earlier evolutionary stages going back even to the reptilian age, so the human psyche is a product of evolution which, when followed back to its origins, shows countless archaic traits.

9:105

Just as a man has a body which is no different in principle from that of an animal, so also his psychology has a whole series of lower storeys in which the spectres from humanity's past epochs still dwell, then the animal souls from the age of Pithecanthropus and the hominids, then the "psyche" of the cold-blooded saurians, and, deepest down of all, the transcendental mystery and paradox of the sympathetic and parasympathetic psychoid systems.

48:279

The psychology of the individual can never be exhaustively explained from himself alone: a clear recognition is needed of the way it is also conditioned by historical and environmental circumstances. His individual psychology is not merely a physiological, biological, or personal problem; it is also a contemporary problem.

69:717

Again, no psychological fact can ever be exhaustively explained in terms of causality alone; as a living phenomenon, it is always indissolubly bound up with the continuity of the vital process, so that it is not only something evolved but also continually evolving and creative. Anything psychic is Janus-faced: it looks both backwards and forwards. Because it is evolving, it is also preparing the future. Were this not so, intentions, aims, plans, calculations, predictions, and premonitions would be psychological impossibilities.

69:717f

Being that has soul is living being. Soul is the living thing in man, that which lives of itself and causes life. Therefore God breathed into Adam a living breath, that he might live. With her cunning play of illusions the soul lures into life the inertness of matter that does not want to live. She makes us believe incredible things, that life may be lived. She is full of snares and traps, in order that man should fall, should reach the earth, entangle himself there, and stay caught, so that life should be lived; as Eve in the garden of Eden could not rest content until she had convinced Adam of the goodness of the forbidden apple. Were it not for the leaping and twinkling of the soul, man would rot away in his greatest passion, idleness.   10:56

The nature of the psyche reaches into obscurities far beyond the scope of our understanding. It contains as many riddles as the universe with its galactic systems, before whose majestic configurations only a mind lacking in imagination can fail to admit its own insufficiency. This extreme uncertainty of human comprehension makes the intellectualistic hubbub not only ridiculous, but also deplorably dull.   90:815

It is true that our religion speaks of an immortal soul; but it has very few kind words to say for the human psyche as such, which would go straight to eternal damnation were it not for a special act of Divine Grace.   74:28

The immortality of the soul insisted upon by dogma exalts it above the transitoriness of mortal man and causes it to partake of some supernatural quality. It thus infinitely surpasses the perishable, conscious individual in significance, so that logically the Christian is forbidden to regard the soul as a "nothing but." As the eye to the sun, so the soul corresponds to God. Since our conscious mind does not comprehend the soul it is ridiculous to speak of the things of the soul in a patronizing or depreciatory manner. Even the believing Christian does not know God's hidden ways and must leave him to decide whether he will work on man from the outside or from within, through the soul.   72:11

To treat a metaphysical statement as a psychic process is not to say that it is "merely psychic," as my critics assert—in the fond belief that the word "psychic" postulates something known. It does not seem to have occurred to these people that when we say "psychic" we are alluding to the densest darkness it is possible to imagine.   103:448

Metaphysical assertions are statements of the psyche, and are therefore psychological. To the Western mind, which compensates its well-known feelings of resentment by a slavish regard for "rational" explanations, this obvious truth seems all too obvious, or else it is seen as an inadmissible negation of metaphysical "truth." Whenever the Westerner hears the word "psychological," it always sounds to him like "*only* psychological." For him the "soul" is something pitifully small, unworthy, personal, subjective, and a lot more besides. He therefore prefers to use the word "mind" instead, though he likes to pretend at the same time that a statement which may in fact be very subjective indeed is made by the "mind," naturally by the "Universal Mind," or even—at a pinch—by the "Absolute" itself. This rather ridiculous presumption is probably a compensation for the regrettable smallness of the soul. It almost seems as if Anatole France had uttered a truth which were valid for the whole Western world when, in his *Penguin Island,* Cathérine d'Alexandrie offers this advice to God: "Donnez-leur une âme, mais une petite!"   22:835

We do not devalue statements that originally were intended to be metaphysical when we demonstrate their psychic nature; on the contrary, we confirm their factual character. But, by treating them as psychic phenomena, we remove them from the inaccessible realm of metaphysics, about which nothing verifiable can be said, and this disposes of the impossible question as to whether they are "true" or not. We take our stand simply and solely on the facts, recognizing that the archetypal structure of the unconscious will produce, over and over again and irrespective of tradition, those figures which reappear in the history of all epochs and all peoples, and will endow them with the same significance and numinosity that have been theirs from the beginning.   48:558

It would be blasphemy to assert that God can manifest himself everywhere save only in the human soul. Indeed the very intimacy of the relationship between God and the soul precludes from the start any devaluation of the latter. It would be going perhaps too far to speak of an affinity; but at all events the soul must contain in itself the faculty of relation to God, i.e., a correspondence, otherwise a connection could never come about.   72:11

I did not attribute a religious function to the soul, I merely produced the facts which prove that the soul is *naturaliter religiosa*, i.e., possesses a religious function. I did not invent or insinuate this function, it produces itself of its own accord without being prompted thereto by any opinions or suggestions of mine. With a truly tragic delusion theologians fail to see that it is not a matter of proving the existence of the light, but of blind people who do not know that their eyes could see. It is high time we realized that it is pointless to praise the light and preach it if nobody can see it. It is much more needful to teach people the art of seeing. For it is obvious that far too many people are incapable of establishing a connection between the sacred figures and their own psyche: they cannot see to what extent the equivalent images are lying dormant in their own unconscious. In order to facilitate this inner vision we must first clear the way for the faculty of seeing. How this is to be done without psychology, that is, without making contact with the psyche, is, frankly, beyond my comprehension.

72:14

The doctrine that all evil thoughts come from the heart and that the human soul is a sink of iniquity must lie deep in the marrow of their bones. Were it so, then God had made a sorry job of creation, and it were high time for us to go over to Marcion the Gnostic and depose the incompetent demiurge. Ethically, of course, it is infinitely more convenient to leave God the sole responsibility for such a Home for Idiot Children, where no one is capable of putting a spoon into his own mouth. But it is worth man's while to take pains with himself, and he has something in his own soul that can grow. It is rewarding to watch patiently the silent happenings in the soul, and the most and the best happens when it is not regulated from outside and from above.

72:126

People will do anything, no matter how absurd, in order to avoid facing their own souls. They will practise Indian yoga and all its exercises, observe a strict regimen of diet, learn the literature of the whole world—all because they cannot get on with themselves and have not the slightest faith that anything useful could ever come out of their own souls. Thus the soul has gradually been turned into a Nazareth from which nothing good can come. Therefore let us fetch it from the four corners of the earth—the more far-fetched and bizarre it is the better!

72:126

Whoever speaks of the reality of the soul or psyche is accused of "psychologism." Psychology is spoken of as if it were "only" psychology and nothing else. The notion that there can be psychic factors which correspond to the divine figures is regarded as a devaluation of the latter. It smacks of blasphemy to think that a religious experience is a psychic process; for, so it is argued, a religious experience "is not *only* psychological." Anything psychic is *only* Nature and therefore, people think, nothing religious can come out of it. At the same time such critics never hesitate to derive all religions—with the exception of their own—from the nature of the psyche.   72:9

I do not underestimate the psyche in any respect whatsoever, nor do I imagine for a moment that psychic happenings vanish into thin air by being explained. Psychologism represents a still primitive mode of magical thinking, with the help of which one hopes to conjure the reality of the soul out of existence, after the manner of the "Proktophantasmist" in *Faust*:

> Are you still there? Nay, it's a thing unheard.
> Vanish at once! We've said the enlightening word.
>
> 7:750

Were it not a fact of experience that supreme values reside in the soul (quite apart from the *antimimon pneuma* who is also there), psychology would not interest me in the least, for the soul would then be nothing but a miserable vapour. I know, however, from hundredfold experience that it is nothing of the sort, but on the contrary contains the equivalents of everything that has been formulated in dogma and a good deal more, which is just what enables it to be an eye destined to behold the light. This requires limitless range and unfathomable depth of vision. I have been accused of "deifying the soul." Not I but God himself has deified it!   72:14

To have soul is the whole venture of life, for soul is a life-giving daemon who plays his elfin game above and below human existence, for which reason—in the realm of dogma—he is threatened and propitiated with superhuman punishments and blessings that go far beyond the possible deserts of human beings. Heaven and hell are the fates meted out to the soul and not to civilized man, who in his nakedness and timidity would have no idea of what to do with himself in a heavenly Jerusalem.   10:56

Consciousness and the Unconscious

Our consciousness does not create itself—it wells up from unknown depths. In childhood it awakens gradually, and all through life it wakes each morning out of the depths of sleep from an unconscious condition.   75:935

Just as conscious contents can vanish into the unconscious, other contents can also arise from it. Besides a majority of mere recollections, really new thoughts and creative ideas can appear which have never been conscious before. They grow up from the dark depths like a lotus.   8:37*

The world comes into being when man discovers it. But he only discovers it when he sacrifices his containment in the primal mother, the original state of unconsciousness.

100:652

If one reflects upon what consciousness really is, one is deeply impressed by the extremely wonderful fact that an event which occurs outside in the cosmos produces simultaneously an inner image. Thus it also occurs within; in other words, it becomes conscious.   11:1*

How else could it have occurred to man to divide the cosmos, on the analogy of day and night, summer and winter, into a bright day-world and a dark night-world peopled with fabulous monsters, unless he had the prototype of such a division in himself, in the polarity between the conscious and the invisible and unknowable unconscious? Primitive man's perception of objects is conditioned only partly by the objective behaviour of the things themselves, whereas a much greater part is often played by intrapsychic facts which are not related to the external objects except by way of projection. This is due to the simple fact that the primitive has not yet experienced that ascetic discipline of mind known to us as the critique of knowledge. To him the world is a more or less fluid phenomenon within the stream of his own fantasy, where subject and object are undifferentiated and in a state of mutual interpenetration.

67:187

The primitive cannot assert that he thinks; it is rather that "something thinks in him." The spontaneity of the act of thinking does not lie, causally, in his conscious mind, but in his unconscious. Moreover, he is incapable of any conscious effort of will; he must put himself beforehand into the "mood of willing," or let himself be put—hence his *rites d'entrée et de sortie.* His consciousness is menaced by an almighty unconscious: hence his fear of magical influences which may cross his path at any moment; and for this reason, too, he is surrounded by unknown forces and must adjust himself to them as best he can. Owing to the chronic twilight state of his consciousness, it is often next to impossible to find out whether he merely dreamed something or whether he really experienced it. The spontaneous manifestation of the unconscious and its archetypes intrudes everywhere into his conscious mind, and the mythical world of his ancestors—for instance, the *aljira* or *bugari* of the Australian aborigines—is a reality equal if not superior to the material world. It is not the world as we know it that speaks out of his unconscious, but the unknown world of the psyche, of which we know that it mirrors out empirical world only in part, and that, for the other part, it moulds this empirical world in accordance with its own psychic assumptions. The archetype does not proceed from physical facts but describes how the psyche experiences the physical fact, and in so doing the psyche often behaves so autocratically that it denies tangible reality or makes statements that fly in the face of it.   76:260

The world is as it ever has been, but our consciousness undergoes peculiar changes. First, in remote times (which can still be observed among primitives living today), the main body of psychic life was apparently in human and in nonhuman objects: it was projected, as we should say now. Consciousness can hardly exist in a state of complete projection. At most it would be a heap of emotions. Through the withdrawal of projections, conscious knowledge slowly developed. Science, curiously enough, began with the discovery of astronomical laws, and hence with the withdrawal, so to speak, of the most distant projections. This was the first stage in the despiritualization of the world. One step followed another: already in antiquity the gods were withdrawn from mountains and rivers, from trees and animals. Modern science has subtilized its projections to an almost unrecognizable degree, but our ordinary life still swarms with them. You can find them spread out in the newspapers, in books, rumours, and ordinary social gossip. All gaps in our actual knowledge are still filled out with projections. We are still so sure we know what other people think or what their true character is.   74:140

Whatever name we may put to the psychic background, the fact remains that our consciousness is influenced by it in the highest degree, and all the more so the less we are conscious of it. The layman can hardly conceive how much his inclinations, moods, and decisions are influenced by the dark forces of his psyche, and how dangerous or helpful they may be in shaping his destiny. Our cerebral consciousness is like an actor who has forgotten that he is playing a role. But when the play comes to an end, he must remember his own subjective reality, for he can no longer continue to live as Julius Caesar or as Othello, but only as himself, from whom he has become estranged by a momentary sleight of consciousness. He must know once again that he was merely a figure on the stage who was playing a piece by Shakespeare, and that there was a producer as well as a director in the background who, as always, will have something very important to say about his acting.   45:332

Since the stars have fallen from heaven and our highest symbols have paled, a secret life holds sway in the unconscious. That is why we have a psychology today, and why we speak of the unconscious. All this would be quite superfluous in an age or culture that possessed symbols. Symbols are spirit from above, and under those conditions the spirit is above too. Therefore it would be a foolish and senseless undertaking for such people to wish to experience or investigate an unconscious that contains nothing but the silent, undisturbed sway of nature. Our unconscious, on the other hand, hides living water, spirit that has become nature, and that is why it is disturbed. Heaven has become for us the cosmic space of the physicists, and the divine empyrean a fair memory of things that once were. But "the heart glows," and a secret unrest gnaws at the roots of our being.   10:50

Empirical psychology loved, until recently, to explain the "unconscious" as mere absence of consciousness—the term itself indicates as much—just as shadow is an absence of light. Today accurate observation of unconscious processes has recognized, with all other ages before us, that the unconscious possesses a creative autonomy such as a mere shadow could never be endowed with.   74:141

Rationalism and superstition are complementary. It is a psychological rule that the brighter the light, the blacker the shadow; in other words, the more rationalistic we are in our conscious minds, the more alive becomes the spectral world of the unconscious.   47:10*

Anyone who penetrates into the unconscious with purely biological assumptions will become stuck in the instinctual sphere and be unable to advance beyond it, for he will be pulled back again and again into physical existence.

22: 843

Just as, in its lower reaches, the psyche loses itself in the organic-material substrate, so in its upper reaches it resolves itself into a "spiritual" form about which we know as little as we do about the functional basis of instinct.

53: 380

Psychic processes therefore behave like a scale along which consciousness "slides." At one moment it finds itself in the vicinity of instinct, and falls under its influence; at another, it slides along to the other end where spirit predominates and even assimilates the instinctual processes most opposed to it.

53: 408

Nowhere and never has man controlled matter without closely observing its behaviour and paying heed to its laws, and only to the extent that he did so could he control it. The same is true of that objective spirit which today we call the unconscious: it is refractory like matter, mysterious and elusive, and obeys laws which are so non-human or suprahuman that they seem to us like a *crimen laesae majestatis humanae*. If a man puts his hand to the opus, he repeats, as the alchemists say, God's work of creation. The struggle with the unformed, with the chaos of Tiamat, is in truth a primordial experience.

92: 286

We know that the mask of the unconscious is not rigid —it reflects the face we turn towards it. Hostility lends it a threatening aspect, friendliness softens its features.

72: 29

The unconscious is not a demoniacal monster, but a natural entity which, as far as moral sense, aesthetic taste, and intellectual judgment go, is completely neutral. It only becomes dangerous when our conscious attitude to it is hopelessly wrong. To the degree that we repress it, its danger increases.   61:329

The unconscious mind of man sees correctly even when conscious reason is blind and impotent.   7:608

In the unconscious is everything that has been rejected by consciousness, and the more Christian one's consciousness is, the more heathenishly does the unconscious behave, if in the rejected heathenism there are values which are important for life.   7:713

The unconscious is the unwritten history of mankind from time unrecorded.   65:280

The conscious mind allows itself to be trained like a parrot, but the unconscious does not—which is why St. Augustine thanked God for not making him responsible for his dreams. The unconscious is an antonomous psychic entity; any efforts to drill it are only apparently successful, and moreover harmful to consciousness. It is and remains beyond the reach of subjective arbitrary control, a realm where nature and her secrets can be neither improved upon nor perverted, where we can listen but may not meddle.

72:51

Any attempt to determine the nature of the unconscious state runs up against the same difficulties as atomic physics: the very act of observation alters the object observed. Consequently, there is at present no way of objectively determining the real nature of the unconscious.   48:88

Nobody can say where man ends. That is the beauty of it. The unconscious of man can reach God knows where. There we are going to make discoveries.   39E:62*

It suits our hypertrophied and hybristic modern consciousness not to be mindful of the dangerous autonomy of the unconscious and to treat it negatively as an absence of consciousness. The hypothesis of invisible gods or daemons would be, psychologically, a far more appropriate formulation, even though it would be an anthropomorphic projection. But since the development of consciousness requires the withdrawal of all the projections we can lay our hands on, it is not possible to maintain any non-psychological doctrine about the gods. If the historical process of world despiritualization continues as hitherto, then everything of a divine or daemonic character outside us must return to the psyche, to the inside of the unknown man, whence it apparently originated.   74:141

Since the gods are without doubt personifications of psychic forces, to assert their metaphysical existence is as much an intellectual presumption as the opinion that they could ever be invented. Not that "psychic forces" have anything to do with the conscious mind, fond as we are of playing with the idea that consciousness and psyche are identical. This is only another piece of intellectual presumption. "Psychic forces" have far more to do with the realm of the unconscious. Our mania for rational explanations obviously has its roots in our fear of metaphysics, for the two were always hostile brothers. Hence anything unexpected that approaches us from that dark realm is regarded either as coming from outside and therefore as real, or else as an hallucination and therefore not true. The idea that anything could be real or true which does *not* come from outside has hardly begun to dawn on contemporary man.   115:387

In the same way that the State has caught the individual, the individual imagines that he has caught the psyche and holds her in the hollow of his hand. He is even making a science of her in the absurd supposition that the intellect, which is but a part and a function of the psyche, is sufficient to comprehend the much greater whole. In reality the psyche is the mother and the maker, the subject and even the possibility of consciousness itself. It reaches so far beyond the boundaries of consciousness that the latter could easily be compared to an island in the ocean. Whereas the island is small and narrow, the ocean is immensely wide and deep and contains a life infinitely surpassing, in kind and degree, anything known on the island—so that if it is a question of space, it does not matter whether the gods are "inside" or "outside." It might be objected that there is no proof that consciousness is nothing more than an island in the ocean. Certainly it is impossible to prove this, since the known range of consciousness is confronted with the unknown extension of the unconscious, of which we only know that it exists and by the very fact of its existence exerts a limiting effect on consciousness and its freedom.   74:141

Man's capacity for consciousness alone makes him man.

53:412

✧

The reason why consciousness exists, and why there is an urge to widen and deepen it, is very simple: without consciousness things go less well. This is obviously the reason why Mother Nature deigned to produce consciousness, that most remarkable of all nature's curiosities. Even the well-nigh unconscious primitive can adapt and assert himself, but only in his primitive world, and that is why under other conditions he falls victim to countless dangers which we on a higher level of consciousness can avoid without effort. True, a higher consciousness is exposed to dangers undreamt of by the primitive, but the fact remains that the conscious man has conquered the earth and not the unconscious one. Whether in the last analysis, and from a superhuman point of view, this is an advantage or a calamity we are not in a position to decide.   5:695

Genesis represents the act of becoming conscious as a taboo infringement, as though knowledge meant that a sacrosanct barrier had been impiously overstepped. I think that Genesis is right in so far as every step towards greater consciousness is a kind of Promethean guilt: through knowledge, the gods are as it were robbed of their fire, that is, something that was the property of the unconscious powers is torn out of its natural context and subordinated to the whims of the conscious mind. The man who has usurped the new knowledge suffers, however, a transformation or enlargement of consciousness, which no longer resembles that of his fellow men. He has raised himself above the human level of his age ("ye shall become like unto God"), but in so doing has alienated himself from humanity. The pain of this loneliness is the vengeance of the gods, for never again can he return to mankind. He is, as the myth says, chained to the lonely cliffs of the Caucasus, forsaken of God and man.   104B:243n

And yet the attainment of consciousness was the most precious fruit of the tree of knowledge, the magical weapon which gave man victory over the earth, and which we hope will give him a still greater victory over himself. 45:289

The man who has attained consciousness of the present is solitary. The "modern" man has at all times been so, for every step towards fuller consciousness removes him further from his original, purely animal *participation mystique* with the herd, from submersion in a common unconsciousness. Every step forward means tearing oneself loose from

the maternal womb of unconsciousness in which the mass
of men dwells.   93:150

Before the bar of nature and fate, unconsciousness is
never accepted as an excuse; on the contrary there are very
severe penalties for it.   7:745

Every advance in culture is, psychologically, an extension
of consciousness, a coming to consciousness that can take
place only through discrimination. Therefore an advance
always begins with individuation, that is to say with the
individual, conscious of his isolation, cutting a new path
through hitherto untrodden territory. To do this he must
first return to the fundamental facts of his own being, irrespective of all authority and tradition, and allow himself
to become conscious of his distinctiveness. If he succeeds
in giving collective validity to his widened consciousness,
he creates a tension of opposites that provides the stimula-
tion which culture needs for its further progress.   54:111

It is just man's turning away from instinct—his opposing himself to instinct—that creates consciousness. Instinct
is nature and seeks to perpetuate nature, whereas consciousness can only seek culture or its denial. Even when we turn
back to nature, inspired by a Rousseauesque longing, we
"cultivate" nature. As long as we are still submerged in
nature we are unconscious, and we live in the security of
instinct which knows no problems. Everything in us that
still belongs to nature shrinks away from a problem, for
its name is doubt, and wherever doubt holds sway there is
uncertainty and the possibility of divergent ways. And
where several ways seem possible, there we have turned
away from the certain guidance of instinct and are handed
over to fear. For consciousness is now called upon to do
that which nature has always done for her children—
namely, to give a certain, unquestionable, and unequivocal

decision. And here we are beset by an all-too-human fear that consciousness—our Promethean conquest—may in the end not be able to serve us as well as nature.   94:750

When we must deal with problems, we instinctively resist trying the way that leads through obscurity and darkness. We wish to hear only of unequivocal results, and completely forget that these results can only be brought about when we have ventured into and emerged again from the darkness. But to penetrate the darkness we must summon all the powers of enlightenment that consciousness can offer.   94:752

If psychic life consisted only of self-evident matters of fact—which on a primitive level is still the case—we could content ourselves with a sturdy empiricism. The psychic life of civilized man, however, is full of problems; we cannot even think of it except in terms of problems. Our psychic processes are made up to a large extent of reflections, doubts, experiments, all of which are almost completely foreign to the unconscious, instinctive mind of primitive man. It is the growth of consciousness which we must thank for the existence of problems; they are the Danaän gift of civilization.   94:750

"Reflection" should be understood not simply as an act of thought, but rather as an attitude. It is a privilege born of human freedom in contradistinction to the compulsion of natural law. As the word itself testifies ("reflection" means literally "bending back"), reflection is a spiritual act that runs counter to the natural process; an act whereby we stop, call something to mind, form a picture, and take up a relation to and come to terms with what we have seen. It should, therefore, be understood as an act of becoming conscious.   65:235n

There is no other way open to us; we are forced to resort to conscious decisions and solutions where formerly we trusted ourselves to natural happenings. Every problem, therefore, brings the possibility of a widening of consciousness, but also the necessity of saying goodbye to childlike unconsciousness and trust in nature. This necessity is a psychic fact of such importance that it constitutes one of the most essential symbolic teachings of the Christian religion. It is the sacrifice of the merely natural man, of the unconscious, ingenuous being whose tragic career began with the eating of the apple in Paradise. The biblical fall of man presents the dawn of consciousness as a curse. And as a matter of fact it is in this light that we first look upon every problem that forces us to greater consciousness and separates us even further from the paradise of unconscious childhood.

94:751

The unconscious is the only available source of religious experience. This in certainly not to say that what we call the unconscious is identical with God or is set up in his place. It is simply the medium from which religious experience seems to flow. As to what the further cause of such experience might be, the answer to this lies beyond the range of human knowledge. Knowledge of God is a transcendental problem.

106:565

Since we cannot imagine—unless we have lost our critical faculties altogether—that mankind today has attained the highest possible degree of consciousness, there must be some potential unconscious psyche left over whose development would result in a further extension and a higher differentiation of consciousness. No one can say how great or small this "remnant" might be, for we have no means of measuring the possible range of conscious development, let alone the extent of the unconscious.

77:387

Gleaming islands, indeed whole continents, can still add themselves to our modern consciousness.   53:387

There are many people who are only partially conscious. Even among absolutely civilized Europeans there is a disproportionately high number of abnormally unconscious individuals who spend a great part of their lives in an unconscious state. They know what happens to them, but they do not know what they do or say. They cannot judge of the consequences of their actions. These are people who are abnormally unconscious, that is, in a primitive state. What then finally makes them conscious? If they get a slap in the face, then they become conscious; something really happens, and that makes them conscious. They meet with something fatal and then they suddenly realize what they are doing.   11:6*

An inflated consciousness is always egocentric and conscious of nothing but its own existence. It is incapable of learning from the past, incapable of understanding contemporary events, and incapable of drawing right conclusions about the future. It is hypnotized by itself and therefore cannot be argued with. It inevitably dooms itself to calamities that must strike it dead.   72:563

Everything that man should, and yet cannot, be or do— be it in a positive or negative sense—lives on as a mythological figure and anticipation alongside his consciousness, either as a religious projection or—what is still more dangerous—as unconscious contents which then project themselves spontaneously into incongruous objects, e.g., hygienic and other "salvationist" doctrines or practices. All these are so many rationalized substitutes for mythology, and their unnaturalness does more harm than good.   76:287

The stirring up of conflict is a Luciferian virtue in the true sense of the word. Conflict engenders fire, the fire of affects and emotions, and like every other fire it has two aspects, that of combustion and that of creating light. On the one hand, emotion is the alchemical fire whose warmth brings everything into existence and whose heat burns all superfluities to ashes (*omnes superfluitates comburit*). But on the other hand, emotion is the moment when steel meets flint and a spark is struck forth, for emotion is the chief source of consciousness. There is no change from darkness to light or from inertia to movement without emotion. 67:179

Since the differentiated consciousness of civilized man has been granted an effective instrument for the practical realization of its contents through the dynamics of his will, there is all the more danger, the more he trains his will, of his getting lost in one-sidedness and deviating further and further from the laws and roots of his being. 76:276

When there is a marked change in the individual's state of consciousness, the unconscious contents which are thereby constellated will also change. And the further the conscious situation moves away from a certain point of equilibrium, the more forceful and accordingly the more dangerous become the unconscious contents that are struggling to restore the balance. This leads ultimately to a dissociation: on the one hand, ego-consciousness makes convulsive efforts to shake off an invisible opponent (if it does not suspect its next-door neighbour of being the devil!), while on the other hand it increasingly falls victim to the tyrannical will of an internal "Government opposition" which displays all the characteristics of a daemonic subman and superman combined. When a few million people get into this state, it produces the sort of situation which has afforded us such an edifying object-lesson every day for the last ten years.* These contemporary events betray their psychological background by their very singularity. The insensate destruction and devastation are a reaction against the deflection of consciousness from the point of equilibrium. For an equilibrium does in fact exist between the psychic ego and non-ego, and that equilibrium is a *religio*, a "careful consideration" of ever-present unconscious forces which we neglect at our peril.   77:394f

Nothing is so apt to challenge our self-awareness and alertness as being at war with oneself. One can hardly think of any other or more effective means of waking humanity out of the irresponsible and innocent half-sleep of the primitive mentality and bringing it to a state of conscious responsibility.   70:964

The hero's main feat is to overcome the monster of darkness: it is the long-hoped-for and expected triumph of consciousness over the unconscious. The coming of consciousness was probably the most tremendous experience of primeval times, for with it a world came into being whose existence no one had suspected before. "And God said, 'Let there be light'" is the projection of that immemorial experience of the separation of consciousness from the unconscious.   76:284

Without consciousness there would, practically speaking, be no world, for the world exists for us only in so far as it is consciously reflected by a psyche. Consciousness is a precondition of being. Thus the psyche is endowed with the dignity of a cosmic principle, which philosophically and in fact gives it a position co-equal with the principle of physical being. The carrier of this consciousness is the individual, who does not produce the psyche of his own voli-

* 1935-1945.

tion but is, on the contrary, preformed by it and nourished by the gradual awakening of consciousness during child-hood. If therefore the psyche is of overriding empirical importance, so also is the individual, who is the only immediate manifestation of the psyche.   106:528

"But why on earth," you may ask, "should it be necessary for man to achieve, by hook or by crook, a higher level of consciousness?" This is truly the crucial question, and I do not find the answer easy. Instead of a real answer I can only make a confession of faith: I believe that, after thousands and millions of years, someone had to realize that this wonderful world of mountains and oceans, suns and moons, galaxies and nebulae, plants and animals, *exists*. From a low hill in the Athi plains of East Africa I once watched the vast herds of wild animals grazing in soundless stillness, as they had done from time immemorial, touched only by the breath of a primeval world. I felt then as if I were the first man, the first creature, to know that all this *is*. The entire world round me was still in its primeval state; it did not know that it *was*. And then, in that one moment in which I came to know, the world sprang into being; without that moment it would never have been. All Nature seeks this goal and finds it fulfilled in man, but only in the most highly developed and most fully conscious man.

67:177

The Archetypes

It is in my view a great mistake to suppose that the psyche of a new-born child is a *tabula rasa* in the sense that there is absolutely nothing in it. In so far as the child is born with a differentiated brain that is predetermined by heredity and therefore individualized, it meets sensory stimuli coming from outside not with *any* aptitudes, but with *specific* ones, and this necessarily results in a particular, individual choice and pattern of apperception. These aptitudes can be shown to be inherited instincts and preformed patterns, the latter being the *a priori* and formal conditions of apperception that are based on instinct. Their presence gives the world of the child and the dreamer its anthropomorphic stamp. They are the archetypes, which direct all fantasy activity into its appointed paths and in this way produce, in the fantasy-images of children's dreams as well as in the delusions of schizophrenia, astonishing mythological parallels such as can also be found, though in lesser degree, in the dreams of normal persons and neurotics. It is not, therefore, a question of inherited *ideas* but of inherited *possibilities* of ideas. 16:136

The original structural components of the psyche are of no less surprising a uniformity than are those of the visible body. The archetypes are, so to speak, organs of the pre-rational psyche. They are eternally inherited forms and ideas which have at first no specific content. Their specific content only appears in the course of the individual's life, when personal experience is taken up in precisely these forms. 22:845

Archetypes are like riverbeds which dry up when the water deserts them, but which it can find again at any time. An archetype is like an old watercourse along which the

water of life has flowed for centuries, digging a deep channel for itself. The longer it has flowed in this channel the
more likely it is that sooner or later the water will return
to its old bed.   115:395

Archetypes were, and still are, living psychic forces that
demand to be taken seriously, and they have a strange way
of making sure of their effect. Always they were the bring-
ers of protection and salvation, and their violation has as
its consequence the "perils of the soul" known to us from
the psychology of primitives. Moreover, they are the infallible causes of neurotic and even psychotic disorders, behav-
ing exactly like neglected or maltreated physical organs or
organic functional systems.   76:266

Our personal psychology is just a thin skin, a ripple on
the ocean of collective psychology. The powerful factor, the
factor which changes our whole life, which changes the
surface of our known world, which makes history, is collective psychology, and collective psychology moves according
to laws entirely different from those of our consciousness.
The archetypes are the great decisive forces, they bring
about the real events, and not our personal reasoning and
practical intellect . . . The archetypal images decide the fate
of man.   6:183*

All the most powerful ideas in history go back to archetypes. This is particularly true of religious ideas, but the
central concepts of science, philosophy, and ethics are no
exception to this rule. In their present form they are variants
of archetypal ideas, created by consciously applying and
adapting these ideas to reality. For it is the function of consciousness not only to recognize and assimilate the external
world through the gateway of the senses, but to translate
into visible reality the world within us.   96:342

❖

I have often been asked where the archetype comes from and whether it is acquired or not. This question cannot be answered directly. Archetypes are, by definition, factors and motifs that arrange the psychic elements into certain images, characterized as archetypal, but in such a way that they can be recognized only from the effects they produce. They exist preconsciously, and presumably they form the structural dominants of the psyche in general. They may be compared to the invisible presence of the crystal lattice in a saturated solution. As *a priori* conditioning factors they represent a special, psychological instance of the biological "pattern of behaviour," which gives all living organisms their specific qualities. Just as the manifestations of this biological ground plan may change in the course of development, so also can those of the archetype. Empirically considered, however, the archetype did not ever come into existence as a phenomenon of organic life, but entered into the picture with life itself.   65: 222n

To the extent that the archetypes intervene in the shaping of conscious contents by regulating, modifying, and motivating them, they act like instincts. It is therefore very natural to suppose that these factors are connected with the instincts and to enquire whether the typical situational patterns which these collective form-principles apparently represent are not in the end identical with the instinctual patterns, namely, with the patterns of behaviour.   53: 404

The archetype or primordial image might suitably be described as the instinct's perception of itself, or as the self-portrait of the instinct, in exactly the same way as consciousness is an inward perception of the objective life-process.   38: 277

We must constantly bear in mind that what we mean

by "archetype" is in itself irrepresentable, but has effects
which make visualizations of it possible, namely, the archetypal images and ideas. We meet with a similar situation
in physics: there the smallest particles are themselves irrepresentable but have effects from the nature of which we
can build up a model. The archetypal image, the motif or
mythologem, is a construction of this kind.   53:417

Sooner or later nuclear physics and the psychology of
the unconscious will draw closer together as both of them,
independently of one another and from opposite directions,
push forward into transcendental territory, the one with
the concept of the atom, the other with that of the
archetype.   3:412

Just as the "psychic infra-red," the biological instinctual
psyche, gradually passes over into the physiology of the
organism and thus merges with its chemical and physical
conditions, so the "psychic ultra-violet," the archetype, describes a field which exhibits none of the peculiarities of the
physiological and yet, in the last analysis, can no longer be
regarded as psychic.   53:420

The archetypal representations (images and ideas) medi-
ated to us by the unconscious should not be confused with
the archetype as such. They are very varied structures
which all point back to one essentially "irrepresentable"
basic form. The latter is characterized by certain formal
elements and by certain fundamental meanings, although
these can be grasped only approximately. The archetype as
such is a psychoid factor that belongs, as it were, to the invisible, ultra-violet end of the psychic spectrum . . . It seems
to me probable that the real nature of the archetype is not
capable of being made conscious, that it is transcendent, on
which account I call it psychoid [quasi-psychic].   53:417

That the world inside and outside us rests on a transcendental background is as certain as our own existence, but it is equally certain that the direct perception of the archetypal world inside us is just as doubtfully correct as that of the physical world outside us.   48:787

In spite or perhaps because of its affinity with instinct, the archetype represents the authentic element of spirit, but a spirit which is not to be identified with the human intellect, since it is the latter's *spiritus rector*. The essential content of all mythologies and all religions and all isms is archetypal. The archetype is spirit or anti-spirit: what it ultimately proves to be depends on the attitude of the human mind. Archetype and instinct are the most polar opposites imaginable, as can easily be seen when one compares a man who is ruled by his instinctual drives with a man who is seized by the spirit. But, just as between all opposites there obtains so close a bond that no position can be established or even thought of without its corresponding negation, so in this case also "les extrêmes se touchent."   53:406

The archetype as an image of instinct is a spiritual goal toward which the whole nature of man strives; it is the sea to which all rivers wend their way, the prize which the hero wrests from the fight with the dragon.   53:415

✧

I can only gaze with wonder and awe at the depths and heights of our psychic nature. Its non-spatial universe conceals an untold abundance of images which have accumulated over millions of years of living development and become fixed in the organism. My consciousness is like an eye that penetrates to the most distant spaces, yet it is the psychic non-ego that fills them with non-spatial images. And these images are not pale shadows, but tremendously powerful psychic factors. The most we may be able to do is misunderstand them, but we can never rob them of their power by denying them. Beside this picture I would like to place the spectacle of the starry heavens at night, for the only equivalent of the universe within is the universe without; and just as I reach this world through the medium of the body, so I reach that world through the medium of the psyche.

42:764

The organism confronts light with a new structure, the eye, and the psyche confronts the natural process with a symbolic image, which apprehends it in the same way as the eye catches the light. And just as the eye bears witness to the peculiar and spontaneous creative activity of living matter, the primordial image expresses the intrinsic and unconditioned creative power of the psyche. The primordial image is thus a condensation of the living process.

69:748f

It is a great mistake in practice to treat an archetype as if it were a mere name, word, or concept. It is far more than that: it is a piece of life, an image connected with the living individual by the bridge of emotion.   8:96*

The so-called "forces of the unconscious" are not intellectual concepts that can be arbitrarily manipulated, but dangerous antagonists which can, among other things, work frightful devastation in the economy of the personality. They are everything one could wish for or fear in a psychic "Thou." The layman naturally thinks he is the victim of some obscure organic disease; but the theologian, who suspects it is the devil's work, is appreciably nearer to the psychological truth.   83:659*

In psychic matters we are dealing with processes of experience, that is, with transformations which should never be given hard and fast names if their living movement is not to petrify into something static. The protean mythologem and the shimmering symbol express the processes of the psyche far more trenchantly and, in the end, far more clearly than the clearest concept; for the symbol not only conveys a visualization of the process but—and this is perhaps just as important—it also brings a re-experiencing of it, of that twilight which we can learn to understand only through inoffensive empathy, but which too much clarity only dispels.   58: 199

The great problems of life, including of course sex, are always related to the primordial images of the collective unconscious. These images are balancing and compensating factors that correspond to the problems which life confronts us with in reality. This is no matter for astonishment, since these images are deposits of thousands of years of experience of the struggle for existence and for adaptation. Every great experience in life, every profound conflict, evokes the accumulated treasure of these images and brings about their inner constellation. But they become accessible to consciousness only when the individual possesses so much self-awareness and power of understanding that he also reflects on what he experiences instead of just living it blindly. In the latter event he actually lives the myth and the symbol without knowing it.   69: 373f

The soul gives birth to images that from the rational standpoint of consciousness are assumed to be worthless. And so they are, in the sense that they cannot immediately be turned to account in the objective world. The first possibility of making use of them is artistic, if one is in any way gifted in that direction; a second is philosophical speculation; a third is quasi-religious, leading to heresy and the founding of sects; and a fourth way of employing the *dynamis* of these images is to squander it in every form of licentiousness.   69: 426

The symbol is a living body, *corpus et anima*; hence the "child" is such an apt formula for the symbol. The uniqueness of the psyche can never enter wholly into reality, it can only be realized approximately, though it still remains the absolute basis of all consciousness. The deeper "layers" of the psyche lose their individual uniqueness as they retreat farther and farther into darkness. "Lower down," that is to say as they approach the autonomous functional systems, they become increasingly collective until they are universalized and extinguished in the body's materiality, i.e., in chemical substances. The body's carbon is simply carbon. Hence "at bottom" the psyche is simply "world." In this sense I hold Kerényi to be absolutely right when he says that in the symbol the *world itself* is speaking. The more archaic and "deeper," that is the more *physiological*, the symbol is, the more collective and universal, the more "material" it is. The more abstract, differentiated, and specific it is, and the more its nature approximates to conscious uniqueness and individuality, the more it sloughs off its universal character. Having finally attained full consciousness, it runs the risk of becoming a mere allegory which nowhere oversteps the bounds of conscious comprehension, and is then exposed to all sorts of attempts at rationalistic and therefore inadequate explanation.

76: 291

Not for a moment dare we succumb to the illusion that an archetype can be finally explained and disposed of. Even the best attempts at explanation are only more or less successful translations into another metaphorical language. (Indeed, language itself is only an image.) The most we can do is to *dream the myth onwards* and give it a modern dress. And whatever explanation or interpretation does to

it, we do to our own souls as well, with corresponding results for our own well-being. The archetype—let us never
forget this—is a psychic organ present in all of us.

76:271

In reality we can never legitimately cut loose from our
archetypal foundations unless we are prepared to pay the
price of a neurosis, any more than we can rid ourselves of
our body and its organs without committing suicide. If we
cannot deny the archetypes or otherwise neutralize them,
we are confronted, at every new stage in the differentiation
of consciousness to which civilization attains, with the task
of finding a new *interpretation* appropriate to this stage,
in order to connect the life of the past that still exists in us
with the life of the present, which threatens to slip away
from it. If this link-up does not take place, a kind of rootless consciousness comes into being no longer oriented to
the past, a consciousness which succumbs helplessly to all
manner of suggestions and, in practice, is susceptible to
psychic epidemics. With the loss of the past, now become
"insignificant," devalued, and incapable of revaluation, the
saviour is lost too, for the saviour either is the insignificant
thing itself or else arises out of it. Over and over again in
the "metamorphosis of the gods," he rises up as the prophet
or first-born of a new generation and appears unexpectedly
in the unlikeliest places (sprung from a stone, tree, furrow,
water, etc.) and in ambiguous form (Tom Thumb, dwarf,
child, animal, and so on).   76:267

All psychic events are so deeply grounded in the archetype and are so much interwoven with it that in every case
considerable critical effort is needed to separate the unique
from the typical with any certainty. Ultimately, every individual life is at the same time the eternal life of the species.
The individual is continuously "historical" because strictly
time-bound; the relation of the type to time, on the other

hand, is irrelevant. Since the life of Christ is archetypal to a high degree, it represents to just that degree the life of the archetype. But since the archetype is the unconscious precondition of every human life, its life, when revealed, also reveals the hidden, unconscious groundlife of every individual. That is to say, what happens in the life of Christ happens always and everywhere. In the Christian archetype all lives of this kind are prefigured and are expressed over and over again or once and for all.   74:146

A symbol loses its magical or, if you prefer, its redeeming power as soon as its liability to dissolve is recognized. To be effective, a symbol must be by its very nature unassailable. It must be the best possible expression of the prevailing worldview, an unsurpassed container of meaning; it must also be sufficiently remote from comprehension to resist all attempts of the critical intellect to break it down; and finally, its aesthetic form must appeal so convincingly to our feelings that no arguments can be raised against it on that score.   69:401

Do we ever understand what we think? We only understand that kind of thinking which is a mere equation, from which nothing comes out but what we have put in. That is the working of the intellect. But besides that there is a thinking in primordial images, in symbols which are older than the historical man, which are inborn in him from the earliest times, and, eternally living, outlasting all generations, still make up the groundwork of the human psyche. It is only possible to live the fullest life when we are in harmony with these symbols; wisdom is a return to them.

94:794

As we can see from the example of Faust, the vision of the symbol is a pointer to the onward course of life, beckoning the libido towards a still distant goal—but a goal that henceforth will burn unquenchably within him, so that his life, kindled as by a flame, moves steadily towards the far-off beacon. This is the specific life-promoting significance of the symbol, and such, too, is the meaning and value of religious symbols. I am speaking, of course, not of symbols that are dead and stiffened by dogma, but of living symbols that rise up from the creative unconscious of the living man. The immense significance of such symbols can be denied only by those for whom the history of the world begins with the present day.   69:202*f*

Why is psychology the youngest of the empirical sciences? Why have we not long since discovered the unconscious and raised up its treasure-house of eternal images? Simply because we had a religious formula for everything psychic—and one that is far more beautiful and comprehensive than immediate experience. Though the Christian view of the world has paled for many people, the symbolic treasure-rooms of the East are still full of marvels that can nourish for a long time to come the passion for show and new clothes. What is more, these images—be they Christian or Buddhist or what you will—are lovely, mysterious, richly intuitive. Naturally, the more familiar we are with them the more does constant usage polish them smooth, so that what remains is only banal superficiality and meaningless paradox.   10:11

The Catholic way of life is completely unaware of psychological problems in this sense. Almost the entire life of the collective unconscious has been channelled into the dogmatic archetypal ideas and flows along like a well-controlled stream in the symbolism of creed and ritual. It manifests itself in the inwardness of the Catholic psyche. The collective unconscious, as we understand it today, was never a matter of "psychology," for before the Christian Church existed there were the antique mysteries, and these reach back into the grey mists of neolithic prehistory. Mankind has never lacked powerful images to lend magical aid against all the uncanny things that live in the depths of the psyche. Always the figures of the unconscious were expressed in protecting and healing images and in this way were expelled from the psyche into cosmic space.   10:21

The gods of Greece and Rome perished from the same disease as did our Christian symbols: people discovered then, as today, that they had no thoughts whatever on the subject. On the other hand, the gods of the strangers still had unexhausted mana. Their names were weird and incomprehensible and their deeds portentously dark—something altogether different from the hackneyed *chronique scandaleuse* of Olympus. At least one couldn't understand the Asiatic symbols, and for this reason they were not banal like the conventional gods. The fact that people accepted the new as unthinkingly as they had rejected the old did not become a problem at that time. Is it becoming a problem today? Shall we be able to put on, like a new suit of clothes, ready-made symbols grown on foreign soil, saturated with foreign blood, spoken in a foreign tongue, nourished by a foreign culture, interwoven with foreign history, and so resemble a beggar who wraps himself in kingly raiment, a king who disguises himself as a beggar? No doubt this is possible. Or is there something in ourselves that commands us to go in for no mummeries, but perhaps even to sew our garment ourselves?   10:26f

Anyone who has lost the historical symbols and cannot be satisfied with substitutes is certainly in a very difficult position today: before him there yawns the void, and he turns away from it in horror. What is worse, the vacuum gets filled with absurd political and social ideas, which one and all are distinguished by their spiritual bleakness. But if he cannot get along with these pedantic dogmatisms, he sees himself forced to be serious for once with his alleged trust in God, though it usually turns out that his fear of things going wrong if he did so is even more persuasive.

10:28

To gain an understanding of religious matters, probably all that is left us today is the psychological approach. That is why I take these thought-forms that have become historically fixed, try to melt them down again and pour them into moulds of immediate experience. It is certainly a difficult undertaking to discover connecting links between dogma and immediate experience of psychological archetypes, but a study of the natural symbols of the unconscious gives us the necessary raw material.   74:148

Reverence for the great mysteries of nature, which the language of religion seeks to express in symbols hallowed by their antiquity, profound significance, and beauty, will not suffer from the extension of psychology to this domain, to which science has hitherto found no access. We only shift the symbols back a little, shedding a little light on their darker reaches, but without succumbing to the erroneous notion that we have created more than merely a new symbol for the same enigma that perplexed all ages before us.

69:428

Eternal truth needs a human language that alters with the spirit of the times. The primordial images undergo ceaseless transformation and yet remain ever the same, but only in a new form can they be understood anew. Always they require a new interpretation if, as each formulation becomes obsolete, they are not to lose their spellbinding power over that *fugax Mercurius* and allow that useful though dangerous enemy to escape. What is that about "new wine in old bottles"? Where are the answers to the spiritual needs and troubles of a new epoch? And where the knowledge to deal with the psychological problems raised by the development of modern consciousness? Never before has "eternal" truth been faced with such a hybris of will and power. 77:396

All the true things must change and only that which changes remains true. 48:503

All ages before us have believed in gods in some form or other. Only an unparalleled impoverishment of symbolism could enable us to rediscover the gods as psychic factors, that is, as archetypes of the unconscious. No doubt this discovery is hardly credible at present. 10:50

It is only through the psyche that we can establish that God acts upon us, but we are unable to distinguish whether these actions emanate from God or from the unconscious. . . Strictly speaking, the God-image does not coincide with the unconscious as such, but with a special content of it, namely the archetype of the self. It is this archetype from which we can no longer distinguish the God-image empirically. We can arbitrarily postulate a difference between these two entities, but that does not help us at all. On the contrary, it only helps us to separate man from God, and prevents God from becoming man. Faith is certainly right when it impresses on man's mind and heart how infinitely far away and inaccessible God is; but it also teaches his nearness, his immediate presence, and it is just this nearness which has to be empirically real if it is not to lose all significance. Only that which acts upon me do I recognize as real and actual. But that which does not act upon me might as well not exist. The religious need longs for wholeness, and therefore lays hold of the images of wholeness offered by the unconscious, which, independently of our conscious mind, rise up from the depths of our psychic nature.

7:757

God has indeed made an inconceivably sublime and mysteriously contradictory image of himself, without the help of man, and implanted it in man's unconscious as an archetype, the archetypal light: not in order that theologians of all times and places should be at one another's throats, but in order that the unpresumptuous man might glimpse an image, in the stillness of his soul, that is akin to him and is wrought of his own psychic substance. This image contains everything which he will ever imagine concerning his gods or concerning the ground of his psyche.

83:661*f**

Dreams

The dream is a little hidden door in the innermost and most secret recesses of the soul, opening into that cosmic night which was psyche long before there was any ego-consciousness, and which will remain psyche no matter how far our ego-consciousness extends. For all ego-consciousness is isolated; because it separates and discriminates, it knows only particulars, and it sees only those that can be related to the ego. Its essence is limitation, even though it reach to the farthest nebulae among the stars. All consciousness separates; but in dreams we put on the likeness of that more universal, truer, more eternal man dwelling in the darkness of primordial night. There he is still the whole, and the whole is in him, indistinguishable from nature and bare of all egohood. It is from these all-uniting depths that the dream arises, be it never so childish, grotesque, and immoral.

45: 304f

No amount of scepticism and criticism has yet enabled me to regard dreams as negligible occurrences. Often enough they appear senseless, but it is obviously we who lack the sense and ingenuity to read the enigmatic message from the nocturnal realm of the psyche. Seeing that at least half our psychic existence is passed in that realm, and that consciousness acts upon our nightly life just as much as the unconscious overshadows our daily life, it would seem all the more incumbent on medical psychology to sharpen its senses by a systematic study of dreams. Nobody doubts the importance of conscious experience; why then should we doubt the significance of unconscious happenings? They also are part of our life, and sometimes more truly a part of it for weal or woe than any happenings of the day.

61: 325

The dream has for the primitive an incomparably higher value than it has for civilized man. Not only does he talk a great deal about his dreams, he also attributes an extraordinary importance to them, so that it often seems as though he were unable to distinguish between them and reality. To the civilized man dreams as a rule appear valueless, though there are some people who attach great significance to certain dreams on account of their weird and impressive character. This peculiarity lends plausibility to the view that dreams are inspirations.   68:574

Dream psychology opens the way to a general comparative psychology from which we may hope to gain the same understanding of the development and structure of the human psyche as comparative anatomy has given us concerning the human body.   30:476

A dream, like every element in the psychic structure, is a product of the total psyche. Hence we may expect to find in dreams everything that has ever been of significance in the life of humanity. Just as human life is not limited to this or that fundamental instinct, but builds itself up from a multiplicity of instincts, needs, desires, and physical and psychic conditions, etc., so the dream cannot be explained by this or that element in it, however beguilingly simple such an explanation may appear to be. We can be certain that it is incorrect, because no simple theory of instinct will ever be capable of grasping the human psyche, that mighty and mysterious thing, nor, consequently, its exponent, the dream. In order to do anything like justice to dreams, we need an interpretive equipment that must be laboriously fitted together from all branches of the humane sciences.

30:527

The dream is often occupied with apparently very silly details, thus producing an impression of absurdity, or else it is on the surface so unintelligible as to leave us thoroughly bewildered. Hence we always have to overcome a certain resistance before we can seriously set about disentangling the intricate web through patient work. But when at last we penetrate to its real meaning, we find ourselves deep in the dreamer's secrets and discover with astonishment that an apparently quite senseless dream is in the highest degree significant, and that in reality it speaks only of important and serious matters. This discovery compels rather more respect for the so-called superstition that dreams have a meaning, to which the rationalistic temper of our age has hitherto given short shrift.   104A:24

Dreams that form logically, morally, or aesthetically satisfying wholes are exceptional. Usually a dream is a strange and disconcerting product distinguished by many "bad" qualities, such as lack of logic, questionable morality, uncouth form, and apparent absurdity or nonsense. People are therefore only too glad to dismiss it as stupid, meaningless, and worthless.   52:532

Dreams are impartial, spontaneous products of the unconscious psyche, outside the control of the will. They are pure nature; they show us the unvarnished, natural truth, and are therefore fitted, as nothing else is, to give us back an attitude that accords with our basic human nature when our consciousness has strayed too far from its foundations and run into an impasse.   45:317

As in our waking state, real people and things enter our field of vision, so the dream-images enter like another kind of reality into the field of consciousness of the dream-ego. We do not feel as if we were producing the dreams, it is rather as if the dreams came to us. They are not subject to our control but obey their own laws. They are obviously autonomous psychic complexes which form themselves out of their own material. We do not know the source of their motives, and we therefore say that dreams come from the unconscious. In saying this, we assume that there are independent psychic complexes which elude our conscious control and come and go according to their own laws.   68:580

In sleep, fantasy takes the form of dreams. But in waking life, too, we continue to dream beneath the threshold of consciousness, especially when under the influence of repressed or other unconscious complexes.   63:125

The dream is specifically the utterance of the unconscious. Just as the psyche has a diurnal side which we call consciousness, so also it has a nocturnal side: the unconscious psychic activity which we apprehend as dreamlike fantasy.

61:317

Dreams contain images and thought associations which we do not create with conscious intent. They arise spontaneously without our assistance and are representatives of a psychic activity withdrawn from our arbitrary will. Therefore the dream is, properly speaking, a highly objective, natural product of the psyche, from which we might expect indications, or at least hints, about certain basic trends in the psychic process. Now, since the psychic process, like any other life-process, is not just a causal sequence, but is also a process with a teleological orientation, we might expect dreams to give us certain *indicia* about the objective causality as well as about the objective tendencies, because they are nothing less than self-portraits of the psychic life-process.   104B:210

❖

The dream rectifies the situation. It contributes the material that was lacking and thereby improves the patient's

attitude. That is the reason we need dream-analysis in our
therapy. 30:482

The dream shows the inner truth and reality of the patient
as it really is: not as I conjecture it to be, and not as
he would like it to be, but *as it is*. 61:304

The unconscious is the unknown at any given moment,
so it is not surprising that dreams add to the conscious
psychological situation of the moment all those aspects
which are essential for a totally different point of view. It is
evident that this function of dreams amounts to a psychological adjustment, a compensation absolutely necessary for
properly balanced action. In a conscious process of reflection
it is essential that, so far as possible, we should realize all
the aspects and consequences of a problem in order to find
the right solution. This process is continued automatically
in the more or less unconscious state of sleep, where, as experience seems to show, all those aspects occur to the
dreamer (at least by way of allusion) that during the day
were insufficiently appreciated or even totally ignored—
in other words, were comparatively unconscious. 30:469

The view that dreams are merely the imaginary fulfil-
ments of repressed wishes is hopelessly out of date. There
are, it is true, dreams which manifestly represent wishes or
fears, but what about all the other things? Dreams may
contain ineluctable truths, philosophical pronouncements, illusions, wild fantasies, memories, plans, anticipations, irrational experiences, even telepathic visions, and heaven
knows what besides. 61:317

As against Freud's view that the dream is essentially a
wish-fulfillment, I hold . . . that the dream is a spontaneous
self-portrayal, in symbolic form, of the actual situation in
the unconscious. 30:505

The psyche is a self-regulating system that maintains its equilibrium just as the body does. Every process that goes too far immediately and inevitably calls forth compensations, and without these there would be neither a normal metabolism nor a normal psyche. In this sense we can take the theory of compensation as a basic law of psychic behaviour. Too little on one side results in too much on the other.

61: 330

The more one-sided his conscious attitude is, and the further it deviates from the optimum, the greater becomes the possibility that vivid dreams with a strongly contrasting but purposive content will appear as an expression of the self-regulation of the psyche.

30: 488

The primitives I observed in East Africa took it for granted that "big" dreams are dreamed only by "big" men —medicine-men, magicians, chiefs, etc. This may be true on a primitive level. But with us these dreams are dreamed also by simple people, more particularly when they have got themselves, mentally or spiritually, in a fix.

45: 324

Never apply any theory, but always ask the patient how *he* feels about his dream images. For dreams are always about a particular problem of the individual about which he has a wrong conscious judgment. The dreams are the reaction to our conscious attitude in the same way that the body reacts when we overeat or do not eat enough or when we ill-treat it in some other way. Dreams are the natural reaction of the self-regulating psychic system.

6: 123*

It is not easy to lay down any special rules for the type of dream-compensation. Its character is always closely bound up with the whole nature of the individual. The possibilities of compensation are without number and inexhaustible, though with increasing experience certain basic features gradually crystallize out. 30:490

Though dreams contribute to the self-regulation of the psyche by automatically bringing up everything that is repressed or neglected or unknown, their compensatory significance is often not immediately apparent because we still have only a very incomplete knowledge of the nature and the needs of the human psyche. There are psychological compensations that seem to be very remote from the problem on hand. In these cases one must always remember that every man, in a sense, represents the whole of humanity and its history. What was possible in the history of mankind at large is also possible on a small scale in every individual. What mankind has needed may eventually be needed by the individual too. It is therefore not surprising that religious compensations play a great role in dreams. That this is increasingly so in our time is a natural consequence of the prevailing materialism of our outlook.

30:483

I would not deny the possibility of *parallel* dreams, i.e., dreams whose meaning coincides with or supports the conscious attitude, but in my experience, at least, these are rather rare. 72:48

To interpret the dream-process as compensatory is in my view entirely consistent with the nature of the biological process in general. Freud's view tends in the same direction, since he too ascribes a compensatory role to dreams in so far as they preserve sleep. . . . As against this, we should not overlook the fact that the very dreams which disturb sleep most—and these are not uncommon—have a dramatic structure which aims logically at creating a highly affective situation, and builds it up so efficiently that it unquestionably wakes the dreamer. Freud explains these dreams by saying that the censor was no longer able to suppress the painful affect. It seems to me that this explanation fails to do justice to the facts. Dreams which concern themselves in a very disagreeable manner with the painful experiences and activities of daily life and expose just the most disturbing thoughts with the most painful distinctness are known to everyone. It would, in my opinion, be unjustified to speak here of the dream's sleep-preserving, affect-disguising function. One would have to stand reality on its head to see in these dreams a confirmation of Freud's view.

30:485f

✧

Much may be said for Freud's view as a scientific explanation of dream psychology. But I must dispute its completeness, for the psyche cannot be conceived merely in causal terms but requires also a final view. Only a combination of points of view—which has not yet been achieved in a scientifically satisfactory manner, owing to the enormous difficulties, both practical and theoretical, that still remain to be overcome—can give us a more complete conception of the nature of dreams.

30:473

Dreams are often anticipatory and would lose their specific meaning on a purely causalistic view. They afford unmistakable information about the analytical situation, the correct understanding of which is of the greatest therapeutic importance.

61:312

The causal point of view tends by its very nature towards uniformity of meaning, that is, towards a fixed significance of symbols. The final point of view, on the other hand, perceives in the altered dream-image the expression of an altered psychological situation. It recognizes no fixed meaning of symbols. From this standpoint, all the dream-images are important in themselves, each one having a special significance of its own, to which, indeed, it owes its inclusion in the dream. . . . The symbol in the dream has more the value of a parable: it does not conceal, it teaches.

30: 471

It is only in exceptional cases that somatic stimuli are the determining factor. Usually they coalesce completely with the symbolical expression of the unconscious dream-content; in other words, they are used as a means of expression. Not infrequently the dreams show that there is a remarkable inner symbolical connection between an undoubted physical illness and a definite psychic problem, so that the physical disorder appears as a direct mimetic expression of the psychic situation.

30: 502

Considering a dream from the standpoint of finality, which I contrast with the causal standpoint of Freud, does not—as I would expressly like to emphasize—involve a denial of the dream's causes, but rather a different interpretation of the associative material gathered round the dream. The material facts remain the same, but the criterion by which they are judged is different. The question may be formulated simply as follows: What is the purpose of this dream? What effect is it meant to have? These questions are not arbitrary inasmuch as they can be applied to every psychic activity. Everywhere the question of the "why" and the "wherefore" may be raised, because every organic structure consists of a complicated network of purposive functions, and each of these functions can be resolved into a series of individual facts with a purposive orientation.

30: 462

The prospective function, on the other hand, is an anticipation in the unconscious of future conscious achievements, something like a preliminary exercise or sketch, or a plan

roughed out in advance. . . . The occurrence of prospective dreams cannot be denied. It would be wrong to call
them prophetic, because at bottom they are no more prophetic than a medical diagnosis or a weather forecast. They
are merely an anticipatory combination of probabilities
which may coincide with the actual behaviour of things
but need not necessarily agree in every detail. Only in the
latter case can we speak of "prophecy." That the prospective function of dreams is sometimes greatly superior
to the combinations we can consciously foresee is not surprising, since a dream results from the fusion of subliminal
elements and is thus a combination of all the perceptions,
thoughts, and feelings which consciousness has not regis-
tered because of their feeble accentuation. In addition,
dreams can rely on subliminal memory traces that are no
longer able to influence consciousness effectively. With regard to prognosis, therefore, dreams are often in a much
more favourable position than consciousness.   30:493

Another dream-determinant that deserves mention is
telepathy. The authenticity of this phenomenon can no
longer be disputed today. It is, of course, very simple to
deny its existence without examining the evidence, but that
is an unscientific procedure which is unworthy of notice.
I have found by experience that telepathy does in fact
influence dreams, as has been asserted since ancient times.
Certain people are particularly sensitive in this respect and
often have telepathically influenced dreams. But in acknowledging the phenomenon of telepathy I am not giving unqualified assent to the popular theory of action at a distance.
The phenomenon undoubtedly exists, but the theory of it
does not seem to me so simple.   61:503

❖

Dream-analysis stands or falls with the hypothesis of the
unconscious. Without it, the dream is a mere freak of

nature, a meaningless conglomeration of fragments left over from the day.   61:294

Anyone who wishes to interpret a dream must himself be on approximately the same level as the dream, for nowhere can he see anything more than what he is himself.

45:324

Dreams are as simple or as complicated as the dreamer is himself, only they are always a little bit ahead of the dreamer's consciousness. I do not understand my own dreams any better than any of you, for they are always somewhat beyond my grasp and I have the same trouble with them as anyone who knows nothing about dream interpretation. Knowledge is no advantage when it is a matter of one's own dreams.   6:122*

On paper the interpretation of a dream may look arbitrary, muddled, and spurious; but the same thing in reality can be a little drama of unsurpassed realism. To *experience* a dream and its interpretation is very different from having a tepid rehash set before you on paper. Everything about this psychology is, in the deepest sense, experience; the entire theory, even where it puts on the most abstract airs, is the direct outcome of something experienced.   104A:199

The art of interpreting dreams cannot be learnt from books. Methods and rules are good only when we can get along without them. Only the man who can do it anyway has real skill, only the man of understanding really understands.   45:325

It is obvious that in handling "big" dreams intuitive guesswork will lead nowhere. Wide knowledge is required, such as a specialist ought to possess. But no dream can be interpreted with knowledge alone. This knowledge, furthermore, should not be dead material that has been memorized; it must possess a living quality, and be infused with the experience of the person who uses it. Of what use is philosophical knowledge in the head, if one is not also a philosopher at heart?

45:324

One would do well to treat every dream as though it were a totally unknown object. Look at it from all sides, take it in your hand, carry it about with you, let your imagination play round it, and talk about it with other people. Primitives tell each other impressive dreams, in a public palaver if possible, and this custom is also attested in late antiquity, for all the ancient peoples attributed great significance to dreams. Treated in this way, the dream suggests all manner of ideas and associations which lead us closer to its meaning. The ascertainment of the meaning is, I need hardly point out, an entirely arbitrary affair, and this is where the hazards begin. Narrower or wider limits will be set to the meaning, according to one's experience, temperament, and taste. Some people will be satisfied with little, for others much is still not enough. Also the meaning of the dream, or our interpretation of it, is largely dependent on the intentions of the interpreter, on what he expects the meaning to be or requires it to do. In eliciting the meaning he will involuntarily be guided by certain presuppositions, and it depends very much on the scrupulousness and honesty of the investigator whether he gains something by his interpretation or perhaps only becomes still more deeply entangled in his mistakes.

45:320

So difficult is it to understand a dream that for a long time I have made it a rule, when someone tells me a dream and asks for my opinion, to say first of all to myself: "I have no idea what this dream means." After that I can begin to examine the dream.

53:533

The psychological context of dream-contents consists in the web of associations in which the dream is naturally embedded. Theoretically we can never know anything in advance about this web, but in practice it is sometimes possible, granted long enough experience. Even so, careful analysis will never rely too much on technical rules; the danger of deception and suggestion is too great. In the analysis of isolated dreams above all, this kind of knowing in advance and making assumptions on the grounds of practical expectation or general probability is positively wrong. It should therefore be an absolute rule to assume that every dream, and every part of a dream, is unknown at the outset, and to attempt an interpretation only after carefully taking up the context. We can then apply the meaning we have thus discovered to the text of the dream itself and see whether this yields a fluent reading, or rather whether a satisfying meaning emerges. 72:48

Everyone who analyses the dreams of others should constantly bear in mind that there is no simple and generally known theory of psychic phenomena, neither with regard to their nature, nor to their causes, nor to their purpose. We therefore possess no general criterion of judgment. We know that there are all kinds of psychic phenomena, but we know nothing certain about their essential nature. We know only that, though the observation of the psyche from any one isolated standpoint can yield very valuable results, it can never produce a satisfactory theory from which one could make deductions. The sexual theory and the wish theory, like the power theory, are valuable points of view without, however, doing anything like justice to the profundity and richness of the human psyche. Had we a theory that did, we could then content ourselves with learning a method mechanically. It would then be simply a matter of reading certain signs that stood for fixed contents, and for this it would only be necessary to learn a few semiotic rules by heart. Knowledge and correct assessment of the conscious situation would then be as superfluous as in the performance of a lumbar puncture.   30:498

One should never forget that one dreams in the first place, and almost to the exclusion of all else, of oneself.   45:321

I call every interpretation which equates the dream images with real objects an *interpretation on the objective level.* In contrast to this is the interpretation which refers every part of the dream and all the actors in it back to the dreamer himself. This I call *interpretation on the subjective level.* Interpretation on the objective level is analytic, be-cause it breaks down the dream content into memory-complexes that refer to external situations. Interpretation on the subjective level is synthetic, because it detaches the underlying memory-complexes from their external causes, regards them as tendencies or components of the subject, and reunites them with that subject. . . . In this case, there-fore, all the contents of the dream are treated as symbols for subjective contents.   104A:130

If our dreams reproduce certain ideas these ideas are pri-marily *our* ideas, in the structure of which our whole being is interwoven. They are subjective factors, grouping them-selves as they do in the dream, and expressing this or that meaning, not for extraneous reasons but from the most intimate promptings of our psyche. The whole dream-work is essentially subjective, and a dream is a theatre in which the dreamer is himself the scene, the player, the prompter, the producer, the author, the public, and the critic.   30:509

The relation between conscious and unconscious is com-pensatory. This is one of the best-proven rules of dream interpretation. When we set out to interpret a dream, it is

always helpful to ask: What conscious attitude does it
compensate? 61:330

If we want to interpret a dream correctly, we need a thorough knowledge of the conscious situation at that moment,
because the dream contains its unconscious complement,
that is, the material which the conscious situation has constellated in the unconscious. Without this knowledge it is
impossible to interpret a dream correctly, except by a lucky
fluke. 30:477

The real difficulty begins when the dreams do not point
to anything tangible, and this they do often enough, especially when they hold anticipations of the future. I do not
mean that such dreams are necessarily prophetic, merely
that they feel the way, they "reconnoitre." These dreams
contain inklings of possibilities and for that reason can never
be made plausible to an outsider. 2:89

Anyone sufficiently interested in the dream problem cannot have failed to observe that dreams also have a continuity *forwards*—if such an expression be permitted—since
dreams occasionally exert a remarkable influence on the
conscious mental life even of persons who cannot be considered superstitious or particularly abnormal. 30:444

It is not denied in medieval ecclesiastical writings that a
divine influx may occur in dreams, but this view is not
exactly encouraged, and the Church reserves the right to
decide whether a revelation is to be considered authentic or
not. In spite of the Church's recognition that certain dreams
are sent by God, she is disinclined, and even averse, to any
serious concern with dreams, while admitting that some
might conceivably contain an immediate revelation. Thus
the change of mental attitude that has taken place in recent
centuries is, from this point of view at least, not wholly un-

welcome to the Church, because it effectively discouraged the earlier introspective attitude which favoured a serious consideration of dreams and inner experiences.   74:32

As individuals we are not completely unique, but are like all other men. Hence a dream with a collective meaning is valid in the first place for the dreamer, but it expresses at the same time the fact that his momentary problem is also the problem of other people. This is often of great practical importance, for there are countless people who are inwardly cut off from humanity and oppressed by the thought that nobody else has their problems. Or else they are those all-too-modest souls who, feeling themselves nonentities, have kept their claim to social recognition on too low a level. Moreover, every individual problem is somehow connected with the problem of the age, so that practically every subjective difficulty has to be viewed from the standpoint of the human situation as a whole. But this is permissible only when the dream really is a mythological one and makes use of collective symbols.   45:323

If, in addition to this, we bear in mind that the unconscious contains everything that is lacking to consciousness, that the unconscious therefore has a compensatory tendency, then we can begin to draw conclusions—provided, of course, that the dream does not come from too deep a psychic level. If it is a dream of this kind, it will as a rule contain mythological motifs, combinations of ideas or images which can be found in the myths of one's own folk or in those of other races. The dream will then have a collective meaning, a meaning which is the common property of mankind.   45:322

It is characteristic that dreams never express themselves in a logical, abstract way but always in the language of parable or simile. This is also a characteristic of primitive languages, whose flowery turns of phrase are very striking. If we remember the monuments of ancient literature, we find that what nowadays is expressed by means of abstractions was then expressed mostly by similes. Even a philosopher like Plato did not disdain to express certain fundamental ideas in this way. 30: 474

Just as the body bears the traces of its phylogenetic development, so also does the human mind. Hence there is nothing surprising about the possibility that the figurative language of dreams is a survival from an archaic mode of thought. 30: 475

As regards the much discussed symbolism of dreams, its evaluation varies according to whether it is considered from the causal or from the final standpoint. The causal approach of Freud starts from a desire or craving, that is, from the repressed dream-wish. This craving is always something comparatively simple and elementary, which can hide itself under manifold disguises. . . . Hence it is that the more rigorous adherents of the Freudian school have come to the point of interpreting—to give a gross example—pretty well all oblong objects in dreams as phallic symbols and all round or hollow objects as feminine symbols. 30: 470

Further researches, expressly referred to by Maeder, have shown that the sexual language of dreams is not always to be interpreted in a concretistic way—that it is, in fact, an archaic language which naturally uses all the analogies readiest to hand without their necessarily coinciding with a real sexual content. It is therefore unjustifiable to take the sexual language of dreams literally under all circumstances, while other contents are explained as symbolical. But as soon as you take the sexual metaphors as symbols for something unknown, your conception of the nature of dreams at once deepens.   30:506

✧

Nature commits no errors.   6:95*

I take the dream for what it is. The dream is such a difficult and complicated thing that I do not dare to make any assumptions about its possible cunning or its tendency to deceive. The dream is a natural occurrence, and there is no earthly reason why we should assume that it is a crafty device to lead us astray. It occurs when consciousness and will are to a large extent extinguished. It seems to be a natural product which is also found in people who are not neurotic. Moreover, we know so little about the psychology of the dream process that we must be more than careful when we introduce into its explanation elements that are foreign to the dream itself.   74:41

Nature is often obscure or impenetrable, but she is not, like man, deceitful. We must therefore take it that the dream is just what it pretends to be, neither more nor less. If it shows something in a negative light, there is no reason for assuming that it is meant positively.   104A:162

When a dream apparently disguises something and a particular person therefore seems indicated, there is an obvious tendency at work not to allow this person to appear, because, in the sense of the dream, he represents a mistaken way of thinking or acting. When, for instance, as not infrequently happens in women's dreams, the analyst is represented as a hairdresser (because he "fixes" the head), the analyst is not being so much disguised as devalued. The patient, in her conscious life, is only too ready to acknowledge any kind of authority because she cannot or will not use her own head. The analyst (says the dream) should have no more significance than the hairdresser who puts her head right so that she can then use it herself.   60:479

I leave theory aside as much as possible when analysing dreams—not entirely, of course, for we always need some theory to make things intelligible. It is on the basis of theory, for instance, that I expect dreams to have a meaning. I cannot prove in every case that this is so, for there are dreams which the doctor and the patient simply do not understand. But I have to make such an hypothesis in order to find courage to deal with dreams at all.   61:318

But in no circumstances may we anticipate that this meaning will fit in with any of our subjective expectations; for quite possibly, indeed very frequently, the dream is saying something surprisingly different from what we would expect. As a matter of fact, if the meaning we find in the dream happens to coincide with our expectations, that is a reason for suspicion; for as a rule the standpoint of the unconscious is complementary or compensatory to consciousness and thus unexpectedly "different."   72:48

Every interpretation is an hypothesis, an attempt to read an unknown text. An obscure dream, taken in isolation, can hardly ever be interpreted with any certainty. For this reason I attach little importance to the interpretation of single dreams. A relative degree of certainty is reached only in the interpretation of a series of dreams, where the later dreams correct the mistakes we have made in handling those that went before. Also, the basic ideas and themes can be recognized much better in a dream-series.   61:322

Seen purely theoretically, a dream image can mean anything or nothing. For that matter, does a thing or a fact ever mean anything in itself? The only certainty is that it is always man who interprets, who assigns meaning. And that is the gist of the matter for psychology.   2:93

Lack of conscious understanding does not mean that the dream has no effect at all. Even civilized man can occasionally observe that a dream which he cannot remember can slightly alter his mood for better or worse. Dreams can be "understood" to a certain extent in a subliminal way, and that is mostly how they work.   8:52*f**

It makes very little difference whether the doctor understands or not, but it makes all the difference whether the patient understands. Understanding should therefore be understanding in the sense of an agreement which is the fruit of joint reflection. The danger of a one-sided understanding is that the doctor may judge the dream from the standpoint of a preconceived opinion. His judgment may be in line with orthodox theory, it may even be fundamentally correct, but it will not win the patient's assent, he will not come to an understanding with him, and that is in the practical sense incorrect—incorrect because it anticipates and thus cripples the patient's development. The patient, that is to say, does not need to have a truth inculcated into him—if we do that, we only reach his head; he needs far more to grow up to this truth, and in that way we reach his heart, and the appeal goes deeper and works more powerfully.   61:314

A dream that is not understood remains a mere occurrence; understood, it becomes a living experience.   29:252

But when, you may rightly ask, is one sure of the interpretation? Is there anything approaching a reliable criterion for the correctness of an interpretation? This question, happily, can be answered in the affirmative. If we have made a wrong interpretation, or if it is somehow incomplete,

we may be able to see it from the next dream. Thus, for
example, the earlier motif will be repeated in clearer form,
or our interpretation may be deflated by some ironic para-
phrase, or it may meet with straightforward violent opposition. Now supposing that these interpretations also go
astray, the general inconclusiveness and futility of our procedure will make itself felt soon enough in the bleakness,
sterility, and pointlessness of the undertaking, so that doctor and patient alike will be suffocated either by boredom
or by doubt. Just as the reward of a correct interpretation
is an uprush of life, so an incorrect one dooms them to
deadlock, resistance, doubt, and mutual desiccation.

104A: 189

If, as happens in long and difficult treatments, the analyst
observes a series of dreams often running into hundreds,
there gradually forces itself upon him a phenomenon which,
in an isolated dream, would remain hidden behind the compensation of the moment. This phenomenon is a kind of
developmental process in the personality itself. At first it
seems that each compensation is a momentary adjustment
of one-sidedness or an equalization of disturbed balance.
But with deeper insight and experience, these apparently
separate acts of compensation arrange themselves into a
kind of plan. They seem to hang together and in the deepest sense to be subordinated to a common goal, so that a
long dream-series no longer appears as a senseless string of
incoherent and isolated happenings, but resembles the suc-
cessive steps in a planned and orderly process of development. I have called this unconscious process spontaneously
expressing itself in the symbolism of a long dream-series the
individuation process.   52: 550

So long as I help the patient to discover the effective elements in his dreams, and so long as I try to get him to see

the general meaning of his symbols, he is still, psychologically speaking, in a state of childhood. For the time being he is dependent on his dreams and is always asking himself whether the next dream will give him new light or not. Moreover, he is dependent on my having ideas about his dreams and on my ability to increase his insight through my knowledge. Thus he is still in an undesirably passive condition where everything is rather uncertain and questionable; neither he nor I know the journey's end. Often it is not much more than a groping about in Egyptian darkness. In this condition we must not expect any very startling results—the uncertainty is too great for that. Besides which there is always the risk that what we have woven by day the night will unravel. The danger is that nothing is achieved, that nothing remains fixed.   2:101

I have no theory about dreams, I do not know how dreams arise. And I am not at all sure that my way of handling dreams even deserves the name of a "method." I share all your prejudices against dream-interpretation as the quintessence of uncertainty and arbitrariness. On the other hand, I know that if we meditate on a dream sufficiently long and thoroughly, if we carry it around with us and turn it over and over, something almost always comes of it. This something is not of course a scientific result to be boasted about or rationalized; but it is an important practical hint which shows the patient what the unconscious is aiming at. Indeed, it ought not to matter to me whether the result of my musings on the dream is scientifically verifiable or tenable, otherwise I am pursuing an ulterior—and therefore autoerotic—aim. I must content myself wholly with the fact that the result means something to the patient and sets his life in motion again. I may allow myself only one criterion for the result of my labours: does it work? As for my scientific hobby—my desire to know *why* it works—this I must reserve for my spare time.   2:86

When we consider the infinite variety of dreams, it is difficult to conceive that there could ever be a method or a technical procedure which would lead to an infallible result. It is, indeed, a good thing that no valid method exists, for otherwise the meaning of the dream would be limited in advance and would lose precisely that virtue which makes dreams so valuable for therapeutic purposes —their ability to offer new points of view.   45:319

The use of dream-analysis in psychotherapy is still a much debated question. Many practitioners find it indispensable in the treatment of neuroses, and consider that the dream is a function whose psychic importance is equal to that of the conscious mind itself. Others, on the contrary, dispute the value of dream-analysis and regard dreams as a negligible by-product of the psyche. Obviously, if a person holds the view that the unconscious plays a decisive part in the aetiology of neuroses, he will attribute a high practical importance to dreams as direct expressions of the unconscious. Equally obviously, if he denies the unconscious or at least thinks it aetiologically insignificant, he will minimize the importance of dream-analysis.   61:294

The evolutionary stratification of the psyche is more clearly discernible in the dream than in the conscious mind. In the dream, the psyche speaks in images, and gives expression to instincts, which derive from the most primitive levels of nature. Therefore, through the assimilation of unconscious contents, the momentary life of consciousness can once more be brought into harmony with the law of nature from which it all too easily departs, and the patient can be led back to the natural law of his own being.
    61:351

The interpretation of dreams enriches consciousness to such an extent that it relearns the forgotten language of the instincts.   8:52*

Many people who know something, but not enough, about dreams and their meaning, and who are impressed by their subtle and apparently intentional compensation, are liable to succumb to the prejudice that the dream actually has a moral purpose, that it warns, rebukes, comforts, foretells the future, etc. If one believes that the unconscious always knows best, one can easily be betrayed into leaving the dreams to take the necessary decisions, and is then disappointed when the dreams become more and more trivial and meaningless. Experience has shown me that a slight knowledge of dream psychology is apt to lead to an overrating of the unconscious which impairs the power of conscious decision. The unconscious functions satisfactorily only when the conscious mind fulfils its tasks to the very limit. A dream may perhaps supply what is then lacking, or it may help us forward where our best conscious efforts have failed.   52:568

In each of us there is another whom we do not know. He speaks to us in dreams and tells us how differently he sees us from the way we see ourselves. When, therefore, we find ourselves in a difficult situation to which there is no solution, he can sometimes kindle a light that radically alters our attitude—the very attitude that led us into the difficult situation.   45:325

Together the patient and I address ourselves to the 2,000,000-year-old man that is in all of us. In the last analysis, most of our difficulties come from losing contact with our instincts, with the age-old unforgotten wisdom stored up in us. And where do we make contact with this old man in us? In our dreams.   39H*

To concern ourselves with dreams is a way of reflecting on ourselves—a way of self-reflection. It is not our ego-consciousness reflecting on itself; rather, it turns its attention to the objective actuality of the dream as a communication or message from the unconscious, unitary soul of humanity. It reflects not on the ego but on the self; it recollects that strange self, alien to the ego, which was ours from the beginning, the trunk from which the ego grew. It is alien to us because we have estranged ourselves from it through the aberrations of the conscious mind.   45:318

A dream is nothing but a lucky idea that comes to us from the dark, all-unifying world of the psyche. What would be more natural, when we have lost ourselves amid the endless particulars and isolated details of the world's surface, than to knock at the door of dreams and inquire of them the bearings which would bring us closer to the basic facts of human existence? Here we encounter the obstinate prejudice that dreams are so much froth, they are not real, they lie, they are mere wish-fulfilments. All this is but an excuse not to take dreams seriously, for that would be uncomfortable. Our intellectual hybris of consciousness loves isolation despite all its inconveniences, and for this reason people will do anything rather than admit that dreams are real and speak the truth. There are some saints who had very rude dreams. Where would their saintliness be, the very thing that exalts them above the vulgar rabble, if the obscenity of a dream were a real truth? But it is just the most squalid dreams that emphasize our blood-kinship with the rest of mankind, and most effectively damp down the arrogance born of an atrophy of the instincts. Even if the whole world were to fall to pieces, the unity of the psyche would never be shattered. And the wider and more numerous the fissures on the surface, the more this unity is strengthened in the depths.   45:305*f*

MAN IN HIS RELATION TO OTHERS

Doctor and Patient

Anyone who wants to know the human psyche will learn next to nothing from experimental psychology. He would be better advised to put away his scholar's gown, bid farewell to his study, and wander with human heart through the world. There, in the horrors of prisons, lunatic asylums and hospitals, in drab suburban pubs, in brothels and gambling-hells, in the salons of the elegant, the Stock Exchanges, Socialist meetings, churches, revivalist gatherings and ecstatic sects, through love and hate, through the experience of passion in every form in his own body, he would reap richer stores of knowledge than text-books a foot thick could give him, and he will know how to doctor the sick with real knowledge of the human soul.

104C: 409

It is enough to drive one to despair that in practical psychology there are no universally valid recipes and rules. There are only individual cases with the most heterogeneous needs and demands—so heterogeneous that we can virtually never know in advance what course a given case will take, for which reason it is better for the doctor to abandon all preconceived opinions. This does not mean that he should throw them overboard, but that in any given case he should use them merely as hypotheses for a possible explanation.

63: 163

Experience has taught me to keep away from therapeutic "methods" as much as from diagnoses. The enormous variation among individuals and their neuroses has set before me the ideal of approaching each case with a minimum of prior assumptions. The ideal would naturally be to have no assumptions at all. But this is impossible even if one exercises the most rigorous self-criticism, for one is *oneself* the biggest of all one's assumptions, and the one with the gravest consequences. Try as we may to have no assumptions and to use no ready-made methods, the assumption that I myself am will determine my method: as I am, so will I proceed.   82:543

An ancient adept has said: "If the wrong man uses the right means, the right means work in the wrong way." This Chinese saying, unfortunately only too true, stands in sharp contrast to our belief in the "right" method irrespective of the man who applies it. In reality, everything depends on the man and little or nothing on the method.

112:4

Nobody should play with analysis as with an easy tool. Those who write superficial and cheap books about the subject are either unconscious of the far-reaching effects of analytical treatment or else ignorant of the real nature of the human soul.   4A:343*

If we have to deal with the human soul we can only meet it on its own ground, and we are bound to do so whenever we are confronted with the real and crushing problems of life.   109:81

We would do well to abandon from the start any attempt to apply ready-made solutions and warmed-up generalities of which the patient knows just as much as the doctor. Long experience has taught me not to know anything in advance and not to know better, but to let the unconscious take precedence. Our instincts have ridden so infinitely many times, unharmed, over the problems that arise [in later] life that we may be sure the transformation processes which make the transition possible have long been prepared in the unconscious and are only waiting to be released.   97:528

The remarkable potency of unconscious contents always indicates a corresponding weakness in the conscious mind and its functions. It is as though the latter were threatened with impotence. For primitive man this danger is one of the most terrifying instances of "magic." So we can understand why this secret fear is also to be found among civilized people. In serious cases it is the secret fear of going mad; in less serious, the fear of the unconscious—a fear which even the normal person exhibits in his resistance to psychological views and explanations. This resistance borders on the grotesque when it comes to scouting all psychological explanations of art, philosophy, and religion, as though the human psyche had, or should have, absolutely nothing to do with these things. The doctor knows these well-defended zones from his consulting hours: they are reminiscent of island fortresses from which the neurotic tries to ward off the octopus. ("Happy neurosis island," as one of my patients called his conscious state!) The doctor is well aware that the patient needs an island and would be lost without it. It serves as a refuge for his consciousness and as the last stronghold against the threatening embrace of the unconscious. The same is true of the normal person's taboo regions which psychology must not touch. But since no war was ever won on the defensive, one must, in order to terminate hostilities, open negotiations with the enemy and see what his terms really are. Such is the intention of the doctor who volunteers to act as a mediator. He is far from wishing to disturb the somewhat precarious island idyll or pull down the fortifications. On the contrary, he is thankful that somewhere a firm foothold exists that does not first have to be fished up out of the chaos, always a desperately difficult task. He knows that the island is a bit cramped and that life on it is pretty meagre and plagued with all sorts of imaginary wants because too much life has been left outside, and that as a result a terrifying monster is created, or rather is roused out of its slumbers. He also knows that this seemingly alarming animal stands in a secret compensatory relationship to the island and could supply everything that the island lacks. 77:374

Practical medicine is and has always been an art, and the same is true of practical analysis. True art is creation, and creation is beyond all theories. That is why I say to any beginner: Learn your theories as well as you can, but put them aside when you touch the miracle of the living soul. Not theories but your own creative individuality alone must decide. 4A:361*

The patient is there to be treated and not to verify a theory. For that matter, there is no single theory in the whole field of practical psychology that cannot on occasion be proved to be basically wrong. In particular, the view that the patient's resistances are in no circumstances justified is completely fallacious. The resistance might very well prove that the treatment rests on false assumptions. 29:237

One has to remind oneself again and again that in therapy it is more important for the patient to understand than for the analyst's theoretical expectations to be satisfied. The patient's resistance to the analyst is not necessarily wrong; it is rather a sign that something does not "click." Either the patient is not yet at a point where he would be able to understand, or the interpretation does not fit. 8:61*

Neither our modern medical training nor academic psychology and philosophy can equip the doctor with the necessary education, or with the means, to deal effectively and understandingly with the often very urgent demands of his psychotherapeutic practice. It therefore behoves us, unembarrassed by our shortcomings as amateurs of history, to go to school once more with the medical philosophers of a distant past, when body and soul had not yet been wrenched asunder into different faculties. Although we are specialists par excellence, our specialized field, oddly enough, drives us to universalism and to the complete overcoming of the specialist attitude, if the totality of body and soul is not to be just a matter of words.   79 : 190

Even the so-called highly scientific suggestion therapy employs the wares of the medicine-man and the exorcising shaman. And why not? The public is not much more advanced either and continues to expect miraculous cures from the doctor. And indeed, we must rate those doctors wise— worldly-wise in every sense—who know how to surround themselves with the aura of a medicine-man. They have not only the biggest practices but also get the best results. This is because, apart from the neuroses, countless physical illnesses are tainted and complicated with psychic material to an unsuspected degree. The medical exorcist betrays by his whole demeanour his full appreciation of that psychic component when he gives the patient the opportunity of fixing his faith firmly on the mysterious personality of the doctor. In this way he wins the sick man's mind, which from then on helps him to restore his body to health. The cure works best when the doctor himself believes in his own formulae, otherwise he may be overcome by scientific doubt and so lose the proper convincing tone.   89 : 578

As a doctor it is my task to help the patient to cope with life. I cannot presume to pass judgment on his final decisions, because I know from experience that all coercion—be it suggestion, insinuation, or any other method of persuasion—ultimately proves to be nothing but an obstacle to the highest and most decisive experience of all, which is to be alone with his own self, or whatever else one chooses to call the objectivity of the psyche. The patient must be alone if he is to find out what it is that supports him when he can no longer support himself. Only this experience can give him an indestructible foundation.   72:32

✧

Natural science is not a science of words and ideas, but of facts. I am no terminological rigorist—call the existing symbols "wholeness," "self," "consciousness," "higher ego," or what you will—it makes little difference. I for my part only try not to give any false or misleading names. All these terms are simply names for the facts that alone carry weight. The names I give do not imply a philosophy, although I cannot prevent people from barking at these terminological phantoms as if they were metaphysical hypostases.   77:537

It is amazing how people get caught in words. They imagine that the name postulates the thing—just as if we were doing the devil a serious wrong when we call him a neurosis!   45:311

Neurosis is intimately bound up with the problem of our time and really represents an unsuccessful attempt on the part of the individual to solve the general problem in his own person. Neurosis is self-division.   104A:18

People whose own temperaments offer problems are often neurotic, but it would be a serious misunderstanding to confuse the existence of problems with neurosis. There is a marked difference between the two in that the neurotic is ill because he is unconscious of his problems, while the person with a difficult temperament suffers from his conscious problems without being ill.   94:763

The greatest mistake an analyst can make is to assume that his patient has a psychology similar to his own.

30:498

No psychotherapist should lack that natural reserve which prevents people from riding roughshod over mysteries they do not understand and trampling them flat. This reserve will enable him to pull back in good time when he encounters the mystery of the patient's difference from himself, and to avoid the danger—unfortunately only too real—of committing psychic murder in the name of therapy. For the ultimate cause of a neurosis is something *positive* which needs to be safeguarded for the patient; otherwise he suffers a psychic loss, and the result of the treatment is at best a defective cure. 82:564

Medicine in the hand of a fool was ever poison and death. Just as we demand from a surgeon, besides his technical knowledge, a skilled hand, courage, presence of mind, and power of decision, so we must expect from an analyst a very serious and thorough psychoanalytic training of his own personality before we are willing to entrust a patient to him. I would even go so far as to say that the acquisition and practice of the psychoanalytic technique presuppose not only a specific psychological gift but in the very first place a serious concern with the moulding of one's own character. 101:450

Each new case that requires thorough treatment is pioneer work, and every trace of routine then proves to be a blind alley. Consequently the higher psychotherapy is a most exacting business, and sometimes it sets tasks which challenge not only our understanding or our sympathy but the whole man. The doctor is inclined to demand this total effort from his patients, yet he must realize that this same demand only works if he is aware that it also applies to himself. 77:367

There are analysts who believe that they can get along with a self-analysis. This is Munchausen psychology, and

they will certainly remain stuck. They forget that one of
the most important therapeutically effective factors is subjecting yourself to the objective judgment of another. As
regards ourselves we remain blind, despite everything and
everybody.   101:449

The object of therapy is not the neurosis but the man who
has the neurosis. We have long known, for instance, that a
cardiac neurosis comes not from the heart, as the old medical mythology would have it, but from the mind of the suf-
ferer. Nor does it come from some obscure corner of the
unconscious, as many psychotherapists still struggle to believe; it comes from the totality of a man's life and from all
the experiences that have accumulated over the years and
decades, and finally, not merely from his life as an individual but from his psychic experience within the family or
even the social group.   95:337

The personality of the patient demands all the resources
of the doctor's personality and not technical tricks.

                                                    95:338

When, as a psychotherapist, I set myself up as a medical
authority over my patient and on that account claim to
know something about his individuality, or to be able to
make valid statements about it, I am only demonstrating
my lack of criticism, for I am in no position to judge the
whole of the personality before me. I cannot say anything
valid about him except in so far as he approximates to the
"universal man." But since all life is to be found only in
individual form, and I myself can assert of another individuality only what I find in my own, I am in constant danger
either of doing violence to the other person or of succumbing to his influence. If I wish to treat another individual

psychologically at all, I must for better or worse give up all pretensions to superior knowledge, all authority and desire to influence. 62:2

An analyst who cannot risk his authority will be sure to lose it. 27:xiii*

Psychotherapy is at bottom a dialectical relationship between doctor and patient. It is an encounter, a discussion between two psychic wholes, in which knowledge is used only as a tool. The goal is transformation—not one that is predetermined, but rather an indeterminable change, the only criterion of which is the disappearance of egohood. No efforts on the part of the doctor can compel this experience. The most he can do is to smooth the path for the patient and help him to attain an attitude which offers the least resistance to the decisive experience. 98:904

Most people need someone to confess to, otherwise the basis of experience is not sufficiently real. They do not "hear" themselves, cannot contrast themselves with something different, and so they have no outside "control." Everything flows inwards and is answered only by oneself, not by another. It makes an enormous difference whether I confess my guilt only to myself or to another person.
20:17*

A general and merely academic "insight into one's mistakes" is ineffectual, for then the mistakes are not really seen at all, only the idea of them. They show up acutely when a human relationship brings them to the fore and when they are noticed by the other person as well as by oneself. Then and then only can they really be felt and their true nature recognized. 77:503

Nobody can meddle with fire or poison without being affected in some vulnerable spot; for the true physician does not stand outside his work but is always in the thick of it.

72:5

An analyst can help his patient just so far as he himself has gone and not a step further. In my practice I have had from the beginning to deal with patients who got "stuck" with their previous analysis, and this always happened at the point where the analyst could make no further progress with himself.

82:545

If the doctor wants to guide another, or even accompany him a step of the way, he must *feel* with that person's psyche. He never feels it when he passes judgment. Whether he puts his judgments into words, or keeps them to himself, makes not the slightest difference.

78:519

Unfortunately far too many of us talk about a man only as it would be desirable for him to be, never about the man as he really is. But the doctor has always to do with the real man, who remains obstinately himself until all sides of his reality are recognized. True education can only start from naked reality, not from a delusive ideal.

104A:93

We cannot change anything unless we accept it. Condemnation does not liberate, it oppresses. I am the oppressor of the person I condemn, not his friend and fellow-sufferer. I do not in the least mean to say that we must never pass judgment when we desire to help and improve. But if the doctor wishes to help a human being he must be able to accept him as he is. And he can do this in reality only when he has already seen and accepted himself as he is.

78:519

So long as you feel the human contact, the atmosphere of mutual confidence, there is no danger; and even if you have to face the terrors of insanity, or the shadowy menace of suicide, there is still that area of human faith, that certainty of understanding and of being understood, no matter how black the night. 4:181

When a patient begins to feel the inescapable nature of his inner development, he may easily be overcome by a panic fear that he is slipping helplessly into some kind of madness he can no longer understand. More than once I have had to reach for a book on my shelves, bring down an old alchemist, and show my patient his terrifying fantasy in the form in which it appeared four hundred years ago. This has a calming effect, because the patient then sees that he is not alone in a strange world which nobody understands, but is part of the great stream of human history, which has experienced countless times the very things that he regards as a pathological proof of his craziness. 60:325

The little word "ought" always proves the helplessness of the therapist; it is an admission that he has come to the end of his resources. 79:178

We can wax indignant over man's notorious lack of spirituality, but when one is a doctor one does not invariably think that the disease is malevolent or the patient morally inferior; instead, one supposes that the negative results may possibly be due to the remedy applied. 77:393

The doctor cannot afford to point, with a gesture of facile moral superiority, to the tablets of the law and say, "Thou shalt not." He has to examine things objectively and weigh up possibilities, for he knows, less from religious training and education than from instinct and experience,

that there is something very like a *felix culpa*. He knows
that one can miss not only one's happiness but also one's
final guilt, without which a man will never reach his wholeness. Wholeness is in fact a charisma which one can manufacture neither by art nor by cunning; one can only grow
into it and endure whatever its advent may bring.   72:36

Modern man has heard enough about guilt and sin. He
is sorely enough beset by his own bad conscience, and
wants rather to know how he is to reconcile himself with
his own nature—how he is to love the enemy in his own
heart and call the wolf his brother.   78:523

It is presumptuous to think we can always say what is
good or bad for the patient. Perhaps he knows something
is really bad and does it anyway and then gets a bad conscience. From the therapeutic, that is to say empirical, point
of view, this may be very good indeed for him. Perhaps he
has to experience the power of evil and suffer accordingly,
because only in that way can he give up his Pharisaic attitude to other people. Perhaps fate or the unconscious or God
—call it what you will—had to give him a hard knock and
roll him in the dirt, because only such a drastic experience
could strike home, pull him out of his infantilism, and
make him more mature. How can anyone find out how
much he needs to be saved if he is quite sure that there is
nothing he needs saving from?   32:867

There is hope of repairing a breakdown whenever a
patient has neurotic symptoms. They indicate that he is
not at one with himself, and the neurotic symptoms usually diagnose what is wrong. Those who have no neurotic
symptoms are probably beyond help by anyone.   39H*

There is no admonition to repentance unless the patient

does it himself, no penance unless—as is almost the rule—he has got himself in a thorough mess, and no absolution unless God has mercy on him. 20:17*

A conscientious doctor must be able to doubt all his skills and all his theories, otherwise he is befooled by a system. But all systems mean bigotry and inhumanity. Neurosis —let there be no doubt about this—may be any number of things, but never a "nothing but." It is the agony of a human soul in all its vast complexity—so vast, indeed, that any and every theory of neurosis is little better than a worthless sketch, unless it be a gigantic picture of the psyche which not even a hundred Fausts could conceive. 95:357

The neurotic is ill not because he has lost his old faith but because he has not yet found a new form for his finest aspirations. 89:669

We cannot demand of our patients a faith which they reject because they do not understand it, or which does not suit them even though we may hold it ourselves. We have to rely on the curative powers inherent in the patient's own nature, regardless of whether the ideas that emerge agree with any known creed or philosophy. 83:664*

There is no illness that is not at the same time an unsuccessful attempt at a cure. Instead of showing up the patient as the secret accomplice of morally inadmissible wishes, one can just as well explain him as the unwitting victim of instinctual problems which he doesn't understand and which nobody in his environment has helped him solve. His dreams, in particular, can be taken as nature's own auguries, having nothing whatever to do with the all-too-human self-deluding operations which Freud insinuates into the dream-process. 37:68

The patient has not to learn how to get rid of his neurosis, but how to bear it. His illness is not a gratuitous and therefore meaningless burden; it is *his own self*, the "other" whom, from childish laziness or fear, or for some other reason, he was always seeking to exclude from his life. In this way, as Freud rightly says, we turn the ego into a "seat of anxiety," which it would never be if we did not defend ourselves against ourselves so neurotically.   95 : 360

When the ego has been made a "seat of anxiety," someone is running away from himself and will not admit it.

95 : 360

In psychology it is very important that the doctor should not strive to heal at all costs. One has to be exceedingly careful not to impose one's own will and conviction on the patient. You have to give him a certain amount of freedom. You can't wrest people away from their fate, just as in medicine you cannot cure a patient if nature means him to die. Sometimes it is really a question whether you are allowed to rescue a man from the fate he must undergo for the sake of his further development.   6 : 147*

We would be doing our neurotic patients a grievous wrong if we tried to force them all into the category of the coerced. Among neurotics, there are not a few who do not require any reminders of their social duties and obligations, but are born and destined rather to be bearers of new cultural ideals. They are neurotic as long as they bow down before authority and refuse the freedom to which they are destined. As long as we look at life only retrospectively, as is the case in the psychoanalytic writings of the Viennese school, we shall never do justice to these persons and never bring them the longed-for deliverance. For in this way we train them only to be obedient children and thereby

strengthen the very forces that made them ill—their conservative backwardness and submission to authority.

89:658

The small world of the child, the family milieu, is the
model for the big world. The more intensely the family sets
its stamp on the child, the more he will be emotionally
inclined, as an adult, to see in the great world his former
small world. Of course this must not be taken as a conscious
intellectual process. On the contrary, the patient feels and
sees the difference between now and then, and tries as well
as he can to adapt himself. Perhaps he will even believe
himself perfectly adapted, since he may be able to grasp
the situation intellectually, but that does not prevent his
emotions from lagging far behind his intellectual insight.

101:312

The childhood experience of a neurotic is not, in itself,
negative; far from it. It becomes negative only when it
finds no suitable place in the life and outlook of the adult.
The real task of analysis, it seems to me, is to bring about
a synthesis between the two.   82:564

Hidden in the neurosis is a bit of still undeveloped personality, a precious fragment of the psyche lacking which
a man is condemned to resignation, bitterness, and everything else that is hostile to life. A psychology of neurosis
that sees only the negative elements empties out the baby
with the bath-water, since it neglects the positive meaning
and value of these "infantile"—i.e., creative—fantasies.

95:355

Infantilism, however, is something extremely ambiguous.
First, it can be either genuine or purely symptomatic; and
second, it can be either residuary or embryonic. There is an
enormous difference between something that has *remained*

infantile and something that is in the process of growth. Both can take an infantile or embryonic form, and more often than not it is impossible to tell at first glance whether we are dealing with a regrettably persistent fragment of infantile life or with a vitally important creative beginning. To deride these possibilities is to act like a dullard who does not know that the future is more important than the past.   95:345

A neurosis is by no means merely a negative thing, it is also something positive. Only a soulless rationalism reinforced by a narrow materialistic outlook could possibly have overlooked this fact. In reality the neurosis contains the patient's psyche, or at least an essential part of it; and if, as the rationalist pretends, the neurosis could be plucked from him like a bad tooth, he would have gained nothing but would have lost something very essential to him. That is to say, he would have lost as much as the thinker deprived of his doubt, or the moralist deprived of his temptation, or the brave man deprived of his fear. To lose a neurosis is to find oneself without an object; life loses its point and hence its meaning. This would not be a cure, it would be a regular amputation.   95:355

✧

What are religions? Religions are psychotherapeutic systems. What are we doing, we psychotherapists? We are trying to heal the suffering of the human mind, of the human psyche or the human soul, and religions deal with the same problem. Therefore our Lord himself is a healer; he is a doctor; he heals the sick and he deals with the troubles of the soul; and that is exactly what we call psychotherapy.   6:181*

The thing that cures a neurosis must be as convincing as the neurosis, and since the latter is only too real, the helpful experience must be equally real. It must be a very real illusion, if you want to put it pessimistically. But what is the difference between a real illusion and a healing religious experience? It is merely a difference of words.   74:167

Healing comes only from what leads the patient beyond himself and beyond his entanglements in the ego.   60:397

A neurosis is truly removed only when it has removed the false attitude of the ego. We do not cure it—it cures us. A man is ill, but the illness is nature's attempt to heal him, and what the neurotic flings away as absolutely worthless contains the true gold we should never have found elsewhere.   95:361

The labours of the doctor as well as the quest of the patient are directed towards that hidden and as yet unmanifest "whole" man, who is at once the greater and the future man. But the right way to wholeness is made up, unfortunately, of fateful detours and wrong turnings. It is a *longissima via*, not straight but snakelike, a path that unites the opposites in the manner of the guiding caduceus, a path whose labyrinthine twists and turns are not lacking in terrors. It is on this *longissima via* that we meet with those experiences which are said to be "inaccessible." Their inaccessibility really consists in the fact that they cost us an enormous amount of effort: they demand the very thing we most fear, namely the "wholeness" which we talk about so glibly and which lends itself to endless theorizing, though in actual life we give it the widest possible berth. It is infinitely more popular to go in for "compartment psychology," where the left-hand pigeon-hole does not know what is in the right.   72:6

If the goal of wholeness and of realizing the personality originally intended for him should grow naturally in the patient, we may sympathetically assist him towards it. But if it does not grow of itself, it cannot be implanted without remaining a permanent foreign body. Therefore we renounce such artifices when nature herself is clearly not working to this end. As a medical art, equipped only with human tools, our psychology does not presume to preach the way to salvation, for that does not lie within its power.   20: 18*

What the physician does is not *his* work [says Paracelsus]: he is "the means by which nature is put to work. . . . Let him not say with desperate Satan: it is impossible." He should put his trust in God.   57: 42

The doctor has to cope with actual suffering for better or worse, and ultimately has nothing to rely on except the mystery of divine Providence.   51: 693*

Man and Woman

Where love reigns, there is no will to power; and where the will to power is paramount, love is lacking. The one is but the shadow of the other.   104A:78

It is hard to believe that this teeming world is too poor to provide an object for human love—it offers boundless opportunities to everyone. It is rather the inability to love which robs a person of these opportunities. The world is empty only to him who does not know how to direct his libido towards things and people, and to render them alive and beautiful. What compels us to create a substitute from within ourselves is not an external lack, but our own inability to include anything outside ourselves in our love. Certainly the difficulties and adversities of the struggle for existence may oppress us, yet even the worst conditions need not hinder love; on the contrary, they often spur us on to greater efforts.   100:253

Unfortunately, it is almost a collective ideal for men and women to be as unconscious as possible in the ticklish affairs of love. But behind the mask of respectability and faithfulness the full fury of neglected love falls upon the children. You cannot blame the ordinary individual, as you cannot expect people to know the attitude they ought to adopt and how they are to solve their love problems within the framework of present-day ideals and conventions. Mostly they know only the negative measures of negligence, procrastination, suppression, and repression.   4:218

The more remote and unreal the personal mother is, the more deeply will the son's yearning for her clutch at his soul, awakening that primordial and eternal image of the mother for whose sake everything that embraces, protects,

nourishes, and helps assumes maternal form, from the
Alma Mater of the university to the personification of
cities, countries, sciences, and ideals.   58:147

A mother-complex is not got rid of by blindly reducing
the mother to human proportions. Besides that we run the
risk of dissolving the experience "Mother" into atoms, thus
destroying something supremely valuable and throwing
away the golden key which a good fairy laid in our cradle.
That is why mankind has always instinctively added the
pre-existent divine pair to the personal parents—the "god"-
father and "god"-mother of the newborn child—so that,
from sheer unconsciousness or shortsighted rationalism, he
should never forget himself so far as to invest his own parents with divinity.   67:172

The overdevelopment of the maternal instinct is identical
with that well-known image of the mother which has been
glorified in all ages and all tongues. This is the mother-
love which is one of the most moving and unforgettable
memories of our lives, the mysterious root of all growth
and change; the love that means homecoming, shelter, and
the long silence from which everything begins and in which
everything ends. Intimately known and yet strange like
Nature, lovingly tender and yet cruel like fate, joyous and
untiring giver of life—*mater dolorosa* and mute implaca-
ble portal that closes upon the dead. Mother is mother-
love, *my* experience and *my* secret. Why risk saying too
much, too much that is false and inadequate and beside the
point, about that human being who was our mother, the
accidental carrier of that great experience which includes
herself and myself and all mankind, and indeed the whole
of created nature, the experience of life whose children we
are? The attempt to say these things has always been made,
and probably always will be; but a sensitive person cannot
in all fairness load that enormous burden of meaning, re-

sponsibility, duty, heaven and hell, on to the shoulders of
one frail and fallible human being—so deserving of love,
indulgence, understanding, and forgiveness—who was our
mother. He knows that the mother carries for us that inborn
image of the *mater natura* and *mater spiritualis,* of the totality of life of which we are a small and helpless part.

67:172

The fact that mothers bear children is not holy but
merely natural. If people say it is holy, then one strongly
suspects that something very unholy has to be covered up
by it. Freud has said out loud "what is behind it," only he
has unfortunately blackened the infant instead of the
mother. 88:50

In spite of all indignant protestations to the contrary, the
fact remains that love (using the word in the wider sense
which belongs to it by right and embraces more than sexuality), its problems and its conflicts, is of fundamental
importance in human life and, as careful inquiry consistently shows, is of far greater significance than the individual
suspects. 104A:14

The love problem is part of mankind's heavy toll of suffering, and nobody should be ashamed of having to pay his
tribute. 4:219

❖

It is difficult to gauge the spirit of one's own time; but,
if we observe the trend of art, of style, and of public taste,
and see what people read and write, what sort of societies
they found, what "questions" are the order of the day, what
the Philistines fight against, we shall find that in the long
catalogue of our present social questions by no means the
last is the so-called "sexual question." This is discussed by

men and women who challenge the existing sexual morality and who seek to throw off the burden of moral guilt which past centuries have heaped upon Eros. One cannot simply deny the existence of these endeavours nor condemn then as indefensible; they exist, and probably have adequate grounds for their existence. It is more interesting and more useful to examine carefully the underlying causes of these contemporary movements than to join in the lamentations of the professional mourners of morality who prophesy the moral downfall of humanity.   104C: 427

We must begin by overcoming our virtuousness, with the justifiable fear of falling into vice on the other side. This danger certainly exists, for the greatest virtuousness is always compensated inwardly by a strong tendency to vice, and how many vicious characters treasure inside themselves sugary virtues and a moral megalomania.

100A: 221*

While we are all agreed that murder, stealing, and ruthlessness of any kind are obviously inadmissible, there is nevertheless what we call a "sexual question." We hear nothing of a murder question or a rage question; social reform is never invoked against those who wreak their bad tempers on their fellow men. Yet these things are all examples of instinctual behaviour, and the necessity for their suppression seems to us self-evident. Only in regard to sex do we feel the need of a question mark. This points to a doubt —the doubt whether our existing moral concepts and the legal institutions founded on them are really adequate and suited to their purpose. No intelligent person will deny that in this field opinion is sharply divided. Indeed, there would be no problem at all if public opinion were united about it. It is obviously a reaction against a too rigorous morality. It is not simply an outbreak of primitive instinctuality; such outbreaks, as we know, have never yet bothered themselves with moral laws and moral problems. There are, rather, serious misgivings as to whether our existing moral views have dealt fairly with the nature of sex. From this doubt there naturally arises a legitimate interest in any attempt to understand the nature of sex more truly and deeply. 54:105

Nowadays we have no real sexual morality, only a legalistic attitude to sexuality; just as the Middle Ages had no real morality of money-making but only prejudices and a legalistic point of view. We are not yet far enough advanced to distinguish between moral and immoral behaviour in the realm of free sexual activity. This is clearly expressed in the customary treatment, or rather ill-treatment, of unmarried mothers. All the repulsive hypocrisy, the high tide of prostitution and of venereal diseases, we owe to the barbarous, wholesale legal condemnation of certain kinds of sexual behaviour, and to our inability to develop a finer moral sense for the enormous psychological differences that exist in the domain of free sexual activity. 89:666

It is a favourite neurotic misunderstanding that the right attitude to the world is found by indulgence in sex.

101:440

Our civilization enormously underestimates the importance of sexuality, but just because of the repressions imposed upon it, sexuality breaks through into every conceivable field where it does not belong, and uses such an indirect mode of expression that we may expect to meet it all of a sudden practically everywhere. Thus the very idea of an intimate understanding of the human psyche, which is actually a very pure and beautiful thing, becomes besmirched and perversely distorted by the intrusion of an indirect sexual meaning. A direct and spontaneous expression of sexuality is a natural occurrence and, as such, never ugly or repulsive. It is "moral" repression that makes sexuality on the one hand dirty and hypocritical, and on the other shameless and blatant. This secondary significance, or rather the misuse which the repressed and suborned sexuality makes of the highest psychic functions, gives certain of our opponents an opportunity to sniff out the prurient eroticism of the confessional in psychoanalysis.   100A: 295*

It is undoubtedly true that instinctuality conflicts with our moral views most frequently and most conspicuously in the realm of sex. The conflict between infantile instinctuality and ethics can never be avoided. It is, it seems to me, the *sine qua non* of psychic energy.   54: 105

The conflict between ethics and sex today is not just a collision between instinctuality and morality, but a struggle to give an instinct its rightful place in our lives, and to recognize in this instinct a power which seeks expression and evidently may not be trifled with, and therefore cannot be made to fit in with our well-meaning moral laws. Sexuality is not mere instinctuality; it is an indisputably creative power that is not only the basic cause of our individual lives, but a very serious factor in our psychic life as well. Today we know only too well the grave consequences that sexual disturbances can bring in their train.

54: 107

Anyone who overlooks the instincts will be ambuscaded by them.   97: 620

Eros is a superhuman power which, like nature herself, allows itself to be conquered and exploited as though it were impotent. But triumph over nature is dearly paid for. Nature requires no explanations of principle, but asks only for tolerance and wise measure. "Eros is a mighty daemon," as the wise Diotima said to Socrates. We shall never get the better of him, or only to our own hurt. He is not the whole of our inward nature, though he is at least one of its essential aspects.   104A: 32*f*

Eros is a questionable fellow and will always remain so, whatever the legislation of the future may have to say about it. He belongs on one side to man's primordial animal nature which will endure as long as man has an animal body. On the other side he is related to the highest forms of the spirit. But he only thrives when spirit and instinct are in right harmony. If one or the other aspect is lacking to him, the result is injury or at least a lopsidedness that may easily veer towards the pathological. Too much of the animal distorts the civilized man, too much civilization makes sick animals.   104A: 32

Normal sex life, as a shared experience with apparently similar aims, further strengthens the feeling of unity and identity. This state is described as one of complete harmony, and is extolled as a great happiness ("one heart and one soul")—not without good reason, since the return to that original condition of unconscious oneness is like a return to childhood. Hence the childish gestures of all lovers. Even more is it a return to the mother's womb, into the teeming depths of an as yet unconscious creativity. It is, in truth, a genuine and incontestable experience of the Divine, whose transcendent force obliterates and consumes everything individual; a real communion with life and the impersonal power of fate.   44: 330

❖

So far as we know, consciousness is always ego-consciousness. In order to be conscious of myself, I must be able to distinguish myself from others. Relationship can only take place where this distinction exists.   44: 326

Although man and woman unite they nevertheless represent irreconcilable opposites which, when activated, degenerate into deadly hostility. This primordial pair of opposites symbolizes every conceivable pair of opposites that may occur; hot and cold, light and dark, north and south, dry and damp, good and bad, conscious and unconscious.

72:192

For two personalities to meet is like mixing two chemical substances: if there is any combination at all, both are transformed.   63:163

[All that pertains to the opposite sex] has a mysterious charm tinged with fear, perhaps even with disgust. For this reason its charm is particularly attractive and fascinating, even when it comes to us not directly from outside, in the guise of a woman, but from within, as a psychic influence—for instance in the form of a temptation to abandon oneself to a mood or an affect.   114:244

It must be admitted that a fit of rage or a sulk has its secret attractions. Were that not so, most people would long since have acquired a little wisdom.   7:619

The young person of marriageable age does, of course, possess an ego-consciousness (girls more than men, as a rule), but, since he has only recently emerged from the mists of original unconsciousness, he is certain to have wide areas which still lie in the shadow and which preclude to that extent the formation of psychological relationship. This means, in practice, that the young man (or woman) can have only an incomplete understanding of himself and others, and is therefore imperfectly informed as to his, and their, motives. As a rule the motives he acts from are largely unconscious. Subjectively, of course, he thinks himself very conscious and knowing, for we constantly overestimate the existing content of consciousness, and it is a great and surprising discovery when we find that what we had supposed to be the final peak is nothing but the first step in a very long climb.   44:327

Why is it that we are especially interested in psychology just now? The answer is that everyone is in desperate need of it. Humanity seems to have reached a point where the concepts of the past are no longer adequate, and we begin to realize that our nearest and dearest are actually strangers to us, whose language we no longer understand. It is beginning to dawn on us that the people living on the other side of the mountain are not made up exclusively of red-headed devils who are responsible for all the evil on this side of the mountain. A little of this uneasy suspicion has filtered through into the relations between the sexes; not everyone is utterly convinced that everything good is in "me" and everything evil in "you." Already we can find super-moderns who ask themselves in all seriousness whether there may not be something wrong with us, whether perhaps we are too unconscious, too antiquated, and whether this may not be the reason why when confronted with difficulties in sexual relationships we still continue to employ with disastrous results the methods of the Middle Ages if not those of the caveman.   33:xi*

Since [in the Middle Ages] the psychic relation to woman was expressed in the collective worship of Mary, the image of woman lost a value to which human beings had a natural right. This value could find its natural expression only through individual choice, and it sank into the unconscious when the individual form of expression was replaced by a collective one. In the unconscious the image of woman received an energy charge that activated the archaic and infantile dominants. And since all unconscious contents, when activated by dissociated libido, are projected upon the external object, the devaluation of the real woman was compensated by daemonic features. She no longer appeared as an object of love, but as a persecutor or witch. The consequence of increasing Mariolatry was the witch hunt, that indelible blot on the later Middle Ages.   69: 399

Although we are still far from having overcome our primitive mentality, which enjoys its most signal triumphs just in the sphere of sex where man is made most vividly aware of his mammalian nature, certain ethical refinements have nevertheless crept in which permit anyone with ten to fifteen centuries of Christian education behind him to progress towards a slightly higher level. On this level the spirit—from the biological point of view an incomprehensible psychic phenomenon—plays a not unimportant role psychologically. It had a weighty word to say on the subject of Christian marriage and it still participates vigorously in the discussion whenever marriage is doubted and depreciated. It appears in a negative capacity as counsel for the instincts, and in a positive one as the defender of human dignity. Small wonder, then, that a wild and confusing conflict breaks out between man as an instinctual creature of nature and man as a spiritual and cultural being. The worst thing about it is that the one is forever trying violently to suppress the other in order to bring about a so-called harmonious solution of the conflict. Unfortunately, too many people still believe in this procedure, which is all-powerful in politics; there are only a few here and there who condemn it as barbaric and would like to set up in its place a just compromise whereby each side of man's nature is given a hearing.   33: xii *f**

What can a man say about woman, his own opposite? I mean of course something sensible, that is outside the sexual programme, free of resentment, illusion, and theory. Where is the man to be found capable of such superiority?

Woman always stands just where the man's shadow falls, so that he is only too liable to confuse the two. Then, when he tries to repair this misunderstanding, he overvalues her and believes her the most desirable thing in the world.

114:236

Generally the proximity as well as the absence of women has a specifically constellating effect on the unconscious of a man. When a woman is absent or unattainable the unconscious produces in him a certain femininity which expresses itself in a variety of ways and gives rise to numerous conflicts. The more one-sided his conscious, masculine, spiritual attitude the more inferior, banal, vulgar, and biological will be the compensating femininity of the unconscious. He will, perhaps, not be conscious at all of its dark manifestations, because they have been so overlaid with saccharine sentimentality that he not only believes the humbug himself but enjoys putting it over on other people. An avowedly biological or coarse-minded attitude to women produces an excessively lofty valuation of femininity in the unconscious, where it is pleased to take the form of Sophia or of the Virgin.

48:221

The elementary fact that a person always thinks another's psychology is identical with his own effectively prevents a correct understanding of feminine psychology.   114:240

Psychology guarantees real knowledge of the other sex instead of arbitrary opinions, which are the source of the uncurable misunderstandings now undermining in increasing numbers the marriages of our time.   33:xiii*

❖

The discussion of the sexual problem is only a somewhat crude prelude to a far deeper question, and that is the question of the psychological relationship between the sexes. In comparison with this the other pales into insignificance, and with it we enter the real domain of woman. Woman's psychology is founded on the principle of Eros, the great binder and loosener, whereas from ancient times the ruling principle ascribed to man is Logos.   114:254f

Whereas logic and objectivity are usually the predominant features of a man's outer attitude, or are at least regarded as ideals, in the case of a woman it is feeling. But in the soul it is the other way round: inwardly it is the man who feels, and the woman who reflects. Hence a man's greater liability to total despair, while a woman can always find comfort and hope; accordingly a man is more likely to put an end to himself than a woman. However much a victim of social circumstances a woman may be, as a prostitute for instance, a man is no less a victim of impulses from the unconscious, taking the form of alcoholism and other vices.   69:805

Women are increasingly aware that love alone can give them full stature, just as men are beginning to divine that only the spirit can give life its highest meaning. Both seek a psychic relationship, because love needs the spirit, and the spirit love, for its completion.   114:269

The love of woman is not sentiment, as is a man's, but a will that is at times terrifyingly unsentimental and can even force her to self-sacrifice. A man who is loved in this way cannot escape his inferior side, for he can only respond to the reality of her love with his own reality.   114:261

As long as a woman is content to be a *femme à homme,* she has no feminine individuality. She is empty and merely glitters—a welcome vessel for masculine projections. Woman as a personality, however, is a very different thing: here illusion no longer works. So that when the question of personality arises, which is as a rule the painful fact of the second half of life, the childish form of the self disappears too.   66:355

The woman who fights against her father still has the possibility of leading an instinctive, feminine existence, because she rejects only what is alien to her. But when she fights against the mother she may, at the risk of injury to her instincts, attain to greater consciousness, because in repudiating the mother she repudiates all that is obscure, instinctive, ambiguous, and unconscious in her own nature.   67:186

Every father is given the opportunity to corrupt his daughter's nature, and the educator, husband, or psychiatrist then has to face the music. For what has been spoiled by the father can only be made good by a father, just as what has been spoiled by the mother can only be repaired by a mother. The disastrous repetition of the family pattern could be described as the psychological original sin, or as the curse of the Atrides running through the generations.
                                        48:232

It is a woman's outstanding characteristic that she can do anything for the love of a man. But those women who can achieve something important for the love of a *thing* are most exceptional, because this does not really agree with their nature. Love for a thing is a man's prerogative. But since masculine and feminine elements are united in our human nature, a man can live in the feminine part of himself, and a woman in her masculine part. None the less the feminine element in man is only something in the background, as is the masculine element in woman. If one lives out the opposite sex in oneself one is living in one's own background, and one's real individuality suffers. A man should live as a man and a woman as a woman.   114:243

The conscious side of woman corresponds to the emotional side of man, not to his "mind." Mind makes up the "soul," or better, the "animus" of woman, and just as the anima of a man consists of inferior relatedness, full of affect, so the animus of woman consists of inferior judgments, or better, opinions.   112:60

For a woman, the typical danger emanating from the unconscious comes from above, from the "spiritual" sphere personified by the animus, whereas for a man it comes from the chthonic realm of the "world and woman," i.e., the anima projected on to the world.   97:559

Unconscious assumptions or opinions are the worst enemy of woman; they can even grow into a positively demonic passion that exasperates and disgusts men, and does the woman herself the greatest injury by gradually smothering the charm and meaning of her femininity and driving it into the background. Such a development naturally ends in profound psychological disunion, in short, in a neurosis.   114:245

As the animus is partial to argument, he can best be seen at work in disputes where both parties know they are right. Men can argue in a very womanish way, too, when they are anima-possessed and have thus been transformed into the animus of their own anima.   3:29

No man can converse with an animus for five minutes without becoming the victim of his own anima. Anyone who still had enough sense of humour to listen objectively to the ensuing dialogue would be staggered by the vast number of commonplaces, misapplied truisms, clichés from newspapers and novels, shop-soiled platitudes of every description interspersed with vulgar abuse and brain-splitting lack of logic. It is a dialogue which, irrespective of its participants, is repeated millions and millions of times in all the languages of the world and always remains essentially the same. 3:29

Indeed, it seems a very natural state of affairs for men to have irrational moods and women irrational opinions. Presumably this situation is grounded on instinct and must remain as it is to ensure that the Empedoclean game of the hate and love of the elements shall continue for all eternity. Nature is conservative and does not easily allow her courses to be altered; she defends in the most stubborn way the inviolability of the preserves where anima and animus roam. . . . And on top of this there arises a profound doubt as to whether one is not meddling too much with nature's business by prodding into consciousness things which it would have been better to leave asleep. 3:35

When animus and anima meet, the animus draws his sword of power and the anima ejects her poison of illusion and seduction. The outcome need not always be negative, since the two are equally likely to fall in love (a special instance of love at first sight). 3:30

No man is so entirely masculine that he has nothing feminine in him. The fact is, rather, that very masculine men have—carefully guarded and hidden—a very soft emotional life, often incorrectly described as "feminine." A man counts it a virtue to repress his feminine traits as much as possible, just as a woman, at least until recently, considered it unbecoming to be "mannish." The repression of feminine traits and inclinations naturally causes these contrasexual demands to accumulate in the unconscious. No less naturally, the imago of woman (the soul-image) becomes a receptacle for these demands, which is why a man, in his love-choice, is strongly tempted to win the woman who best corresponds to his own unconscious femininity—a woman, in short, who can unhesitatingly receive the projection of his soul. Although such a choice is often regarded and felt as altogether ideal, it may turn out that the man has manifestly married his own worst weakness.

104B:297

Every man carries within him the eternal image of woman, not the image of this or that particular woman, but a definite feminine image. This image is fundamentally unconscious, an hereditary factor of primordial origin engraved in the living organic system of the man, an imprint or "archetype" of all the ancestral experiences of the female, a deposit, as it were, of all the impressions ever made by woman—in short, an inherited system of psychic adaptation. Even if no women existed, it would still be possible, at any given time, to deduce from this unconscious image exactly how a woman would have to be constituted psychically. The same is true of the woman: she too has her inborn image of man.   44:338

Every mother and every beloved is forced to become the carrier and embodiment of this omnipresent and ageless image, which corresponds to the deepest reality in a man. It belongs to him, this perilous image of Woman; she stands for the loyalty which in the interests of life he must sometimes forgo; she is the much needed compensation for the risks, struggles, sacrifices that all end in disappointment; she is the solace for all the bitterness of life. And, at the same time, she is the great illusionist, the seductress, who draws him into life with her Maya—and not only into life's reasonable and useful aspects, but into its frightful paradoxes and ambivalences where good and evil, success and ruin, hope and despair, counterbalance one another.

Because she is his greatest danger she demands from a man his greatest, and if he has it in him she will receive it.

3:24

The persona, the ideal picture of a man as he should be, is inwardly compensated by feminine weakness, and as the individual outwardly plays the strong man, so he becomes inwardly a woman, i.e., the anima, for it is the anima that reacts to the persona. But because the inner world is dark and invisible to the extraverted consciousness, and because a man is all the less capable of conceiving his weaknesses the more he is identified with the persona, the persona's counterpart, the anima, remains completely in the dark and is at once projected, so that our hero comes under the heel of his wife's slipper. If this results in a considerable increase of her power, she will acquit herself none too well. She becomes inferior, thus providing her husband with the welcome proof that it is not he, the hero, who is inferior in private, but his wife. In return the wife can cherish the illusion, so attractive to many, that at least she has married a hero, unperturbed by her own uselessness. This little game of illusion is often taken to be the whole meaning of life.

104B: 309

The psychiatrist knows only too well how each of us becomes the helpless but not pitiable victim of his own sentiments. Sentimentality is the superstructure erected upon brutality.

105: 184

Archetypes are complexes of experience that come upon us like fate, and their effects are felt in our most personal life. The anima no longer crosses our path as a goddess, but, it may be, as an intimately personal misadventure, or perhaps as our best venture. When, for instance, a highly esteemed professor in his seventies abandons his family and runs off with a young red-headed actress, we know that the gods have claimed another victim.   10:62

If you take a typical intellectual who is terribly afraid of falling in love, you will think his fear very foolish. But he is most probably right, because he will very likely make foolish nonsense when he falls in love. He will be caught most certainly, because his feeling only reacts to an archaic or to a dangerous type of woman. This is why many intellectuals are inclined to marry beneath them. They are caught by the landlady perhaps, or by the cook, because they are unaware of their archaic feeling through which they get caught. But they are right to be afraid, because their undoing will be in their feeling. Nobody can attack them in their intellect. There they are strong and can stand alone, but in their feelings they can be influenced, they can be caught, they can be cheated, and they know it. Therefore never force a man into his feeling when he is an intellectual. He controls it with an iron hand because it is very dangerous.   6:20*

Most of what men say about feminine eroticism, and particularly about the emotional life of women, is derived from their own anima projections and distorted accordingly.
                    44:338

Perfection is a masculine desideratum, while woman inclines by nature to *completeness* . . . a man can stand a relative state of perfection much better and for a longer period than a woman, while as a rule it does not agree with women and may even be dangerous for them. If a woman strives for perfection she forgets the complementary role of completeness, which, though imperfect by itself, forms the necessary counterpart to perfection.   7:620

Woman's consciousness has a lunar rather than a solar character. Its light is the "mild" light of the moon, which merges things together rather than separates them. It does not show up objects in all their pitiless discreteness and separateness, like the harsh, glaring light of day, but blends in a deceptive shimmer the near and the far, magically transforming little things into big things, high into low, softening all colour into a bluish haze, and blending the nocturnal landscape into an unsuspected unity.

48:223

It needs a very moon-like consciousness indeed to hold a large family together regardless of all the differences, and to talk and act in such a way that the harmonious relation of the parts to the whole is not only not disturbed but is actually enhanced. And where the ditch is too deep, a ray of moonlight smoothes it over.

48:227

The moon-nature is its own best camouflage, as at once becomes apparent when a woman's unconscious masculinity breaks through into her consciousness and thrusts her Eros aside. Then it is all up with her charm and the mitigating half-darkness; she takes a stand on some point or other and captiously defends it, although each barbed remark tears her own flesh, and with brutal short-sightedness she jeopardizes everything that is the dearest goal of womanhood.

48:228

The Sol who personifies the feminine unconscious is not the sun of the day but corresponds rather to the *Sol niger*....
It is as void of light and charm as the gentling moonlight is all heavenly peace and magic. It protests too much that it is a light, because it is no light, and a great truth, because it invariably misses the mark, and a high authority, which nevertheless is always wrong, or is only as right as the blind tom-cat who tried to catch imaginary bats in broad

daylight, but one day caught a real one by mistake and thereafter became completely unteachable.   48:229*f*

All that feminine indefiniteness is the longed-for counterpart of male decisiveness and single-mindedness, which can be satisfactorily achieved only if a man can get rid of everything doubtful, ambiguous, vague, and muddled by projecting it upon some charming example of feminine innocence. Because of the woman's characteristic passivity, and the feelings of inferiority which make her continually play the injured innocent, the man finds himself cast in an attractive role: he has the privilege of putting up with the familiar feminine foibles with real superiority, and yet with forbearance, like a true knight.   67:169

Emptiness is a great feminine secret. It is something absolutely alien to man; the chasm, the unplumbed depths, the *yin*. The pitifulness of this vacuous nonentity goes to his heart (I speak here as a man), and one is tempted to say that this constitutes the whole "mystery" of woman. Such a female is fate itself. A man may say what he likes about it; be for it or against it, or both at once; in the end he falls, absurdly happy, into this pit, or, if he doesn't, he has missed and bungled his only chance of making a man of himself. In the first case one cannot disprove his foolish good luck to him, and in the second one cannot make his misfortune seem plausible. "The Mothers, the Mothers, how eerily it sounds!"   67:183

The girl's notorious helplessness is a special attraction. She is so much an appendage of her mother that she can only flutter confusedly when a man approaches. She just doesn't know a thing. She is so inexperienced, so terribly in need of help, that even the gentlest swain becomes a daring abductor who brutally robs a loving mother of her daughter. Such a marvellous opportunity to pass himself

off as a gay Lothario does not occur every day and therefore acts as a strong incentive. This was how Pluto ab-
ducted Persephone from the inconsolable Demeter. But, by
a decree of the gods, he had to surrender his wife every
year to his mother-in-law for the summer season.   67:169

❖

Human relationship leads into the world of the psyche,
into that intermediate realm between sense and spirit, which
contains something of both and yet forfeits nothing of its
own unique character. Into this territory a man must venture if he wishes to meet woman half way. Circumstances
have forced her to acquire a number of masculine traits, so
that she shall not remain caught in an antiquated, purely
instinctual femininity, lost and alone in the world of men.
So, too, man will be forced to develop his feminine side, to
open his eyes to the psyche and to Eros. It is a task he cannot avoid, unless he prefers to go trailing after woman in a
hopelessly boyish fashion, worshipping from afar but always in danger of being stowed away in her pocket.
                                                114:258*f*

The masculinity of the woman and the femininity of the
man *are* inferior, and it is regrettable that the full value of
their personalities should be contaminated by something
that is less valuable. On the other hand, the shadow belongs to the wholeness of the personality: the strong man
must somewhere be weak, somewhere the clever man must
be stupid, otherwise he is too good to be true and falls
back on pose and bluff. Is it not an old truth that woman
loves the weaknesses of the strong man more than his
strength, and the stupidity of the clever man more than
his cleverness?   114:261

It is an almost regular occurrence for a woman to be
wholly contained, spiritually, in her husband, and for a

husband to be wholly contained, emotionally, in his wife. One could describe this as the problem of the "contained" and the "container." 44:331c

The question of relationship borders on a region that for a man is dark and painful. He can face this question only when the woman carries the burden of suffering, that is, when he is the "contained"—in other words, when she can imagine herself having a relationship with another man, and as a consequence suffering disunion within herself. Then it is she who has the painful problem, and he is not obliged to see his own, which is a great relief to him. In this situation he is not unlike a thief who, quite undeservedly, finds himself in the enviable position of having been forestalled by another thief who has been caught by the police. Suddenly he becomes an honourable, impartial onlooker. In any other situation a man always finds the discussion of personal relations painful and boring, just as his wife would find it boring if he examined her on the *Critique of Pure Reason*. For him, Eros is a shadowland which entangles him in his feminine unconscious, in something "psychic," while for woman Logos is a deadly boring kind of sophistry if she is not actually repelled and frightened by it. 114:256

In the eyes of the ordinary man, love in its true sense coincides with the institution of marriage, and outside marriage there is only adultery or "platonic" friendship. For woman, marriage is not an institution at all but a human love-relationship. 114:255

Relationship is possible only if there is a psychic distance between people, in the same way that morality presupposes freedom. For this reason the unconscious tendency of woman aims at loosening the marriage structure, but not at the destruction of marriage and the family. 114:273

[In America] the men and women are giving their vital energy to everything except the relation between themselves. In that relation all is confusion. The women are the mothers of their husbands as well as of their children, yet at the same time there is in them the old primitive desire to be possessed, to yield, to surrender. And there is nothing in the man for her to surrender to except his kindness, his courtesy, his generosity, his chivalry. His competitor, his rival in business must yield, but she need not.   39a*

We deceive ourselves greatly if we think that many married women are neurotic merely because they are unsatisfied sexually or because they have not found the right man or because they have an infantile sexual fixation. The real reason in many cases is that they cannot recognize the cultural task that is waiting for them. We all have far too much the standpoint of the "nothing but" psychology, that is, we still think that the new future which is pressing in at the door can be squeezed into the framework of what is already known.   89:668

Most men are erotically blinded—they commit the unpardonable mistake of confusing Eros with sex. A man thinks he possesses a woman if he has her sexually. He never possesses her less, for to a woman the Eros-relationship is the real and decisive one. For her, marriage is a relationship with sex thrown in as an accompaniment.

114:255

Traditionally, man is regarded as the marriage breaker. This legend comes from times long past, when men still had leisure to pursue all sorts of pastimes. But today life makes so many demands on men that the noble hidalgo, Don Juan, is to be seen nowhere save in the theatre. More than ever man loves his comfort, for ours is an age of neurasthenia, impotence, and easy chairs. There is no

energy left for window-climbing and duels. If anything is
to happen in the way of adultery it must not be too difficult.
In no respect must it cost too much, hence the adventure
can only be of a transitory kind. The man of today is thoroughly scared of jeopardizing marriage as an institution.

114:248

Woman nowadays feels that there is no real security in
marriage, for what does her husband's faithfulness mean
when she knows that his feelings and thoughts are running
after others and that he is merely too calculating or too
cowardly to follow them? What does her own faithfulness
mean when she knows that she is simply using it to ex-
ploit her legal right of possession, and warping her own
soul? She has intimations of a higher fidelity to the spirit
and to a love beyond human weakness and imperfection.

114:270

Do our legislators really know what "adultery" is? Is
their definition of it the final embodiment of the truth?
From the psychological standpoint, the only one that counts
for a woman, it is a wretched piece of bungling, like
everything else contrived by men for the purpose of codify-
ing love. For a woman, love has nothing to do with "marital
misconduct," "extramarital intercourse," "deception of the
husband," or any of the less savoury formulas invented by
the erotically blind masculine intellect and echoed by the
self-opinionated demon in woman. Nobody but the absolute believer in the inviolability of traditional marriage
could perpetrate such breaches of good taste, just as only
the believer in God can really blaspheme. Whoever
doubts marriage in the first place cannot infringe against
it; for him the legal definition is invalid because, like St.
Paul, he feels himself beyond the law, on the higher plane
of love. But because the believers in the law so frequently

trespass against their own laws, whether from stupidity, temptation, or mere viciousness, the modern woman begins to wonder whether she too may not belong to the same category. 114:265

Secretaries, typists, shop-girls, all are agents of this process, and through a million subterranean channels creeps the influence that is undermining marriage. For the desire of all these women is not to have sexual adventures— only the stupid could believe that—but to get married. The possessors of that bliss must be ousted, not as a rule by naked force, but by that silent, obstinate desire which, as we know, has magical effects, like the fixed stare of a snake. This was ever the way of women. 114:251

It is no longer a question of a few dozen voluntary or involuntary old maids here and there, but of millions. Our legislation and our social morality give no answer to this question. Or can the Church provide a satisfactory answer? Should we build gigantic nunneries to accommodate all these women? Or should tolerated prostitution be increased? Obviously this is impossible, since we are dealing neither with saints nor sinners but with ordinary women who cannot register their spiritual requirements with the police. They are decent women who want to marry, and if this is not possible, well—the next best thing. 114:248

It is a bad sign when doctors begin writing books of advice on how to achieve the "perfect marriage." Healthy people need no doctors. Marriage today has indeed become rather precarious. In America about a quarter of the marriages end in divorce. And the remarkable thing is that this time the scapegoat is not the man but the woman. She is the one who doubts and feels uncertain. It is not surprising that this is so, for in post-war Europe there is such an alarming surplus of unmarried women that it would be inconceivable if there were no reaction from that quarter.

114:248

Since the aims of the second half of life are different from those of the first, to linger too long in the youthful attitude produces a division of the will. Consciousness still presses forward in obedience, as it were, to its own inertia, but the unconscious lags behind, because the strength and inner resolve needed for further expansion have been sapped. This disunity with oneself begets discontent, and since one is not conscious of the real state of things one generally projects the reasons for it upon one's partner. A critical atmosphere thus develops, the necessary prelude to conscious realization.

44:331b

Seldom or never does a marriage develop into an individual relationship smoothly and without crises. There is no birth of consciousness without pain.

44:331

Youth and Age

To speak of the morning and spring, of the evening and the autumn of life is not mere sentimental jargon. We thus give expression to psychological truths, and even more to physiological facts.   94:780

Our life is like the course of the sun. In the morning it gains continually in strength until it reaches the zenith-heat of high noon. Then comes the enantiodromia: the steady forward movement no longer denotes an increase, but a decrease, in strength. Thus our task in handling a young person is different from the task of handling an older person. In the former case, it is enough to clear away all the obstacles that hinder expansion and ascent; in the latter, we must nurture everything that assists the descent.
                                                                  104A:114

The high ideal of educating the personality is not for children: for what is usually meant by personality—a well-rounded psychic whole that is capable of resistance and abounding in energy—is an *adult ideal*. It is only in an age like ours, when the individual is unconscious of the problems of adult life, or—what is worse—when he consciously shirks them, that people could wish to foist this ideal on to childhood.   21:286

If there is anything that we wish to change in our children, we should first examine it and see whether it is not something that could better be changed in ourselves. Take our enthusiasm for pedagogics. It may be that the boot is on the other leg. It may be that we misplace the pedagogical need because it would be an uncomfortable reminder that we ourselves are still children in many respects and still need a vast amount of educating.   21:287

Our whole educational problem suffers from a one-sided approach to the child who is to be educated, and from an equally one-sided lack of emphasis on the uneducatedness of the educator.   21:284

I therefore suspect that the *furor paedogogicus* is a god-sent method of by-passing the central problem touched on by Schiller, namely the education of the educator. Children are educated by what the grown-up *is* and not by what he *says*.   76:293

A child certainly allows himself to be impressed by the grand talk of his parents, but do they really imagine he is educated by it? Actually it is the parents' lives that educate the child—what they add by word and gesture at best serves only to confuse him. The same holds good for the teacher. But we have such a belief in method that, if only the method be good, the practice of it seems to sanctify the teacher.   69:665

An inferior man is never a good teacher. But he can conceal his pernicious inferiority, which secretly poisons the pupil, behind an excellent method or an equally brilliant gift of gab. Naturally the pupil of riper years desires nothing better than the knowledge of useful methods, because he is already defeated by the general attitude, which believes in the all-conquering method. He has learnt that the emptiest head, correctly echoing a method, is the best pupil. His whole environment is an optical demonstration that all success and all happiness are outside, and that only the right method is needed to attain the haven of one's desires. Or does, perchance, the life of his religious instructor demonstrate the happiness which radiates from the treasure of the inner vision?   69:665

One looks back with appreciation to the brilliant teachers, but with gratitude to those who touched our human feelings. The curriculum is so much necessary raw material, but warmth is the vital element for the growing plant and for the soul of the child. 31:249

Psychoanalysis cannot be considered a method of education, if by education we mean the topiary art of clipping a tree into a beautiful artificial shape. But those who have a higher conception of education will prize most the method of cultivating a tree so that it fulfils to perfection its own natural conditions of growth. 101:442

Aestheticism is not fitted to solve the exceedingly serious and difficult task of educating man, for it always presupposes the very thing it should create—the capacity to love beauty. It actually hinders a deeper investigation of the problem, because it always averts its face from anything evil, ugly, and difficult, and aims at pleasure, even though it be of an edifying kind. Aestheticism therefore lacks all moral force, because *au fond* it is still only a refined hedonism. 69:194

Children have an almost uncanny instinct for the teacher's personal shortcomings. They know the false from the true far better than one likes to admit. Therefore the teacher should watch his own psychic condition, so that he can spot the source of the trouble when anything goes wrong with the children entrusted to his care. He himself may easily be the unconscious cause of evil. Naturally we must not be too naïve in this matter: there are people, doctors as well as teachers, who secretly believe that a person in authority has the right to behave just as he likes, and that it is up to the child to adapt as best he may, because sooner or later he will have to adapt to real life which will treat him no better. Such people are convinced at heart that the only thing that matters is material success, and that the only real and effective moral restraint is the policeman behind the penal code. Where unconditional adaptation to the powers of this world is accepted as the supreme principle of belief, it would of course be vain to expect psychological insight from a person in authority as a moral obligation. But anyone who professes a democratic view of the world cannot approve of such an authoritarian attitude, believing as he does in a fair distribution of burdens and advantages. It is not true that the educator is always the one who educates, and the child always the one to be educated. The educator, too, is a fallible human being, and the child he educates will reflect his failings. Therefore it is wise to be as clear-sighted as possible about one's subjective views, and particularly about one's faults. As a man is, so will be his ultimate truth, and so also his strongest effect on others.

4:211

No doubt we are right to open the eyes and ears of our young people to the wide world, but it is the maddest of delusions to think that this really equips them for the task of living. It is the kind of training that enables a young person to adapt himself outwardly to the world and reality, but no one gives a thought to the necessity of adapting to the self, to the powers of the psyche, which are far mightier than all the Great Powers of the earth. A system of education does indeed exist, but it has its origins partly in antiquity and partly in the early Middle Ages. It styles itself the Christian Church. But it cannot be denied that in the course of the last two centuries Christianity, no less than Confucianism in China and Buddhism in India, has largely forfeited its educative activity. Human iniquity is not to blame for this, but rather a gradual and widespread spiritual change, the first symptom of which was the Reformation. It shattered the authority of the Church as a teacher, and thereafter the authoritarian principle itself began to crumble away. The inevitable consequence was an increase in the importance of the individual, which found expression in the modern ideals of humanity, social welfare, democracy, and equality. 45: 326

The fact that by far the greater part of humanity not only needs guidance, but wishes for nothing better than to be guided and held in tutelage, justifies, in a sense, the moral value which the Church sets on confession. The priest, equipped with all the insignia of paternal authority, becomes the responsible leader and shepherd of his flock. He is the father confessor and the members of his parish are his penitent children.

Thus priest and Church replace the parents, and to that extent they free the individual from the bonds of the family. In so far as the priest is a morally elevated personality with a natural nobility of soul and a mental culture to match, the institution of confession may be commended as a brilliant method of social guidance and education, which did in fact perform a tremendous educative task for more than fifteen hundred years. So long as the medieval Church knew how to be the guardian of art and science—a role in which her success was due, in part, to her wide tolerance of worldly interests—confession was an admirable instrument of education. But it lost its educative value, at least for more highly developed people, as soon as the Church proved incapable of maintaining her leadership in the intellectual sphere—the inevitable consequence of spiritual rigidity. 101: 433*f*

❖

Side by side with the biological, the spiritual, too, has its inviolable rights. It is assuredly no accident that primitive peoples, even in adult life, make the most fantastic assertions about well-known sexual processes, as for instance that coitus has nothing to do with pregnancy. From this it has been concluded that these people do not even know there is such a connection. But more accurate investigation has shown that they know very well that with animals copulation is followed by pregnancy. Only for human beings is it denied—not *not known*, but flatly *denied*—that this is so, for the simple reason that they prefer a mythological explanation which has freed itself from the trammels of concretism. It is not hard to see that in these facts, so frequently observed among primitives, there lie the beginnings of *abstraction*, which is so very important for culture. We have every reason to suppose that this is also true of the psychology of the child.   64:79

Childhood is important not only because various warpings of instinct have their origin there, but because this is the time when, terrifying or encouraging, those far-seeing dreams and images appear before the soul of the child, shaping his whole destiny, as well as those retrospective intuitions which reach back far beyond the range of childhood experience into the life of our ancestors. Thus in the child-psyche the natural condition is already opposed by a "spiritual" one.   54:98

Fairytales seem to be the myths of childhood and they therefore contain among other things the mythology which children weave for themselves concerning sexual processes. The poetry of fairytale, whose magic is felt even by the adult, rests not least upon the fact that some of the old theories are still alive in our unconscious. We experience a strange and mysterious feeling whenever a fragment of our remotest youth stirs into life again, not actually reaching consciousness, but merely shedding a reflection of its emotional intensity on the conscious mind.   64:44

An individual is infantile because he has freed himself insufficiently, or not at all, from his childish environment and his adaptation to his parents, with the result that he has a false reaction to the world: on the one hand he reacts as a child towards his parents, always demanding love and immediate emotional rewards, while on the other hand he is so identified with his parents through his close ties with them that he behaves like his father or his mother. He is incapable of living his own life and finding the character that belongs to him. 100:431

Nothing exerts a stronger psychic effect upon the human environment, and especially upon children, than the life which the parents have not lived. 56:4

All the life which the parents could have lived, but of which they thwarted themselves for artificial motives, is passed on to the children in substitute form. That is to say, the children are driven unconsciously in a direction that is intended to compensate for everything that was left unfulfilled in the lives of their parents. Hence it is that excessively moral-minded parents have what are called "unmoral" children, or an irresponsible wastrel of a father has a son with a positively morbid amount of ambition, and so on. 44:328

To remain a child too long is childish, but it is just as childish to move away and then assume that childhood no longer exists because we do not see it. But if we return to the "children's land" we succumb to the fear of becoming childish, because we do not understand that everything of psychic origin has a double face. One face looks forward, the other back. It is ambivalent and therefore symbolic, like all living reality. 72:74

It is not possible to live too long amid infantile surroundings, or in the bosom of the family, without endangering one's psychic health. Life calls us forth to independence, and anyone who does not heed this call because of childish laziness or timidity is threatened with neurosis. And once this has broken out, it becomes an increasingly valid reason for running away from life and remaining forever in the morally poisonous atmosphere of infancy.   100:461

The psychic health of the adult individual, who in childhood was a mere particle revolving in a rotary system, demands that he should himself become the centre of a new system.   100:644

It is part of the business of growing up to listen to the fearful discords which real life grinds out and to include them among the images of reality. Truth and reality are assuredly no music of the spheres—they are the beauty and terror of Nature herself.   14:13*

✧

If we try to extract the common and essential factors from the almost inexhaustible variety of individual problems found in the period of youth, we meet in all cases with one particular feature: a more or less patent clinging to the childhood level of consciousness, a resistance to the fateful forces in and around us which would involve us in the world. Something in us wishes to remain a child, to be unconscious or, at most, conscious only of the ego; to reject everything strange, or else subject it to our will; to do nothing, or else indulge our own craving for pleasure or power. In all this there is something of the inertia of matter; it is a persistence in the previous state whose range of consciousness is smaller, narrower, and more egoistic than that of the dualistic phase. For here the individual is faced with the necessity of recognizing and accepting what is different and strange as a part of his own life, as a kind of "also-I." 94:764

Obviously it is in the youthful period of life that we have most to gain from a thorough recognition of the instinctual side. A timely recognition of sexuality, for instance, can prevent that neurotic suppression of it which keeps a man unduly withdrawn from life, or else forces him into a wretched and unsuitable way of living with which he is bound to come into conflict. Proper recognition and appreciation of normal instincts leads the young person into life and entangles him with fate, thus involving him in life's necessities and the consequent sacrifices and efforts through which his character is developed and his experience matured. For the mature person, however, the continued expansion of life is obviously not the right principle, because the descent towards life's afternoon demands simplification, limitation, and intensification—in other words, individual culture. 54:113

It even seems as if young people who have had a hard struggle for existence are spared inner problems, while those who for some reason or other have no difficulty with adaptation run into problems of sex or conflicts arising from a sense of inferiority. 94:762

The solution of the problems of youth by restricting ourselves to the attainable is only temporarily valid and not lasting in a deeper sense. Of course, to win for oneself a place in society and to transform one's nature so that it is more or less fitted to this kind of existence is in all cases a considerable achievement. It is a fight waged within oneself as well as outside, comparable to the struggle of the child for an ego. That struggle is for the most part unobserved because it happens in the dark; but when we see how stubbornly childish illusions and assumptions and egoistic habits are still clung to in later years we can gain some idea of the energies that were needed to form them. And so it is with the ideals, convictions, guiding ideas and attitudes which in the period of youth lead us out into life, for which we struggle, suffer, and win victories: they grow together with our own being, we apparently change into them, we seek to perpetuate them indefinitely and as a matter of course, just as the young person asserts his ego in spite of the world and often in spite of himself.

94:771

Achievement, usefulness and so forth are the ideals that seem to point the way out of the confusions of the problematical state. They are the lodestars that guide us in the adventure of broadening and consolidating our physical existence; they help us to strike our roots in the world, but they cannot guide us in the development of that wider consciousness to which we give the name of culture. In the period of youth, however, this course is the normal one and in all circumstances preferable to merely tossing about in a welter of problems.

94:769

The nearer we approach to the middle of life, and the better we have succeeded in entrenching ourselves in our personal attitudes and social positions, the more it appears as if we had discovered the right course and the right ideals and principles of behaviour. For this reason we suppose them to be eternally valid, and make a virtue of unchangeably clinging to them. We overlook the essential fact that the social goal is attained only at the cost of a diminution of personality. Many—far too many—aspects of life which should also have been experienced lie in the lumber-room among dusty memories; but sometimes, too, they are glowing coals under grey ashes.

94:772

The discovery of the value of human personality is reserved for a riper age. For young people the search for personality values is very often a pretext for evading their biological duty. Conversely, the exaggerated longing of an older person for the sexual values of youth is a short-sighted and often cowardly evasion of a duty which demands recognition of the value of personality and submission to the hierarchy of cultural values. The young neurotic shrinks back in terror from the expansion of life's duties, the old one from the dwindling of the treasures he has attained.

89:664

The psyche does not merely *react*, it gives its own specific answer to the influences at work upon it, and at least half the resulting formation is entirely due to the psyche and the determinants inherent within it. Culture can never be understood as reaction to environment. That shallow explanation can safely be left to the past century. It is just these determinants that appear as psychological imperatives, and we have daily proof of their compelling power. What I call "biological duty" is identical with these determinants.

89:665

It is of the greatest importance for the young person, who is still unadapted and has as yet achieved nothing, to shape his conscious ego as effectively as possible, that is, to educate his will. Unless he is a positive genius he cannot, indeed he should not, believe in anything active within him that is not identical with his will. He must feel himself a man of will, and may safely depreciate everything else in him and deem it subject to his will, for without this illusion he could not succeed in adapting himself socially. It is otherwise with a person in the second half of life who no longer needs to educate his conscious will, but who, to understand the meaning of his individual life, needs to experience his own inner being. Social usefulness is no longer an aim for him, although he does not deny its desirability. Fully aware as he is of the social unimportance of his creative activity, he feels it more as a way of working at himself to his own benefit. Increasingly, too, this activity frees him from morbid dependence, and he thus acquires an inner stability and a new trust in himself.

2: 109*f*

❖

The middle period of life is a time of enormous psychological importance. The child begins its psychological life within very narrow limits, inside the magic circle of the mother and the family. With progressive maturation it widens its horizon and its own sphere of influence; its hopes and intentions are directed to extending the scope of personal power and possessions; desire reaches out to the world in ever-widening range; the will of the individual becomes more and more identical with the natural goals pursued by unconscious motivations. Thus man breathes his own life into things, until finally they begin to live of themselves and to multiply; and imperceptibly he is overgrown by them. Mothers are overtaken by their children, men by their own creations, and what was originally brought into being only with labour and the greatest effort can no longer be held in check. First it was passion, then it became duty, and finally an intolerable burden, a vampire that battens on the life of its creator.

44: 331a

Middle life is the moment of greatest unfolding, when a man still gives himself to his work with his whole strength and his whole will. But in this very moment evening is born, and the second half of life begins. Passion now changes her face and is called duty; "I want" becomes the inexorable "I must," and the turnings of the pathway that once brought surprise and discovery become dulled by custom. The wine has fermented and begins to settle and clear. Conservative tendencies develop if all goes well; instead of looking forward one looks backward, most of the time involuntarily, and one begins to take stock, to see how one's life has developed up to this point. The real motivations are sought and real discoveries are made. The critical survey of himself and his fate enables a man to recognize his peculiarities. But these insights do not come to him easily; they are gained only through the severest shocks.

44:331a

Take for comparison the daily course of the sun—but a sun that is endowed with human feeling and man's limited consciousness. In the morning it rises from the nocturnal sea of unconsciousness and looks upon the wide, bright world which lies before it in an expanse that steadily widens the higher it climbs in the firmament. In this extension of its field of action caused by its own rising, the sun will discover its significance; it will see the attainment of the greatest possible height, and the widest possible dissemination of its blessings, as its goal. In this conviction the sun pursues its course to the unforeseen zenith—unforeseen, because its career is unique and individual, and the culminating point could not be calculated in advance. At the stroke of noon the descent begins. And the descent means the reversal of all the ideals and values that were cherished in the morning.

94:778

The wine of youth does not always clear with advancing years; sometimes it grows turbid. 94:774

Wholly unprepared, we embark upon the second half of life. Or are there perhaps colleges for forty-year-olds which prepare them for their coming life and its demands as the ordinary colleges introduce our young people to a knowledge of the world? No, thoroughly unprepared we take the step into the afternoon of life; worse still, we take this step with the false assumption that our truths and ideals will serve us as hitherto. But we cannot live the afternoon of life according to the programme of life's morning; for what was great in the morning will be little at evening, and what in the morning was true will at evening have become a lie.   94:784

I said just now that we have no schools for forty-year olds. That is not quite true. Our religions were always such schools in the past, but how many people regard them like that today? How many of us older ones have been brought up in such a school and really prepared for the second half of life, for old age, death and eternity?   94:786

An inexperienced youth thinks one can let the old people go, because not much more can happen to them anyway: they have their lives behind them and are no better than petrified pillars of the past. But it is a great mistake to suppose that the meaning of life is exhausted with the period of youth and expansion; that, for example, a woman who has passed the menopause is "finished." The afternoon of life is just as full of meaning as the morning; only, its meaning and purpose are different.   104A:114

Ageing people should know that their lives are not mounting and expanding, but that an inexorable inner process enforces the contraction of life. For a young person it is almost a sin, or at least a danger, to be too preoccupied with himself; but for the ageing person it is a duty and a necessity to devote serious attention to himself. After having lavished its light upon the world, the sun withdraws its rays in order to illuminate itself. Instead of doing likewise, many old people prefer to be hypochondriacs, niggards, pedants, applauders of the past or else eternal adolescents —all lamentable substitutes for the illumination of the self, but inevitable consequences of the delusion that the second half of life must be governed by the principles of the first. 94:785

If we wish to stay on the heights we have reached, we must struggle all the time to consolidate our consciousness and its attitude. But we soon discover that this praise-worthy and apparently unavoidable battle with the years leads to stagnation and desiccation of soul. Our convictions become platitudes ground out on a barrel-organ, our ideals become starchy habits, enthusiasm stiffens into automatic gestures. The source of the water of life seeps away. We ourselves may not notice it, but everybody else does, and that is even more painful. If we should risk a little introspection, coupled perhaps with an energetic attempt to be honest for once with ourselves, we may get a dim idea of all the wants, longings, and fears that have accumulated down there—a repulsive and sinister sight. The mind shies away, but life wants to flow down into the depths. Fate itself seems to preserve us from this, for each of us has a tendency to become an immovable pillar of the past. 100:553

The very frequent neurotic disturbances of adult years all have one thing in common: they want to carry the psychology of the youthful phase over the threshold of the so-called years of discretion. Who does not know those touching old gentlemen who must always warm up the dish of their student days, who can fan the flame of life only by reminiscences of their heroic youth, but who, for the rest, are stuck in a hopelessly wooden Philistinism? As a rule, to be sure, they have this one merit which it would be wrong to undervalue: they are not neurotic, but only boring and stereotyped. The neurotic is rather a person who can never have things as he would like them in the present, and who can therefore never enjoy the past either. 94:776

In my naturally limited experience there are, among people of maturer age, very many for whom the development of individuality is an indispensable requirement. Hence I am privately of the opinion that it is just the mature person who, in our times, has the greatest need of some further education in individual culture after his youthful education in school or university has moulded him on exclusively collective lines and thoroughly imbued him with the collective mentality.   54:112

From the middle of life onward, only he remains vitally alive who is ready to *die with life*.   90:800

✧

Being old is highly unpopular. Nobody seems to consider that not being able to grow old is just as absurd as not being able to outgrow child's-size shoes. A still infantile man of thirty is surely to be deplored, but a youthful septuagenarian—isn't that delightful? And yet both are perverse, lacking in style, psychological monstrosities. A young man who does not fight and conquer has missed the best part of his youth, and an old man who does not know how to listen to the secrets of the brooks, as they tumble down from the peaks to the valleys, makes no sense; he is a spiritual mummy who is nothing but a rigid relic of the past. He stands apart from life, mechanically repeating himself to the last triviality!   90:801

To the psychotherapist an old man who cannot bid farewell to life appears as feeble and sickly as a young man who is unable to embrace it. And as a matter of fact, it is in many cases a question of the selfsame childish greediness, the same fear, the same defiance and wilfulness, in the one as in the other.   94:792

A human being would certainly not grow to be seventy or eighty years old if this longevity had no meaning for the species. The afternoon of human life must also have a significance of its own and cannot be merely a pitiful appendage to life's morning. The significance of the morning undoubtedly lies in the development of the individual, our entrenchment in the outer world, the propagation of our kind, and the care of our children. This is the obvious purpose of nature. But when this purpose has been attained —and more than attained—shall the earning of money, the extension of conquests, and the expansion of life go steadily on beyond the bounds of all reason and sense? Whoever carries over into the afternoon the law of the morning, or the natural aim, must pay for it with damage to his soul, just as surely as a growing youth who tries to carry over his childish egoism into adult life must pay for this mistake with social failure.   94:787

We must not forget that only a very few people are artists in life; that the art of life is the most distinguished and rarest of all the arts. Who ever succeeded in draining the whole cup with grace?   94:789

Just as the childish person shrinks back from the unknown in the world and in human existence, so the grown man shrinks back from the second half of life. It is as if unknown and dangerous tasks awaited him, or as if he were threatened with sacrifices and losses which he does not wish to accept, or as if his life up to now seemed to him so fair and precious that he could not relinquish it. Is it perhaps at bottom the fear of death? That does not seem to me very probable, because as a rule death is still far in the distance and therefore somewhat abstract. Experience shows us, rather, that the basic cause of all the difficulties of this transition is to be found in a deep-seated and peculiar change within the psyche.   94:777f

Our personality develops in the course of our life from germs that are hard or impossible to discern, and it is only our deeds that reveal who we are. We are like the sun, which nourishes the life of the earth and brings forth every kind of strange, wonderful, and evil thing; we are like the mothers who bear in their wombs untold happiness and suffering. At first we do not know what deeds or misdeeds, what destiny, what good and evil we have in us, and only the autumn can show what the spring has engendered, only in the evening will it be seen what the morning began.   21:290

Everything young grows old, all beauty fades, all heat cools, all brightness dims, and every truth becomes stale and trite. For all these things have taken on shape, and all shapes are worn thin by the working of time; they age, sicken, crumble to dust—unless they change. But change they can, for the invisible spark that generated them is potent enough for infinite generation. No one should deny the danger of the descent, but it *can* be risked. No one *need* risk it, but it is certain that some will. And let those who go down the sunset way do so with open eyes, for it is a sacrifice which daunts even the gods. Yet every descent is followed by an ascent; the vanishing shapes are shaped anew, and a truth is valid in the end only if it suffers change and bears witness in new images, in new tongues, like a new wine that is put into new bottles.   100:553

Man has two aims: the first is the natural aim, the begetting of children and the business of protecting the brood; to this belongs the acquisition of money and social position. When this aim has been reached a new phase begins: the cultural aim. For the attainment of the former we have the help of nature and, on top of that, education;

for the attainment of the latter, little or nothing helps. Often, indeed, a false ambition survives, in that an old man wants to be a youth again, or at least feels he must behave like one, although in his heart he can no longer make believe. This is what makes the transition from the natural to the cultural phase so terribly difficult and bitter for many people; they cling to the illusion of youth or to their children, hoping to salvage in this way a last little scrap of youth. One sees it especially in mothers, who find their sole meaning in their children and imagine they will sink into a bottomless void when they have to give them up. No wonder that so many bad neuroses appear at the onset of life's afternoon. It is a sort of second puberty, another "storm and stress" period, not infrequently accompanied by tempests of passion—the "dangerous age." But the problems that crop up at this age are no longer to be solved by the old recipes: the hand of this clock cannot be put back. What youth found and must find outside, the man of life's afternoon must find within himself.   104A:114

There is no human horror or fairground freak that has not lain in the womb of a loving mother. As the sun shines upon the just and the unjust, and as women who bear and give suck tend God's children and the devil's brood with equal compassion, unconcerned about the possible consequences, so we also are part and parcel of this amazing nature, and, like it, carry within us the seeds of the unpredictable.   21:289

It is the way of moralists not to put the slightest trust in God, as if they thought that the good tree of humanity flourished only by dint of being pruned, tied back, and trained on a trellis; whereas in fact Father Sun and Mother Earth have allowed it to grow for their delight in accordance with deep, wise laws.   104C:427

The rapid development of the towns, with the specialization of work brought about by the extraordinary division of labour, the increasing industrialization of the countryside, and the growing sense of insecurity, deprive men of many opportunities for giving vent to their affective energies. The peasant's alternating rhythm of work secures him unconscious satisfactions through its symbolical content—satisfactions which the factory workers and office employees do not know and can never enjoy. What do these know of his life with nature, of those grand moments when, as lord and fructifier of the earth, he drives his plough through the soil, and with a kingly gesture scatters the seed for the future harvest; of his rightful fear of the destructive power of the elements, of his joy in the fruitfulness of his wife, who bears him the daughters and sons who mean increased working-power and prosperity? From all this we city-dwellers, we modern machine-minders, are far removed. Is not the fairest and most natural of all satisfactions beginning to fail us, when we can no longer regard with unmixed joy the harvest of our own sowing, the "blessing" of children? 104C: 428

Nature has the primary claim on mankind, and only long after that comes the luxury of reason. The medieval ideal of a life lived for death should gradually be replaced by a more natural attitude to life, in which the natural claims of man are fully acknowledged, so that the desires of the animal sphere need no longer drag down the higher values of the spiritual sphere in order to be able to function at all. 100A: 295*

We should not rise above the earth with the aid of "spiritual" intuitions and run away from hard reality, as so often happens with people who have brilliant intuitions. We can never reach the level of our intuitions and should therefore not identify ourselves with them. Only the gods

can pass over the rainbow bridge; mortal men must stick
to the earth and are subject to its laws.   72:148

Reduction to the natural condition is neither an ideal state
nor a panacea. If the natural state were really the ideal one,
then the primitive would be leading an enviable existence.
But that is by no means so, for aside from all the other sorrows and hardships of human life the primitive is tor-
mented by superstitions, fears, and compulsions to such a
degree that, if he lived in our civilization, he could not be
described as other than profoundly neurotic, if not mad.

54:94

In the light of the possibilities revealed by intuition,
man's earthliness is certainly a lamentable imperfection;
but this very imperfection is part of his innate being, of his
reality. He is compounded not only of his best intuitions,
his highest ideals and aspirations, but also of the odious
conditions of his existence, such as heredity and the indelible sequence of memories which shout after him: "You did
it, and that's what you are!" Man may have lost his ancient
saurian's tail, but in its stead he has a chain hanging on
to his psyche which binds him to the earth—an anything-
but-Homeric chain* of given conditions which weigh so
heavy that it is better to remain bound to them, even at
the risk of becoming neither a hero nor a saint. (History
gives us some justification for not attaching any absolute
value to these collective norms.) That we are bound to the
earth does not mean that we cannot grow; on the contrary
it is the *sine qua non* of growth. No noble, well-grown
tree ever disowned its dark roots, for it grows not only up-
wards but downwards as well.   72:148

* The Homeric chain (*catena Homeri*) in alchemy is the series
of great wise men, beginning with Hermes Trismegistus, which
links earth with heaven.

Both these necessities exist in ourselves: nature and culture. We cannot only be ourselves, we must also be related to others. Hence a way must be found that is not a mere rational compromise; it must be a state or process that is wholly consonant with the living being, "a highway and a holy way," as the prophet says, "a straight way, so that fools shall not err therein" (Isaiah 35:8).   69:135

No man can begin with the present; he must slowly grow into it, for there would be no present but for the past. A young person has not yet acquired a past, therefore he has no present either. He does not create culture, he merely exists. It is the privilege and the task of maturer people, who have passed the meridian of life, to create culture.

114:272

When Nature is left to herself, energy is transformed along the line of its natural "gradient." In this way natural phenomena are produced, but not "work." So also man when left to himself lives as a natural phenomenon, and, in the proper meaning of the word, produces no work. It is culture that provides the machine whereby the natural gradient is exploited for the performance of work. That man should ever have invented this machine must be due to something rooted deep in his nature, indeed in the nature of the living organism as such. For living matter is itself a transformer of energy, and in some way as yet unknown life participates in the transformation process. Life proceeds, as it were, by making use of natural physical and chemical conditions as a means to its own existence.

54:80

Conscious capacity for one-sidedness is a sign of the highest culture, but involuntary one-sidedness, i.e., inability to be anything but one-sided, is a sign of barbarism. Hence the most one-sided differentiations are found among semi-barbarians—for instance, certain aspects of Christian asceticism that are an affront to good taste, and parallel phenomena among the yogis and Tibetan Buddhists. For the barbarian, this tendency to fall a victim to one-sidedness in one way or another, thus losing sight of his total personality, is a great and constant danger.   69:346

The greater the tension, the greater is the potential. Great energy springs from a correspondingly great tension between opposites.   58:154

No culture is ever really complete, for it always swings more towards one side or the other. Sometimes the cultural idea is extraverted, and then the chief value lies with the object and man's relation to it; sometimes it is introverted, and then the chief value lies with the subject and his relation to the idea. In the former case, culture takes on a collective character, in the latter an individual one.   69:110

No one can make history who is not willing to risk everything for it, to carry the experiment with his own life through to the bitter end, and to declare that his life is not a continuation of the past, but a new beginning. Mere continuation can be left to the animals, but inauguration is the prerogative of man, the one thing he can boast of that lifts him above the beasts.   114:268

Money-making, social achievement, family and posterity are nothing but plain nature, not culture. Culture lies outside the purpose of nature. Could by any chance culture be the meaning and purpose of the second half of life?

94:787

We Westerners knew only how to tame and subdue the pysche; we knew nothing about its methodical development and its functions. Our civilization is still young, and young civilizations need all the arts of the animal-tamer to make the defiant barbarian and the savage in us more or less tractable. But at a higher cultural level we must forgo compulsion and turn to self-development. 63: 174

We obviously need both civilization *and* culture. . . . We cannot create one without the other, and we must admit, unfortunately, that modern humanity lacks both. Where there is too much of the one there is too little of the other, if we want to put it more cautiously. The continual harping on progress has by now become rather suspect. 69: 477

Civilization does not consist in progress as such and in mindless destruction of the old values, but in developing and refining the good that has been won. 65: 292

What aroused a feeling of horror in the Greeks still remains true, but it is true for us only if we give up the vain illusion that we are *different*, i.e., morally better, than the ancients. We have merely succeeded in forgetting that an indissoluble link binds us to the men of antiquity. This truth opens the way to an understanding of the classical spirit such as has never existed before—the way of inner sympathy on the one hand and of intellectual comprehension on the other. By penetrating into the blocked subterranean passages of our own psyches we grasp the living meaning of classical civilization, and at the same time we establish a firm foothold outside our own culture from which alone it is possible to gain an objective understanding of its foundations. That at least is the hope we draw from the rediscovery of the immortality of the Oedipus problem. 100: 1

Doubt about our civilization and its values is the contemporary neurosis. If our convictions were really indubitable nobody would ever doubt them. 37: 69

One of the most fundamental characteristics of every civilization is the quality of permanence, something created by man and wrested from the meaningless flux of nature. Every house, every bridge, every street, is a witness to the value of duration in the midst of change. 99:923

He who is rooted in the soil endures. Alienation from the unconscious and from its historical conditions spells rootlessness. That is the danger that lies in wait for the conqueror of foreign lands, and for every individual who, through one-sided allegiance to any kind of -ism, loses touch with the dark, maternal, earthy ground of his being.
46:103

The essence of culture is continuity and conservation of the past; craving for novelty produces only anti-culture and ends in barbarism. 84:6*

Sooner or later it will be found that nothing really new happens in history. There could be talk of something really novel only if the unimaginable happened: if reason, humanity and love won a lasting victory. 84:56*

The idea wants changelessness and eternity. Whoever lives under the supremacy of the idea strives for permanence; hence everything that pushes towards change must be opposed to the idea. 69:153

In confinio mortis and in the evening of a long and eventful life a man will often see immense vistas of time stretching out before him. Such a man no longer lives in the everyday world and in the vicissitudes of personal relationships, but in the sight of many aeons and in the movement of ideas as they pass from century to century. 7:717

The Individual and the Community

It is one of the most difficult and thankless of tasks to say anything of importance about the civilized man of today . . . for the speaker finds himself caught in the same presuppositions and is blinded by the same prejudices as those whom he wishes to view from a superior standpoint.

9: 104

The man we call modern, the man who is aware of the immediate present, is by no means the average man. He is rather the man who stands upon a peak, or at the very edge of the world, the abyss of the future before him, above him the heavens, and below him the whole of mankind with a history that disappears in primeval mists. The modern man—or, let us say again, the man of the immediate present—is rarely met with, for he must be conscious to a superlative degree. Since to be wholly of the present means to be fully conscious of one's existence as a man, it requires the most intensive and extensive consciousness, with a minimum of unconsciousness. It must be clearly understood that the mere fact of living in the present does not make a man modern, for in that case everyone at present alive would be so. He alone is modern who is fully conscious of the present.

93: 149

We always find in the patient a conflict which at a certain point is connected with the great problems of society. Hence, when the analysis is pushed to this point, the apparently individual conflict of the patient is revealed as a universal conflict of his environment and epoch. Neurosis is thus nothing less than an individual attempt, however unsuccessful, to solve a universal problem; indeed it cannot be otherwise, for a general problem, a "question," is not an *ens per se,* but exists only in the hearts of individuals.

104c: 438

In the case of psychological suffering, which always isolates the individual from the herd of so-called normal people, it is of the greatest importance to understand that the conflict is not a personal failure only, but at the same time a suffering common to all and a problem with which the whole epoch is burdened. This general point of view lifts the individual out of himself and connects him with humanity.   6: 116*

A man can find satisfaction and fulfilment only in what he does not yet possess, just as he can never be satisfied with something of which he has already had too much. To be a social and adapted person has no charms for one to whom such an aspiration is child's play. Always to do the right thing becomes a bore for the man who knows how, whereas the eternal bungler cherishes a secret longing to be right for once in some distant future. The needs and necessities of mankind are manifold. What sets one man free is another man's prison. So also with normality and adaptation. Even if it be a biological axiom that man is a herd animal who only finds optimum health in living as a social being, the very next case may quite possibly invert this axiom and show us that he is completely healthy only when leading an abnormal and unsocial life.   63: 162*f*

Man is not a machine in the sense that he can consistently maintain the same output of work. He can meet the demands of outer necessity in an ideal way only if he is also adapted to his own inner world, that is, if he is in harmony with himself. Conversely, he can only adapt to his inner world and achieve harmony with himself when he is adapted to the environmental conditions.   54: 75

The old religions with their sublime and ridiculous, their friendly and fiendish symbols did not drop from the blue, but were born of this human soul that dwells within us at this moment. All those things, their primal forms, live on in us and may at any time burst in upon us with annihilating force, in the guise of mass-suggestions against which the individual is defenceless. Our fearsome gods have only changed their names: they now rhyme with *ism*. Or has anyone the nerve to claim that the World War or Bolshevism was an ingenious invention? Just as outwardly we live in a world where a whole continent may be submerged at any moment, or a pole be shifted, or a new pestilence break out, so inwardly we live in a world where at any moment something similar may occur, albeit in the form of an idea, but no less dangerous and untrustworthy for that. Failure to adapt to this inner world is a negligence entailing just as serious consequences as ignorance and ineptitude in the outer world.   104B: 326

The mere act of enlightenment may have destroyed the spirits of nature, but not the psychic factors that correspond to them, such as suggestibility, lack of criticism, fearfulness, propensity to superstition and prejudice—in short, all those qualities which make possession possible. Even though nature is depsychized, the psychic conditions which breed demons are as actively at work as ever. The demons have not really disappeared but have merely taken on another form: they have become unconscious psychic forces.

1: 431

No, the demons are not banished; that is a difficult task that still lies ahead. Now that the angel of history has abandoned the Germans,* the demons will seek a new victim. And that won't be difficult. Every man who loses his shadow, every nation that falls into self-righteousness, is their prey. . . . We should not forget that exactly the same fatal tendency to collectivization is present in the victorious

* Written 1945.

nations as in the Germans, that they can just as suddenly become a victim of the demonic powers.   39G*

Just as we tend to assume that the world is as we see it, we naïvely suppose that people are as we imagine them to be. In this latter case, unfortunately, there is no scientific test that would prove the discrepancy between perception and reality. Although the possibility of gross deception is infinitely greater here than in our perception of the physical world, we still go on naïvely projecting our own psychology into our fellow human beings. In this way everyone creates for himself a series of more or less imaginary relationships based essentially on projection.   30:507

The vast majority of people are quite incapable of putting themselves individually into the mind of another. This is indeed a singularly rare art, and, truth to tell, it does not take us very far. Even the man whom we think we know best and who assures us himself that we understand him through and through is at bottom a stranger to us. He is *different*. The most we can do, and the best, is to have at least some inkling of his otherness, to respect it, and to guard against the outrageous stupidity of wishing to interpret it.   104B:363

For the primitive anything strange is hostile and evil. This line of division serves a purpose, which is why the normal person feels under no obligation to make these projections conscious, although they are dangerously illusory. War psychology has made this abundantly clear: everything my country does is good, everything the others do is bad. The centre of all iniquity is invariably found to lie a few miles behind the enemy lines. Because the individual has this same primitive psychology, every attempt to bring these age-old projections to consciousness is felt as irritating. Naturally one would like to have better relations with one's fellows, but only on the condition that *they* live up to *our* expectations—in other words, that they become willing carriers of our projections. Yet if we make ourselves conscious of these projections, it may easily act as an impediment to our relations with others, for there is then no bridge of illusion across which love and hate can stream off so relievingly, and no way of disposing so simply and satisfactorily of all those alleged virtues that are intended to edify and improve others.   30:517

It is so much easier to preach the universal panacea to everybody else than it is to take it oneself, and, as we all know, things are never so bad when everybody is in the same boat. No doubts can exist in the herd; the bigger the crowd the better the truth—and the greater the catastrophe.
                                                                72:563

Whatever we fight about in the outside world is also a battle in our inner selves. For we must finally admit that mankind is not just an accumulation of individuals utterly different from one another, but possesses such a high degree of psychological collectivity that in comparison the individual appears merely as a slight variant. How shall we judge of this matter fairly if we cannot admit that it is also our own problem? Anyone who can admit this will first seek the solution in himself, and this in fact is the way all the great solutions begin.   113:313*

What is true of humanity in general is also true of each individual, for humanity consists only of individuals. And as is the psychology of humanity so also is the psychology of the individual. The [first] World War brought a terrible reckoning with the rational intentions of civilization. What is called "will" in the individual is called "imperialism" in nations; for all will is a demonstration of power over fate, i.e., the exclusion of chance. Civilization is the rational, "purposeful" sublimation of free energies, brought about by will and intention. It is the same with the individual; and just as the idea of a world civilization received a fearful correction at the hands of war, so the individual must often learn in his life that so-called "disposable" energies are not his to dispose.   104A:74

We shall probably get nearest to the truth if we think of the conscious and personal psyche as resting upon the broad basis of an inherited and universal psychic disposition which is as such unconscious, and that our personal psyche bears the same relation to the collective psyche as the individual to society.   104B:234

All human control comes to an end when the individual is caught in a mass movement. Then the archetypes begin to function, as happens also in the lives of individuals when they are confronted with situations that cannot be dealt with in any of the familiar ways.   115:395

This war* has pitilessly revealed to civilized man that he is still a barbarian, and has at the same time shown what an iron scourge lies in store for him if ever again he should be tempted to make his neighbour responsible for his own evil qualities. The psychology of the individual is reflected in the psychology of the nation. What the nation does is done also by each individual, and so long as the individual continues to do it, the nation will do likewise. Only a change in the attitude of the individual can initiate a change in the psychology of the nation.   104A:4*

When fate, for four whole years, played out a war* of monumental frightfulness on the stage of Europe—a war that nobody wanted—nobody dreamt of asking exactly

* World War I.

who or what had caused the war and its continuation. Nobody realized that European man was possessed by something that robbed him of all free will. And this state of unconscious possession will continue undeterred until we Europeans become scared of our "god-almightiness." Such a change can begin only with individuals, for the masses are blind brutes, as we know to our cost.   72:563

Not nature but the "genius of mankind" has knotted the hangman's noose with which it can execute itself at any moment.
                                                                                7:734

When a problem that is at bottom personal, and therefore apparently subjective, coincides with external events that contain the same psychological elements as the personal conflict, it is suddenly transformed into a general question embracing the whole of society. In this way the personal problem acquires a dignity it lacked hitherto, since a state of inner discord always has something humiliating and degrading about it, so that one sinks into an ignominious condition both without and within, like a state dishonoured by civil war. It is this that makes one shrink from displaying before the public a purely personal conflict, provided of course that one does not suffer from an overdose of self-esteem. But if the connection between the personal problem and the larger contemporary events is discerned and understood, it brings release from the loneliness of the purely personal, and the subjective problem is magnified into a general question of our society.   69:119

The great events of world history are, at bottom, profoundly unimportant. In the last analysis, the essential thing is the life of the individual. This alone makes history, here alone do the great transformations first take place, and the whole future, the whole history of the world, ultimately spring as a gigantic summation from these hidden sources in individuals. In our most private and most subjective lives we are not only the passive witnesses of our age, and its sufferers, but also its makers.   45:315

Incisive changes in history are generally attributed exclusively to external causes. It seems to me, however, that external circumstances often serve merely as occasions for a new attitude to life and the world, long prepared in the unconscious, to become manifest. Social, political, and religious conditions affect the collective unconscious in the sense that all those factors which are suppressed by the prevailing views or attitudes in the life of a society gradually accumulate in the collective unconscious and activate its contents. Certain individuals gifted with particularly strong intuition then become aware of the changes going on in it and translate these changes into communicable ideas. The new ideas spread rapidly because parallel changes have been taking place in the unconscious of other people. There is a general readiness to accept the new ideas, although on the other hand they often meet with violent resistance. New ideas are not just the enemies of the old; they also appear as a rule in an extremely unacceptable form.   68:594

The ego lives in space and time and must adapt itself to their laws if it is to exist at all. If it is absorbed by the unconscious to such an extent that the latter alone has the power of decision, then the ego is stifled, and there is no longer any medium in which the unconscious could be integrated and in which the work of realization could take place. The separation of the empirical ego from the "eternal" and universal man is therefore of vital importance, particularly today, when mass-degeneration of the personality is making such threatening strides. Mass-degeneration does not come only from without: it also comes from within, from the collective unconscious. Against the outside, some protection was afforded by the *droits de l'homme* which at present are lost to the greater part of Europe, and even where they are not actually lost we see political parties, as naïve as they are powerful, doing their best to abolish them in favour of the slave state, with the bait of social security. Against the dæmonism from within, the Church offers some protection so long as it wields authority. But protection and security are only valuable when not excessively cramping to our existence; and in the same way the superiority of consciousness is desirable only if it does not suppress and shut out too much life. As always, life is a voyage between Scylla and Charybdis.   77:502

It is, unfortunately, only too clear that if the individual is not truly regenerated in spirit, society cannot be either, for society is the sum total of individuals in need of redemption. I can therefore see it only as a delusion when the Churches try—as apparently they do—to rope the individual into some social organization and reduce him to a condition of diminished responsibility, instead of raising him out of the torpid, mindless mass and making clear to him that he is the one important factor and that the salvation of the world consists in the salvation of the individual soul.   106:536

Resistance to the organized mass can be effected only by the man who is as well organized in his individuality as the mass itself.   106:540

Dionysus is the abyss of impassioned dissolution, where all human distinctions are merged in the animal divinity of the primordial psyche—a blissful and terrible experience. Humanity, huddling behind the walls of its culture, believes it has escaped this experience, until it succeeds in letting loose another orgy of bloodshed. All well-meaning people are amazed and blame high finance, the armaments industry, the Jews, or the Freemasons.   72:118

The catastrophe of the first World War and the extraordinary manifestations of profound spiritual malaise that came afterwards were needed to arouse a doubt as to whether all was well with the white man's mind. Before the war broke out in 1914 we were all quite certain that the world could be righted by rational means. Now we behold the amazing spectacle of states taking over the age-old totalitarian claims of theocracy, which are inevitably accompanied by suppression of free opinion. Once more we see people cutting each other's throats in support of childish theories of how to create paradise on earth. It is not very difficult to see that the powers of the underworld—not to say of hell—which in former times were more or less successfully chained up in a gigantic spiritual edifice where they could be of some use, are now creating, or trying to create, a State slavery and a State prison devoid of any mental or spiritual charm. There are not a few people nowadays who are convinced that mere human reason is not entirely up to the enormous task of putting a lid on the volcano.   74:83

Instead of being at the mercy of wild beasts, earthquakes, landslides, and inundations, modern man is battered by the elemental forces of his own psyche. This is the World Power that vastly exceeds all other powers on earth. The Age of Enlightenment, which stripped nature and human institutions of gods, overlooked the God of Terror who dwells in the human soul.   21:302

There is indeed reason enough for man to be afraid of the impersonal forces lurking in his unconscious. We are blissfully unconscious of these forces because they never, or almost never, appear in our personal relations or under ordinary circumstances. But if people crowd together and form a mob, then the dynamisms of the collective man are let loose—beasts or demons that lie dormant in every person until he is part of a mob. Man in the mass sinks unconsciously to an inferior moral and intellectual level, to that level which is always there, below the threshold of consciousness, ready to break forth as soon as it is activated by the formation of a mass.   74:23

The change of character brought about by the uprush of collective forces is amazing. A gentle and reasonable being can be transformed into a maniac or a savage beast. One is always inclined to lay the blame on external circumstances, but nothing could explode in us if it had not been there. As a matter of fact, we are constantly living on the edge of a volcano, and there is, so far as we know, no way of protecting ourselves from a possible outburst that will destroy everybody within reach. It is certainly a good thing to preach reason and common sense, but what if you have a lunatic asylum for an audience or a crowd in a collective frenzy? There is not much difference between them because the madman and the mob are both moved by impersonal, overwhelming forces.   74:25

It is quite natural that with the triumph of the Goddess of Reason a general neuroticizing of modern man should set in, a dissociation of personality analogous to the splitting of the world today by the Iron Curtain. This boundary line bristling with barbed wire runs through the psyche of modern man, no matter on which side he lives.   106:544

If only a world-wide consciousness could arise that all division and all fission are due to the splitting of opposites in the psyche, then we should know where to begin.   106:575

It is the face of our own shadow that glowers at us across the Iron Curtain.   8:85*

✧

No one can claim to be immune to the spirit of his own epoch or to possess anything like a complete knowledge of it. Regardless of our conscious convictions, we are all without exception, in so far as we are particles in the mass, gnawed at and undermined by the spirit that runs through the masses. Our freedom extends only as far as our consciousness reaches. 58:153

In any age the vast majority of men are called upon to preserve and praise the *status quo*, thus helping to bring about the disastrous consequences which the prescience of the creative spirit had sought to avert. 69:434

The fact that individual consciousness means separation and opposition is something that man has experienced countless times in his long history. And just as for the individual a time of dissociation is a time for sickness, so it is in the life of nations. We can hardly deny that ours is a time of dissociation and sickness. The political and social conditions, the fragmentation of religion and philosophy, the contending schools of modern art and modern psychology all have one meaning in this respect. And does anyone who is endowed with the slightest sense of responsibility feel any satisfaction at this turn of events? If we are honest, we must admit that no one feels quite comfortable in the present-day world; indeed, it becomes increasingly uncomfortable. The word "crisis," so often heard, is a medical expression which always tells us that the sickness has reached a dangerous climax. 45:290

Loss of roots and lack of tradition neuroticize the masses and prepare them for collective hysteria. Collective hysteria calls for collective therapy, which consists in abolition of liberty and terrorization. Where rationalistic materialism holds sway, states tend to develop less into prisons than into lunatic asylums. 3:282

Whenever contents of the collective unconscious become activated, they have a disturbing effect on the conscious mind, and confusion ensues. If the activation is due to the collapse of the individual's hopes and expectations, there is a danger that the collective unconscious may take the place of reality. This state would be pathological. If, on the other hand, the activation is the result of psychological processes in the unconscious of the people, the individual may feel threatened or at any rate disoriented, but the resultant state is not pathological, at least so far as the individual is concerned. Nevertheless, the mental state of the people as a whole might well be compared to a psychosis.

68:595

Masses are always breeding grounds of psychic epidemics.

17:227

Who are we to imagine that "it couldn't happen here"? We have only to multiply the population of Switzerland by twenty to become a nation of eighty millions, and our public intelligence and morality would then be automatically divided by twenty in consequence of the devastating moral and psychic effects of living together in huge masses. Such a state of things provides the basis for collective crime, and it is then really a miracle if the crime is not committed . . . . It has filled us with horror to realize all that man is capable of, and of which, therefore, we too are capable. Since then a terrible doubt about humanity, and about ourselves, gnaws at our hearts.

1:412

The "common man," who is predominantly a mass man, acts on the principle of realizing nothing, nor does he need to, because for him the only thing that commits mistakes is that vast anonymity conventionally known as the "State" or "Society." But once a man knows that he is, or should be, responsible, he feels responsible also for his psychic constitution, the more so the more clearly he sees what he would have to be in order to become healthier, more stable, and more efficient. Once he is on the way to assimilating the unconscious he can be certain that he will escape no difficulty that is an integral part of his nature.

53:410

If a man is capable of leading a responsible life himself, then he is also conscious of his duties to the community.

84:56*

Since everybody is blindly convinced that he is nothing more than his own extremely unassuming and insignificant conscious self, which performs its duties decently and earns a moderate living, nobody is aware that this whole rationalistically organized conglomeration we call a state or a nation is driven on by seemingly impersonal, invisible but terrifying power which nobody and nothing can check. This ghastly power is mostly explained as fear of the neighbouring nation, which is supposed to be possessed by a malevolent fiend. Since nobody is capable of recognizing just where and how much he himself is possessed and unconscious, he simply projects his own condition upon his neighbour, and thus it becomes a sacred duty to have the biggest guns and the most poisonous gas. The worst of it is that he is quite right. All one's neighbours are in the grip of some uncontrolled and uncontrollable fear, just like oneself. In lunatic asylums it is a well-known fact that patients are far more dangerous when suffering from fear than when moved by rage or hatred. 74:85

The mass is swayed by *participation mystique*, which is nothing other than an unconscious identity. Supposing, for example, you go to the theatre: glance meets glance, everybody observes everybody else, so that all those who are present are caught up in an invisible web of mutual unconscious relationship. If this condition increases, one literally feels borne along by the universal wave of identity with others. It may be a pleasant feeling—one sheep among ten thousand! Again, if I feel that this crowd is a great and wonderful unity, I am a hero, exalted along with the group. When I am myself again, I discover that I am Mr. So-and-So, and that I live in such and such a street, on the third floor. I also find that the whole affair was really most delightful, and I hope it will take place again tomorrow so that I may once more feel myself to be a whole nation, which is much better than being just plain Mr. X. Since this is such an easy and convenient way of raising one's personality to a more exalted rank, mankind has always formed groups which made collective experiences of transformation—often of an ecstatic nature—possible. The regressive identification with lower and more primitive states of consciousness is invariably accompanied by a heightened sense of life.   17:226

Human beings have one faculty which, though it is of the greatest utility for collective purposes, is most pernicious for individuation, and that is the faculty of imitation. Collective psychology cannot dispense with imitation, for without it all mass organizations, the State and the social order, are impossible. Society is organized, indeed, less by law than by the propensity to imitation, implying equally suggestibility, suggestion, and mental contagion. But we see every day how people use, or rather abuse, the mechanism of imitation for the purpose of personal differentiation: they are content to ape some eminent personality, some striking characteristic or mode of behaviour, thereby achieving an outward distinction from the circle in which they move. We could almost say that as a punishment for this the uniformity of their minds with those of their neighbours, already real enough, is intensified into an unconscious, compulsive bondage to the environment. As a rule these specious attempts at individual differentiation stiffen into a pose, and the imitator remains at the same level as he always was, only several degrees more sterile than before.

104B: 242

❖

The element of differentiation is the individual. All the highest achievements of virtue, as well as the blackest villainies, are individual. The larger a community is, and the more the sum total of collective factors peculiar to every large community rests on conservative prejudices detrimental to individuality, the more will the individual be morally and spiritually crushed, and, as a result, the one source of moral and spiritual progress for society is choked up. Naturally the only thing that can thrive in such an atmosphere is sociality and whatever is collective in the individual. Everything individual in him goes under, i.e., is doomed to repression. The individual elements lapse into the unconscious, where, by the law of necessity, they are transformed into something essentially baleful, destructive, and anarchical. Socially, this evil principle shows itself in the spectacular crimes—regicide and the like—perpetrated by certain prophetically-inclined individuals; but in the great mass of the community it remains in the background, and only manifests itself indirectly in the inexorable moral degeneration of society. 104B: 240

It is a notorious fact that the morality of society as a whole is in inverse ratio to its size; for the greater the aggregation of individuals, the more the individual factors are blotted out, and with them morality, which rests entirely on the moral sense of the individual and the freedom necessary for this. Hence every man is, in a certain sense, unconsciously a worse man when he is in society than when acting alone; for he is carried by society and to that extent relieved of his individual responsibility. 104B: 240

Any large company composed of wholly admirable persons has the morality and intelligence of an unwieldy, stupid, and violent animal. The bigger the organization, the more unavoidable is its immorality and blind stupidity (*Senatus bestia, senatores boni viri*). Society, by automatically stressing all the collective qualities in its individual representatives, puts a premium on mediocrity, on everything that settles down to vegetate in an easy, irresponsible way. Individuality will inevitably be driven to the wall. This process begins in school, continues at the university, and rules all departments in which the State has a hand. In a small social body, the individuality of its members is better safeguarded; and the greater is their relative freedom and the possibility of conscious responsibility. Without freedom there can be no morality.

104B: 240

The heaping together of paintings by Old Masters in museums is a catastrophe; likewise, a collection of a hundred Great Brains makes one big fathead.   41: 944

A million zeros joined together do not, unfortunately, add up to one.   106: 535

Our admiration for great organizations dwindles when once we become aware of the other side of the wonder: the tremendous piling up and accentuation of all that is primitive in man, and the unavoidable destruction of his individuality in the interests of the monstrosity that every great organization in fact is. The man of today, who resembles more or less the collective ideal, has made his heart into a den of murderers.   104B: 240

The levelling down of the masses through suppression of the aristocratic or hierarchical structure natural to a community is bound, sooner or later, to lead to disaster. For, when everything outstanding is levelled down, the sign-posts are lost, and the longing to be led becomes an urgent necessity. 31:248

Nature cares nothing whatsoever about a higher level of consciousness; quite the contrary. And then society does not value these feats of the psyche very highly; its prizes are always given for achievement and not for personality, the latter being rewarded for the most part posthumously. 94:768

The present attempts to achieve full individual conscious-ness and to mature the personality are, socially speaking, still so feeble that they carry no weight at all in relation to our historic needs. If our European social order is not to be shaken to its foundations, authority must be restored at all costs. This is probably one reason for the efforts now be-ing made in Europe to replace the collectivity of the Church by the collectivity of the State. 80:221*f*

The increasing dependence on the State is anything but a healthy symptom; it means that the whole nation is in a fair way to becoming a herd of sheep, constantly relying on a shepherd to drive them into good pastures. The shep-herd's staff soon becomes a rod of iron, and the shepherds turn into wolves. 1:413

Far too little attention has been paid to the fact that, for all our irreligiousness, the distinguishing mark of the Christian epoch, its highest achievement, has become the congenital vice of our age: the supremacy of the word, of the Logos, which stands for the central figure of our Christian faith. The word has literally become our god, and so it has re-mained, even if we knew of Christianity only by hearsay. Words like "Society" and "State" are so concretized that they are almost personified. In the opinion of the man in the street, the "State," far more than any king in history, is the inexhaustible giver of all good; the "State" is invoked, made responsible, grumbled at, and so on and so forth. Society is elevated to the rank of a supreme ethical principle; indeed, it is even credited with positively creative capacities. No one seems to notice that this worship of the word, which was necessary at a certain phase of man's mental development, has a perilous shadow side. That is to say, the moment the word, as a result of centuries of education, attains universal validity, it severs its original connection with the divine Person. There is then a personified Church, a personified State; belief in the word becomes credulity, and the word itself an infernal slogan capable of any deception.   106: 554

Childlike faith, when it comes naturally, is certainly a charisma. But when "joyful faith" and "childlike trust" are instilled by religious education, they are no charisma but a gift of the ambiguous gods, because they can be manipulated only too easily and with greater effect by other "saviours" as well.   43*

Our blight is ideologies—they are the long-expected Antichrist!   23:778

What is the use of technological improvements when mankind must still tremble before those infantile tyrants, ridiculous yet terrible, in the style of Hitler? Figures like these owe their power only to the frightening immaturity of the man of today, and to his barbarous unconsciousness. Truly we can no longer afford to underestimate the importance of the psychic factor in world affairs.   14:11*

The mass as such is always anonymous and always irresponsible. So-called leaders are the inevitable symptoms of a mass movement. The true leaders of mankind are always those who are capable of self-reflection, and who relieve the dead weight of the masses at least of their own weight, consciously holding aloof from the blind momentum of the mass in movement. But who can resist this all-engulfing force of attraction, when each man clings to the next and each drags the other with him? Only one who is firmly rooted not only in the outside world but also in the world within.   45:326*f*

The wise man who is not heeded is counted a fool, and the fool who proclaims the general folly first and loudest passes for a prophet and Führer, and sometimes it is luckily the other way round as well, or else mankind would long since have perished of stupidity.   48:783

What depths of despair are still needed to open the eyes of the world's responsible leaders, so that at least they can refrain from leading themselves into temptation?

59:455

✧

One might expect, perhaps, that a man of genius would luxuriate in the greatness of his own thoughts and renounce the cheap approbation of the rabble he despises; yet he succumbs to the more powerful impulse of the herd instinct. His seeking and his finding, his heart's cry, are meant for the herd and must be heeded by them.   100:14

The importance of personal prestige can hardly be overestimated, because the possibility of regressive dissolution in the collective psyche is a very real danger, not only for the outstanding individual but also for his followers. This possibility is most likely to occur when the goal of prestige —universal recognition—has been reached. The person then becomes a collective truth, and that is always the beginning of the end. To gain prestige is a positive achievement not only for the oustanding individual but also for the clan. The individual distinguishes himself by his deeds, the many by their renunciation of power. So long as this attitude needs to be fought for and defended against hostile influences, the achievement remains positive; but as soon as there are no more obstacles and universal recognition has been attained, prestige loses its positive value and usually becomes a dead letter. A schismatic movement then sets in, and the whole process begins again from the beginning.   104B:238

The office I hold is certainly my special activity; but it is also a collective factor that has come into existence historically through the cooperation of many people and whose dignity rests solely on collective approval. When, therefore, I identify myself with my office or title, I behave as though I myself were the whole complex of social factors of which that office consists, or as though I were not only the bearer of the office, but also and at the same time the approval of society. I have made an extraordinary extension of myself and have usurped qualities which are not in me but outside me.   104B:227

There is a deep gulf between what a man is and what he represents, between what he is as an individual and what he is as a collective being. His function is developed at the expense of the individuality. Should he excel, he is merely identical with his collective function; but should he not, then, though he may be highly esteemed as a function in society, his individuality is wholly on the level of his inferior, undeveloped functions, and he is simply a barbarian, while in the former case he has happily deceived himself as to his actual barbarism.   69:111

Through his identification with the collective psyche a patient will infallibly try to force the demands of his unconscious upon others, for identity with the collective psyche always brings with it a feeling of universal validity—"god-likeness"—which completely ignores all differences in the personal psyche of his fellows. (The feeling of universal validity comes, of course, from the universality of the collective psyche.) A collective attitude naturally presupposes this same collective psyche in others. But that means a ruthless disregard not only of individual differences but also of differences of a more general kind within the collective psyche itself, as for example differences of race. This disregard for individuality obviously means the suffocation of the single individual, as a consequence of which the element of differentiation is obliterated from the community.

104B:240

If man cannot exist without society, neither can he exist without oxygen, water, albumen, fat, and so forth. Like these, society is one of the necessary conditions of his existence. It would be ludicrous to maintain that man lives in order to breathe air. It is equally ludicrous to say that the individual exists for society. "Society" is nothing more than a term, a concept for the symbiosis of a group of human beings. A concept is not a carrier of life. The sole and natural carrier of life is the individual, and that is so throughout nature.

80:224

Although biological instinctive processes contribute to the formation of personality, individuality is nevertheless essentially different from collective instincts; indeed, it stands in the most direct opposition to them, just as the individual as a personality is always distinct from the collective. His essence consists precisely in this distinction. Every ego-psychology must necessarily exclude and ignore just the collective element that is bound to a psychology of instinct, since it describes that very process by which the ego becomes differentiated from collective drives.   69:88

To find out what is truly individual in ourselves, profound reflection is needed; and suddenly we realize how uncommonly difficult the discovery of individuality in fact is.   104B:242

On closer examination one is always astonished to see how much of our so-called individual psychology is really collective. So much, indeed, that the individual traits are completely overshadowed by it. Since, however, individuation is an ineluctable psychological necessity, we can see from the ascendancy of the collective what very special attention must be paid to this delicate plant "individuality" if it is not to be completely smothered.   104B:241

We yield too much to the ridiculous fear that we are at bottom quite impossible beings, that if everyone were to appear as he really is a frightful social catastrophe would ensue. Many people today take "man as he really is" to mean merely the eternally discontented, anarchic, rapacious element in human beings, quite forgetting that these same human beings have also erected those firmly established forms of civilization which possess greater strength and stability than all the anarchic undercurrents. The strengthening of his social personality is one of the essential conditions for man's existence. Were it not so, humanity would cease to be. The selfishness and rebelliousness we meet in the neurotic's psychology are not "man as he really is" but an infantile distortion. In reality the normal man is "civic-minded and moral"; he created his laws and observes them, not because they are imposed on him from without—that is a childish delusion—but because he loves law and order more than he loves disorder and lawlessness.   101:442

No social legislation will ever be able to overcome the psychological differences between men, this most necessary factor for generating the vital energy of a human society. It may serve a useful purpose, therefore, to speak of the heterogeneity of men. These differences involve such different requirements for happiness that no legislation, however perfect, could afford them even approximate satisfaction. No outward form of life could be devised, however equitable and just it might appear, that would not involve injustice for one or the other human type. That, in spite of this, every kind of enthusiast—political, social, philosophical, and religious—is busily endeavouring to find those uniform external conditions which would bring with them greater opportunities for the happiness of all seems to me connected with a general attitude to life too exclusively oriented by the outer world. 69:845

Although it is certainly a fine thing that every man should stand equal before the law, that every man should have his political vote, and that no man, through hereditary social position and privilege, should have unjust advantage over his brother, it is distinctly less fine when the idea of equality is extended to other walks of life. A man must have a very clouded vision, or view human society from a very misty distance, to cherish the notion that the uniform regulation of life would automatically ensure a uniform distribution of happiness. He must be pretty far gone in delusion if he imagines that equality of income, or equal opportunities for all, would have approximately the same value for everyone. But, if he were a legislator, what would he do about all those people whose greatest opportunities lie not without, but within? If he were just, he would have to give at least twice as much money to the one as to the other, since to the one it means much, to the other little.

69:845

The individual ego could be conceived as the commander of a small army in the struggle with his environment—a war not infrequently on two fronts, before him the struggle

for existence, in the rear the struggle against his own rebel-
lious instinctual nature. Even to those of us who are not
pessimists our existence feels more like a struggle than
anything else. The state of peace is a desideratum, and
when a man has found peace with himself and the world
it is indeed a noteworthy event.   5:693

The optimum of life is not to be found in crude egoism,
for fundamentally man is so constituted that the pleasure
he gives his neighbour is something essential to him. Nor
can the optimum be reached by an unbridled craving for
individualistic supremacy, for the collective element in man
is so powerful that his longing for fellowship would destroy
all pleasure in naked egoism. The optimum can be reached
only through obedience to the tidal laws of the libido, by
which systole alternates with diastole—laws which bring
pleasure and the necessary limitations of pleasure, and also
set us those individual life-tasks without whose accom-
plishment the vital optimum can never be attained.

69:356

✧

We need not be ashamed of ourselves as a nation, nor
can we alter its character. Only the individual can alter or
improve himself, provided he can outgrow his national
prejudices in the course of his psychic development. The
national character is imprinted on a man as a fate he has
not chosen—like a beautiful or an ugly body. It is not the
will of individuals that moulds the destinies of nations,
but suprapersonal factors, the spirit and the earth, which
work in mysterious ways and in unfathomable darkness.

99:921

The mystery of the earth is no joke and no paradox. One
only needs to see how, in America, the skull and pelvis
measurements of all the European races begin to indianize

themselves in the second generation of immigrants. That is the mystery of the American earth. The soil of every country holds some such mystery. We have an unconscious reflection of this in the psyche: just as there is a relationship of mind to body, so there is a relationship of body to earth.

85: 18*f*

The Swiss national character that has been built up over the centuries was not formed by chance; it is a meaningful response to the dangerously undermining influence of the environment. We Swiss should certainly understand why a mind like Keyserling's judges us so harshly, but he should also understand that the very things he taxes us with belong to our most necessary possessions.   99: 924

Our loveliest mountain, which dominates Switzerland far and wide, is called the Jungfrau—the "Virgin." The Virgin Mary is the female patron saint of the Swiss. Of her Tertullian says: ". . . that virgin earth, not yet watered by the rains," and Augustine: "Truth has arisen from the earth, because Christ is born of a virgin." These are living reminders that the virgin mother is the earth. From olden times the astrological sign for Switzerland was either Virgo or Taurus; both are earth-signs, a sure indication that the earthy character of the Swiss had not escaped the old astrologers. From the earth-boundness of the Swiss come all their bad as well as their good qualities: their down-to-earthness, their limited outlook, their non-spirituality, their parsimony, stolidity, stubbornness, dislike of foreigners, mistrustfulness, as well as that awful *Schwizerdütsch* and their refusal to be bothered, or to put it in political terms, their neutrality. Switzerland consists of numerous valleys, depressions in the earth's crust, in which the settlements of man are embedded. Nowhere are there measureless plains, where it is a matter of indifference where a man lives; nowhere is there a coast against which the ocean beats with its lore of distant lands. Buried deep in the backbone of the continent, sunk in the earth, the Alpine dweller lives like a troglodyte, surrounded by more powerful nations that are linked with the wide world, that expand into colonies or can grow rich on the treasures of their soil. The Swiss cling to what they have, for the others, the more powerful ones, have grabbed everything else. Under no circumstances will the Swiss be robbed of their own. Their country is small, their possessions limited. If they lose what they have, what is going to replace it?   99:914

We are in reality unable to borrow or absorb anything from outside, from the world, or from history. What is essential to us can only grow out of ourselves. When the white man is true to his instincts, he reacts defensively against any advice that one might give him. What he has already swallowed he is forced to reject again as if it were a foreign body, for his blood refuses to assimilate anything sprung from foreign soil.   97A:31*

Does neutral Switzerland, with its backward, earthy nature, fulfil any meaningful function in the European system? I think we must answer this question affirmatively. The answer to political or cultural questions need not be only: Progress and Change, but also: Stand still! Hold fast! These days one can doubt in good faith whether the condition of Europe shows any change for the better since the war. Opinions, as we know, are very divided, and we have just heard Spengler's lamentations on the decline of the West. Progress can occasionally go down-hill, and in the face of a dangerously rapid tempo standing still can be a life-saver. Nations, too, get tired and long for political and social stabilization. The Pax Romana meant a good deal to the Roman Empire.   99:922

There are two kinds of interference which cause the hackles of the Swiss to rise: political and spiritual. Everyone can understand why they should defend themselves to the utmost against political interference, and this utmost is the art of neutrality born of necessity. But why they should defend themselves against spiritual interference is rather more mysterious. It is, however, a fact, as I can confirm from my own experience. English, American, and German patients are far more open to new ideas than the Swiss. A new idea for the Swiss is always something of a risk; it is like an unknown, dangerous animal, which must if possible be circumvented or else approached with extreme caution.   99:916

If it be true that we are the most backward, conservative, stiff-necked, self-righteous, smug, and churlish of all European nations, this would mean that in Switzerland the European is truly at home in his geographical and psychological centre. There he is attached to the earth, unconcerned, self-reliant, conservative, and backward—in other words, still intimately connected with the past, occupying a neutral position between the fluctuating and contradictory aspirations and opinions of the other nations or functions. That wouldn't be a bad role for the Swiss: to act as Europe's centre of gravity.   99:920

We do not sufficiently distinguish between individualism and individuation. Individualism means deliberately stressing and giving prominence to some supposed peculiarity, rather than to collective considerations and obligations. But individuation means precisely the better and more complete fulfilment of the collective qualities of the human being, since adequate consideration of the peculiarity of the individual is more conducive to better social achievement than when the peculiarity is neglected or suppressed.

104B:267

Nobody can know himself and differentiate himself from his neighbours if he has a distorted picture of him, just as no one can understand his neighbour if he has no relationship to himself.   48:739

The revolution in our conscious outlook, brought about by the catastrophic results of the [first] World War, shows itself in our inner life by the shattering of our faith in ourselves and our own worth. We used to regard foreigners as political and moral reprobates, but the modern man is forced to recognize that he is politically and morally just like anyone else. Whereas formerly I believed it was my bounden duty to call others to order, I must now admit I need calling to order myself.   93:162

The horror which the dictator States have of late brought upon mankind is nothing less than the culmination of all those atrocities of which our ancestors made themselves guilty in the not so distant past. Quite apart from the barbarities and blood baths perpetrated by the Christian nations among themselves throughout European history, the European has also to answer for all the crimes he has committed against the coloured races during the process of colonization. In this respect the white man carries a very heavy burden indeed. It shows us a picture of the common human shadow that could hardly be painted in blacker colours. The evil that comes to light in man and that undoubtedly dwells within him is of gigantic proportions.

106:571

The principal and indeed the only thing that is wrong with the world is man.   1:441

Today humanity, as never before, is split into two apparently irreconcilable halves. The psychological rule says that when an inner situation is not made conscious, it happens outside, as fate. That is to say, when the individual remains undivided and does not become conscious of his inner opposite, the world must perforce act out the conflict and be torn into opposing halves.   3:126

THE WORLD OF VALUES

Awareness and Creative Living

Knowledge rests not upon truth alone, but on error also.
28:774

Mistakes are, after all, the foundations of truth, and if a man does not know what a thing *is*, it is at least an increase in knowledge if he knows what it is *not*.   3:429

I do not call the man who admits his ignorance an obscurantist; I think it is much rather the man whose consciousness is not sufficiently developed to be aware of his ignorance.   72:564

I do not take kindly to the argument that because certain working hypotheses may not possess eternal validity or may possibly be erroneous, they must be withheld from the public.   100:685

One of the greatest obstacles to psychological understanding is the inquisitive desire to know whether the psychological factor adduced is "true" or "correct." If the description of it is not erroneous or false, then the factor is valid in itself and proves its validity by its very existence. One might just as well ask if the duck-billed platypus is a "true" or "correct" invention of the Creator's will.

102:192

The ideal and aim of science do not consist in giving the most exact possible description of the facts—science cannot compete as a recording instrument with the camera and the gramophone—but in establishing certain laws, which are merely abbreviated expressions for many diverse processes that are yet conceived to be somehow correlated. This aim goes beyond the purely empirical realm by means of the *concept*, which, though it may have general and proved validity, will always be a product of the subjective psychological constellation of the investigator. In the making of scientific theories and concepts many personal and accidental factors are involved. There is also a personal equation that is psychological and not merely psychophysical.   69:9

We see colours but not wave-lengths. This well-known fact must nowhere be taken to heart more seriously than in psychology. The effect of the personal equation begins already in the act of observation. One sees what one can best see oneself. Thus, first and foremost, one sees the mote in one's brother's eye. No doubt the mote is there, but the beam sits in one's own—and may considerably hamper the act of seeing. I mistrust the principle of "pure observation" in so-called objective psychology unless one confines oneself to the eyepieces of chronoscopes and tachistoscopes and suchlike "psychological" apparatus. With such methods one also guards against too embarrassing a yield of empirical psychological facts. But the personal equation asserts itself even more in the presentation and communication of one's own observations, to say nothing of the interpretation and abstract exposition of the empirical material. Nowhere is the basic requirement so indispensable as in psychology that the observer should be adequate to his object, in the sense of being able to see not only subjectively but also objectively. The demand that he should see *only* objectively is quite out of the question, for it is impossible. We must be satisfied if he does not see *too* subjectively.   69:9*f*

Never in any circumstances should one indulge in the unscientific illusion that one's own subjective prejudice is a universal and fundamental psychological truth. No true science can spring from this, only a faith whose shadow is intolerance and fanaticism. Contradictory views are necessary for the evolution of any science, only they must not be set up in rigid opposition to each other but should strive for the earliest possible synthesis.   35:639*

Ultimate truth, if there be such a thing, demands the concert of many voices.   50:xiv*

Today we are convinced that in all fields of knowledge psychological premises exist which exert a decisive influence upon the choice of material, the method of investigation, the nature of the conclusions, and the formulation of hypotheses and theories. We have even come to believe that Kant's personality was a decisive conditioning factor of his *Critique of Pure Reason*. Not only our philosophers, but our own predilections in philosophy, and even what we are fond of calling our "best" truths are affected, if not dangerously undermined, by this recognition of a personal premise. All creative freedom, we cry out, is taken away from us! What? Can it be possible that a man only thinks or says or does what he himself *is*?   67:150

What to the causal view is *fact* to the final view is *symbol*, and vice versa. Everything that is real and essential to the one is unreal and inessential to the other. We are therefore forced to resort to the antinomian postulate and must view the world, too, as a psychic phenomenon. Certainly it is necessary for science to know how things are "in themselves," but even science cannnot escape the psychological conditions of knowledge, and psychology must be peculiarly alive to these conditions.   54:45

I am an empiricist, not a philosopher; I cannot let myself presuppose that my peculiar temperament, my own attitude to intellectual problems, is universally valid. Apparently this is an assumption in which only the philosopher may indulge, who always takes it for granted that his own disposition and attitude are universal, and will not recognize the fact, if he can avoid it, that his "personal equation" conditions his philosophy.   67:149

The tragic thing is that psychology has no self-consistent mathematics at its disposal, but only a calculus of subjective prejudices. Also, it lacks the immense advantage of an Archimedean point such as physics enjoys. The latter observes the physical world from the psychic standpoint and can translate it into psychic terms. The psyche, on the other hand, observes itself and can only translate the psychic back into the psychic.   53:421

The latest developments in psychology show with ever increasing clarity not only that there are no simple formulas from which the world of the psyche might be derived, but that we have never yet succeeded in defining the field of psychic experience with sufficient exactitude. Despite the immense area it covers on the surface, scientific psychology has not even begun to demolish the mountain of prejudices that permanently block the way to the psyche as it really is. Psychology is the youngest of the sciences and is suffering from all those childhood ailments which afflicted the adolescence of other sciences in the late Middle Ages. Psychologies still exist which limit the field of psychic experience to consciousness and its contents, or understand the psyche as a purely reactive phenomenon without any trace of autonomy. The idea of an unconscious psyche has not yet gained undisputed currency, despite the existence of an overwhelming mass of empirical material which proves beyond all doubt that there can be no psychology of consciousness without a recognition of the unconscious. Lacking this foundation, it is impossible to deal with any psychological datum that is in any way complex, and the actual psyche we have to deal with in real life is complexity itself.   33:ix *f**

It is really high time academic psychologists came down to earth and wanted to hear about the human psyche as it really is and not merely about laboratory experiments. It is insufferable that professors should forbid their students to have anything to do with analytical psychology, that they should prohibit the use of analytical concepts and accuse our psychology of taking account, in an unscientific manner, of "everyday experiences." I know that psychology in general could derive the greatest benefit from a serious study of the dream problem once it could rid itself of the unjustified lay prejudice that dreams are caused solely by somatic stimuli. This overrating of the somatic factor in psychiatry is one of the basic reasons why psychopathology has made no advances unless directly fertilized by analytical procedures. The dogma that "mental diseases are diseases of the brain" is a hangover from the materialism of the 1870's. It has become a prejudice which hinders all progress.   30:529

However indignant people may get about "metaphysical phantoms" when cell-processes are explained vitalistically, they nevertheless continue to regard the physical hypothesis as "scientific," although it is no less fantastic. But it fits in with the materialistic prejudice, and therefore every bit of nonsense, provided only that it turns the psychic into the physical, becomes scientifically sacrosanct. Let us hope that the time is not far off when this antiquated relic of ingrained and thoughtless materialism will be eradicated from the minds of our scientists.   30:529

Only those who regard the happenings in this world as a concatenation of errors and accidents, and who therefore believe that the pedagogic hand of the rationalist is constantly needed to guide us, can ever imagine that this path [of psychoanalysis] was an aberration from which we should have been warned off with a signboard. Besides the deeper insight into psychological determination, we owe to this "error" a method of inquiry of incalculable importance. It is for us to rejoice and be thankful that Freud had the courage to let himself be guided along this path. Not thus is the progress of science hindered, but rather by blind adherence to insights once gained, by the typical conservatism of authority, by the childish vanity of the savant and his fear of making mistakes. This lack of courage is considerably more injurious to the name of science than an honest error. When will there be an end to the incessant squabbling about who is right? One has only to look at the history of science: how many have *been* right, and how few have *remained* right!   101:302

Every victory contains the germ of future defeat.

67:150

✧

Nothing is more vulnerable and ephemeral than scientific theories, which are mere tools and not everlasting truths.   8:92*

Theories in psychology are the very devil. It is true that we need certain points of view for their orienting and heuristic value; but they should always be regarded as mere auxiliary concepts that can be laid aside at any time. We still know so very little about the psyche that it is positively grotesque to think we are far enough advanced to frame general theories. We have not even established the empirical extent of the psyche's phenomenology: how then can we dream of general theories? No doubt theory is the best cloak for lack of experience and ignorance, but the consequences are depressing: bigotedness, superficiality, and scientific sectarianism.   64:7*

Psychology, as one of the many expressions of psychic life, operates with ideas which in their turn are derived from archetypal structures and thus generate a somewhat more abstract kind of myth. Psychology therefore translates the archaic speech of myth into a modern mythologem—not yet, of course, recognized as such—which constitutes one element of the myth "science." 76: 302

It is impossible to derive any philosophical system from the fundamental thoughts of primitive man. They provide only antinomies, but it is just these that are the inexhaustible source of all spiritual problems in all times and in all civilizations. 9: 144

We have to learn to think in antinomies, constantly bearing in mind that every truth turns into an antinomy if it is thought out to the end. 49: 14*

Medieval alchemy prepared the way for the greatest intervention in the divine world order that man has ever attempted: alchemy was the dawn of the scientific age, when the daemon of the scientific spirit compelled the forces of nature to serve man to an extent that had never been known before. It was from the spirit of alchemy that Goethe wrought the figure of the "superman" Faust, and this superman led Nietzsche's Zarathustra to declare that God was dead and to proclaim the will to give birth to the superman, to "create a god for yourself out of your seven devils." Here we find the true roots, the preparatory processes deep in the psyche, which unleashed the forces at work in the world today. Science and technology have indeed conquered the world, but whether the psyche has gained anything is another matter. 58: 163

Science comes to a stop at the frontiers of logic, but nature does not—she thrives on ground as yet untrodden by theory. *Venerabilis natura* does not halt at the opposites; she uses them to create, out of opposition, a new birth.

77:524

A man is a philosopher of genius only when he succeeds in transforming the primitive and wholly natural vision into an abstract idea belonging to the common stock of consciousness. This achievement, and this alone, constitutes his personal value, for which he may take credit without necessarily succumbing to inflation. . . . The personal value lies entirely in the philosophical achievement, not in the primary vision. To the philosopher this vision comes as so much increment, and is simply a part of the common property of mankind, in which, in principle, everyone has a share. The golden apples drop from the same tree, whether they be gathered by an imbecile locksmith's apprentice or by a Schopenhauer.   104B:229

I do not regard the pursuit of science as a bickering about who is right, but as an endeavour to augment and deepen human knowledge.   100:685

Our psychology is a science that can at most be accused of having discovered the dynamite terrorists work with. What the moralist and the general practitioner do with it is none of our business and we have no intention of interfering. Plenty of unqualified persons are sure to push their way in and commit the greatest follies, but that too does not concern us. Our aim is simply and solely scientific knowledge, and we do not have to bother with all the uproar it has provoked. If religion and morality are blown to pieces in the process, so much the worse for them for not having more stamina. Knowledge is a force of nature that goes its way irresistibly from inner necessity.   113:314*

Until recently psychology was a special branch of philosophy, but now we are coming to something which Nietzsche foresaw—the rise of psychology in its own right, so much so that it is even threatening to swallow philosophy. The inner resemblance between the two disciplines consists in this, that both are systems of opinion about objects which cannot be fully experienced and therefore cannot be adequately comprehended by a purely empirical approach. Both fields of study thus encourage speculation, with the result that opinions are formed in such variety and profusion that many heavy volumes are needed to contain them all. Neither discipline can do without the other, and the one invariably furnishes the unspoken—and generally unconscious—assumptions of the other.   12:659

There is not *one* modern psychology—there are dozens of them. This is curious enough when we remember that there is only one science of mathematics, of geology, zoology, botany, and so forth. But there are so many psychologies that an American university was able to publish a thick volume under the title *Psychologies of 1930*. I believe there are as many psychologies as philosophies, for there is also no single philosophy, but many. I mention this for the reason that philosophy and psychology are linked by indissoluble bonds which are kept in being by the interrelation of their subject-matters. Psychology takes the psyche for its subject, and philosophy—to put it briefly —takes the world.   12:659

It should not be forgotten that science is not the *summa* of life, that it is actually only one of the psychological attitudes, only one of the forms of human thought.   69:60

Has it ever—except in the most benighted periods of history—been observed that a scientific truth needed to be elevated to the rank of a dogma? Truth can stand on its own

feet, only shaky opinions require the support of dogmatiza-
tion. Fanaticism is ever the brother of doubt.   95:335

Never do human beings speculate more, or have more
opinions, than about things which they do not understand.

48:737

Dogma and science are incommensurable quantities
which damage one another by mutual contamination. Dogma as a factor in religion is of inestimable value precisely
because of its absolute standpoint. But when science dis-
penses with criticism and scepticism it degenerates into a
sickly hot-house plant. One of the elements necessary to science is extreme uncertainty. Whenever science inclines towards dogma and shows a tendency to be impatient and
fanatical, it is concealing a doubt which in all probability
is justified and explaining away an uncertainty which is
only too well founded.   42:746

Doubt alone is the mother of scientific truth. Whoever
fights against dogma in high places falls victim, tragically
enough, to the tyranny of a partial truth.   37:70

Not all are vouchsafed the grace of a faith that anticipates
all solutions, nor is it given to all to rest content with the
sun of revealed truth. The light that is lighted in the heart
by the grace of the Holy Spirit, that same light of nature,
however feeble it may be, is more important to them than
the great light which shines in the darkness and which
the darkness comprehended not. They discover that in
the very darkness of nature a light is hidden, a little spark
without which the darkness would not be darkness.

58:197

One-sidedness appears over and over again in the history
of science. I am not saying this as a reproach: on the con-

trary, we must be glad that there are people who are courageous enough to be immoderate and one-sided. It is to them that we owe our discoveries. What is regrettable is that each should defend his one-sidedness so passionately. Scientific theories are merely suggestions as to how things might be observed.   101:241

Science *qua* science has no boundaries, and there is no speciality whatever that can boast of complete self-sufficiency. Any speciality is bound to spill over its borders and to encroach on adjoining territory if it is to lay serious claim to the status of a science.   80:212

When one unconsciously works against oneself, the result is impatience, irritability, and an impotent longing to get one's opponent down whatever the means. Generally certain symptoms appear, among them a peculiar use of language: one wants to speak forcefully in order to impress one's opponent, so one employs a special, "bombastic" style full of neologisms which might be described as "power-words." This symptom is observable not only in the psychiatric clinic but also among certain modern philosophers, and, above all, whenever anything unworthy of belief has to be insisted on in the teeth of inner resistance: the language swells up, overreaches itself, sprouts grotesque words distinguished only by their needless complexity. The word is charged with the task of achieving what cannot be done by honest means. It is the old word magic, and sometimes it can degenerate into a regular disease.   58:155

The danger that faces us today is that the whole of reality will be replaced by words. This accounts for that terrible lack of instinct in modern man, particularly the city-dweller. He lacks all contact with life and the breath of nature. He knows a rabbit or a cow only from the illustrated paper, the dictionary, or the movies, and thinks he knows what it is really like—and is then amazed that cowsheds "smell," because the dictionary didn't say so. 32:882

Science as an end in itself is assuredly a high ideal, yet its consistent fulfilment brings about as many "ends in themselves" as there are sciences and arts. Naturally this leads to a high differentiation and specialization of the particular functions concerned, but also to their detachment from the world and from life, as well as to a multiplication of specialized fields which gradually lose all connection with one another. The result is an impoverishment and desiccation not merely in the specialized fields but also in the psyche of every man who has differentiated himself up or sunk down to the specialist level. Science must prove her value for life; it is not enough that she be the mistress, she must also be the maid. By so serving she in no way dishonours herself. 69:84

Science is not indeed a perfect instrument, but it is a superb and invaluable tool that works harm only when it is taken as an end in itself. Science must serve; it errs when it usurps the throne. It must be ready to serve all its branches, for each, because of its insufficiency, has need of support from the others. Science is the tool of the Western mind, and with it one can open more doors than with bare hands. It is part and parcel of our understanding, and it obscures our insight only when it claims that the understanding it conveys is the only kind there is. 112:2

Anyone who belittles the merits of Western science is undermining the foundations of the Western mind. 112:2

❖

All the worlds that have ever existed before man were physically *there*. But they were a nameless happening, not a definite actuality, for there did not yet exist that minimal concentration of the psychic factor, which was also present, to speak the word that outweighed the whole of Creation: That is the world, and this is I! That was the first morning of the world, the first sunrise after the primal darkness, when that inchoately conscious complex, the ego, knowingly sundered subject and object, and thus precipitated the world and itself into definite existence, giving it and itself a voice and a name.   48: 129

When I speak of the relation of psychology to art we are outside [art's] sphere, and it is impossible for us not to speculate. We must interpret, we must find meanings in things, otherwise we would be quite unable to think about them. We have to break down life and events, which are self-contained processes, into meanings, images, concepts, well knowing that in doing so we are getting further away from the living mystery. As long as we ourselves are caught up in the process of creation, we neither see nor understand; indeed we ought not to understand, for nothing is more injurious to immediate experience than cognition. But for the purpose of cognitive understanding we must detach ourselves from the creative process and look at it from the outside; only then does it become an image that expresses what we are bound to call "meaning."   55: 121

Perhaps art has no "meaning," at least not as we understand meaning. Perhaps it is like nature, which simply *is* and "means" nothing beyond that. Is "meaning" necessarily more than mere interpretation—an interpretation secreted into something by an intellect hungry for meaning? Art, it has been said, is beauty, and "a thing of beauty is a joy for ever." It needs no meaning, for meaning has nothing to do with art.   55: 121

A great work of art is like a dream; for all its apparent obviousness it does not explain itself and is always ambiguous. A dream never says "you ought" or "this is the truth." It presents an image in much the same way as nature allows a plant to grow, and it is up to us to draw conclusions. If a person has a nightmare, it means he is either too much given to fear or too exempt from it; if he dreams of a wise old man, it means he is either too much of a pedant or else in need of a teacher. In a subtle way both meanings come to the same thing, as we realize when we let a work of art act upon us as it acted upon the artist. To grasp its meaning, we must allow it to shape us as it shaped him. Then we also understand the nature of his primordial experience. He has plunged into the healing and redeeming depths of the collective psyche, where man is not lost in the isolation of consciousness and its errors and sufferings, but where all men are caught in a common rhythm which allows the individual to communicate his feelings and strivings to mankind as a whole.   73:161

The unborn work in the psyche of the artist is a force of nature that achieves its end either with tyrannical might or with the subtle cunning of nature herself, quite regardless of the personal fate of the man who is its vehicle. The creative urge lives and grows in him like a tree in the earth from which it draws its nourishment. We would do well, therefore, to think of the creative process as a living thing implanted in the human psyche.   55:115

Only that aspect of art which consists in the process of artistic creation can be a subject for psychological study, but not that which constitutes its essential nature. The question of what art is in itself can never be answered by the psychologist, but must be approached from the side of aesthetics.   55:97

Personal causes have as much or as little to do with a work of art as the soil with the plant that springs from it. We can certainly learn to understand some of the plant's peculiarities by getting to know its habitat, and for the botanist this is an important part of his equipment. But nobody will maintain that everything essential has then been discovered about the plant itself. The personal orientation which the doctor needs when confronted with the question of aetiology in medicine is quite out of place in dealing with a work of art, just because a work of art is not a human being, but is something supra-personal. It is a thing and not a personality; hence it cannot be judged by personal criteria. Indeed, the special significance of a true work of art resides in the fact that it has escaped from the limitations of the personal and has soared beyond the personal concerns of its creator. 55:107

The essence of a work of art is not to be found in the personal idiosyncrasies that creep into it—indeed, the more there are of them, the less it is a work of art—but in its rising above the personal and speaking from the mind and heart of the artist to the mind and heart of mankind. The personal aspect of art is a limitation and even a vice. 73:156

The creative process has a feminine quality, and the creative work arises from unconscious depths—we might truly say from the realm of the Mothers. Whenever the creative force predominates, life is ruled and shaped by the unconscious rather than by the conscious will, and the ego is swept along on an underground current, becoming nothing more than a helpless observer of events. The progress of the work becomes the poet's fate and determines his psychology. It is not Goethe that creates *Faust*, but *Faust* that creates Goethe. And what is *Faust*? *Faust* is essentially a symbol. By this I do not mean that it is an allegory pointing to something all too familiar, but the expression of something profoundly alive in the soul of every German, which Goethe helped to bring to birth.   73:159

A sign is always less than the thing it points to, and a symbol is always more than we can understand at first sight. Therefore we never stop at the sign but go on to the goal it indicates; but we remain with the symbol because it promises more than it reveals.   8*

Nothing would be more mistaken than to suppose that the poet is working with second-hand material. On the contrary, the primordial experience is the source of his creativeness, but it is so dark and amorphous that it requires the related mythological imagery to give it form. In itself it is wordless and imageless, for it is a vision seen "as in a glass, darkly." It is nothing but a tremendous intuition striving for expression. It is like a whirlwind that seizes everything within reach and assumes visible form as it swirls upward. Since the expression can never match the richness of the vision and can never exhaust its possibilities, the poet must have at his disposal a huge store of material if he is to communicate even a fraction of what he has glimpsed, and must make use of difficult and contradictory images in order to express the strange paradoxes of his vision. Dante decks out his experience in all the imagery of heaven, purgatory, and hell; Goethe brings in the Blocksberg and the Greek underworld; Wagner needs the whole corpus of Nordic myth, including the Parsifal saga; Nietzsche resorts to the hieratic style of the bard and legendary seer; Blake presses into his service the phantasmagoric world of India, the Old Testament, and the Apocalypse; and Spitteler borrows old names for the new figures that pour in alarming profusion from his muse's cornucopia. Nothing is missing in the whole gamut that ranges from the ineffably sublime to the perversely grotesque.   73: 151

The love-episode is a real experience really suffered, and so is the vision. It is not for us to say whether its content is of a physical, psychic, or metaphysical nature. In itself it had psychic reality, and this is no less real than physical reality. Human passion falls within the sphere of conscious experience, while the object of the vision lies beyond it. Through our senses we experience the known, but our intuitions point to things that are unknown and hidden, that by their very nature are secret. If ever they become conscious, they are intentionally kept secret and concealed, for which reason they have been regarded from earliest times as mysterious, uncanny, and deceptive. They are hidden from man, and he hides himself from them out of religious awe, protecting himself with the shield of science and reason. The ordered cosmos he believes in by day is meant to protect him from the fear of chaos that besets him by night —his enlightenment is born of night-fears!   73: 148

✧

If psychology remains for us only a science, we do not penetrate into life—we merely serve the absolute aim of science. It leads us, certainly, to a knowledge of the objective situation, but it always opposes every other aim but its own. The intellect remains imprisoned in itself just so long as it does not willingly sacrifice its supremacy by acknowledging the value of other aims. It shrinks from the step which takes it out of itself and which denies its universal validity, since from the standpoint of the intellect everything else is nothing but fantasy. But what great thing ever came into existence that was not first fantasy?   69: 86

We know that every good idea and all creative work are the offspring of the imagination, and have their source in what one is pleased to call infantile fantasy. Not the artist alone but every creative individual whatsoever owes all that is greatest in his life to fantasy. The dynamic principle of fantasy is play, a characteristic also of the child, and as such it appears inconsistent with the principle of serious work. But without this playing with fantasy no creative work has ever yet come to birth. The debt we owe to the play of imagination is incalculable. It is therefore short-sighted to treat fantasy, on account of its daring or objectionable nature, as a thing of little worth.   69: 93

Fantasy is not a sickness but a natural and vital activity which helps the seeds of psychic development to grow.
110: viii*

Why do we always forget that there is nothing majestic or beautiful in the wide domain of human culture that did not grow originally from a lucky idea? What would become of mankind if nobody had lucky ideas any more? It would be far truer to say that our consciousness is a sack which has nothing in it except what chances to fall into it. We never appreciate how dependent we are on lucky ideas—until we find to our distress that they will not come.   45: 305

Out of a playful movement of elements whose interrelations are not immediately apparent, patterns arise which an observant and critical intellect can only evaluate afterwards. The creation of something new is not accomplished by the intellect but by the play instinct acting from inner necessity. The creative mind plays with the objects it loves.
69: 197

Often the hands know how to solve a riddle with which the intellect has wrestled in vain.   102: 180

Fantasy is the maternally creative side of the masculine mind. When all is said and done, we can never rise above fantasy. It is true that there are unprofitable, futile, morbid, and unsatisfying fantasies whose sterile nature is immediately recognized by every person endowed with common sense; but the faulty performance proves nothing against the normal performance. All the works of man have their origin in creative imagination. What right, then, have we to disparage fantasy? In the normal course of things, fantasy does not easily go astray; it is too deep for that and too closely bound up with the tap-root of human and animal instinct. It has a surprising way of always coming out right in the end. The creative activity of imagination frees man from his bondage to the "nothing but" and raises him to the status of one who plays. As Schiller says, man is completely human only when he is at play.   2:98

Concepts are coined and negotiable values; images are life.   48:226

Every period has its bias, its particular prejudice, and its psychic malaise. An epoch is like an individual; it has its own limitations of conscious outlook, and therefore requires a compensatory adjustment. This is effected by the collective unconscious when a poet or seer lends expression to the unspoken desire of his times and shows the way, by word or deed, to its fulfilment—regardless whether this blind collective need results in good or evil, in the salvation of an epoch or its destruction.   73:153

Re-immersion in the state of *participation mystique* is the secret of artistic creation and of the effect which great art has upon us, for at that level of experience it is no longer the weal or woe of the individual that counts, but the life of the collective. That is why every great work of art is objective and impersonal, and yet profoundly moving. And that is also why the personal life of the artist is at most a help or a hindrance, but is never essential to his creative task. He may go the way of the Philistine, a good citizen, a fool, or a criminal. His personal career may be interesting and inevitable, but it does not explain his art.　　73:162

The true genius nearly always intrudes and disturbs. He speaks to a temporal world out of a world eternal. He says the wrong things at the right time. Eternal truths are never true at any given moment in history. The process of transformation has to make a halt in order to digest and assimilate the utterly impractical things that the genius has produced from the storehouse of eternity. Yet the genius is the healer of his time, because anything he reveals of eternal truth is healing.　　108:1004

Whoever speaks in primordial images speaks with a thousand voices; he enthrals and overpowers, while at the same time he lifts the idea he is seeking to express out of the occasional and the transitory into the realm of the ever-enduring. He transmutes our personal destiny into the destiny of mankind, and evokes in us all those beneficent forces that ever and anon have enabled humanity to find a refuge from every peril and to outlive the longest night.

55:129

✧

There are no inborn ideas, but there are inborn possibilities of ideas that set bounds to even the boldest fantasy and keep our fantasy activity within certain categories: *a priori* ideas, as it were, the existence of which cannot be ascertained except from their effects. They appear only in the shaped material of art as the regulative principles that shape it.　　55:126

The creative process, so far as we are able to follow it at all, consists in the unconscious activation of an archetypal image, and in elaborating and shaping this image into the finished work. By giving it shape, the artist translates it into the language of the present, and so makes it possible for us to find our way back to the deepest springs of life. Therein lies the social significance of art: it is constantly at work educating the spirit of the age, conjuring up the forms in which the age is most lacking. The unsatisfied yearning of the artist reaches back to the primordial image in the unconscious which is best fitted to compensate the inadequacy and one-sidedness of the present. The artist seizes on this image, and in raising it from deepest unconsciousness he brings it into relation with conscious values, thereby transforming it until it can be accepted by the minds of his contemporaries according to their powers.   55:130

Being essentially the instrument of his work, [the artist] is subordinate to it, and we have no right to expect him to interpret it for us. He has done his utmost by giving it form, and must leave the interpretation to others and to the future.
                    73:161

Art is a kind of innate drive that seizes a human being and makes him its instrument. The artist is not a person endowed with free will who seeks his own ends, but one who allows art to realize its purposes through him. As a human being he may have moods and a will and personal aims, but as an artist he is "man" in a higher sense—he is "collective man," a vehicle and moulder of the unconscious psychic life of mankind. That is his office, and it is sometimes so heavy a burden that he is fated to sacrifice happiness and everything that makes life worth living for the ordinary human being.   73:157

It makes no difference whether the artist knows that his work is generated, grows and matures within him, or whether he imagines that it is his own invention. In reality it grows out of him as a child its mother.   73:159

A gift develops in inverse ratio to the maturation of the personality as a whole, and often one has the impression that a creative personality grows at the expense of the human being. Sometimes, indeed, there is such a discrepancy between the genius and his human qualities that one has to ask oneself whether a little less talent might not have been better. What after all is great talent beside moral inferiority? There are not a few gifted persons whose usefulness is paralyzed, not to say perverted, by their human shortcomings. A gift is not an absolute value, or rather, it is such a value only when the rest of the personality keeps pace with it.   31:244

Nature, as we know, is not so lavish with her boons that she joins to a high intelligence the gifts of the heart also. As a rule, where one is present the other is missing, and where one capacity is present in perfection it is generally at the cost of all the others.   106:569

The "best" can be produced only by the best in man, by his conscientiousness and devotion. Cultural products can therefore easily stand for the psychological conditions of their production, that is, for those human virtues which alone make man capable of civilization.   103:383

The genius will come through despite everything, for there is something absolute and indomitable in his nature. The so-called "misunderstood genius" is rather a doubtful phenomenon. Generally he turns out to be a good-for-nothing who is forever seeking a soothing explanation of himself.   31:248

Talent, on the other hand, can either be hampered, crippled, and perverted, or fostered, developed, and improved. The genius is as rare a bird as the phoenix, an apparition not to be counted upon. Consciously or unconsciously, genius is something that by God's grace is there from the start, in full strength. But talent is a statistical regularity and does not always have a dynamism to match.   31:248

To rush ahead is to invite blows, and if you don't get them from the teacher, you will get them from fate, and generally from both. The gifted child will do well to accustom himself early to the fact that any excellence puts him in an exceptional position and exposes him to a great many risks, the chief of which is an exaggerated self-confidence. Against this the only protection is humility and obedience, and even these do not always work.   31:246

The artist's relative lack of adaptation turns out to his advantage; it enables him to follow his own yearnings far from the beaten path, and to discover what it is that would meet the unconscious needs of his age. Thus, just as the one-sidedness of the individual's conscious attitude is corrected by reactions from the unconscious, so art represents a process of self-regulation in the life of nations and epochs.

55:131

To be "normal" is the ideal aim for the unsuccessful, for all those who are still below the general level of adaptation. But for people of more than average ability, people who never found it difficult to gain successes and to accomplish their share of the world's work—for them the moral compulsion to be nothing but normal signifies the bed of Procrustes—deadly and insupportable boredom, a hell of sterility and hopelessness.   63:161

The greatness of historical personalities has never lain in their abject submission *to* convention, but, on the contrary, in their deliverance *from* convention. They towered up like mountain peaks above the mass that still clung to its collective fears, its beliefs, laws, and systems, and boldly chose their own way. To the man in the street it has always seemed miraculous that anyone should turn aside from the beaten track with its known destinations, and strike out on the steep and narrow path leading into the unknown. Hence it was always believed that such a man, if not actually crazy, was possessed by a daemon or a god; for the miracle of a man being able to act otherwise than as humanity has always acted could only be explained by the gift of daemonic power or divine spirit.   21:298

Only the mystics bring creativity into religion.   48:530

Creative life always stands outside convention. That is why, when the mere routine of life predominates in the form of convention and tradition, there is bound to be a destructive outbreak of creative energy. This outbreak is a catastrophe only when it is a mass phenomenon, but never in the individual who consciously submits to these higher powers and serves them with all his strength.   21:305

Every creative person is a duality or a synthesis of contradictory qualities. On the one side he is a human being with a personal life, while on the other he is an impersonal creative process. As a human being he may be sound or morbid, and his personal psychology can and should be explained in personal terms. But he can be understood as an artist only in terms of his creative achievement.   73:157

The distortion of beauty and meaning by grotesque objectivity or equally grotesque irreality is, in the insane, a consequence of the destruction of the personality; in the artist it has a creative purpose. Far from his work being an expression of the destruction of his personality, the modern artist finds the unity of his artistic personality in destructiveness.   105:175

What the artist and the insane have in common is common also to every human being—a restless creative fantasy which is constantly engaged in smoothing away the hard edges of reality. Anyone who observes himself, carefully and unsparingly, will know that there is something within him which would gladly hide and cover up all that is difficult and questionable in life, in order to smooth a path for itself. Insanity gives it a free hand. And once it has gained the ascendency, reality is veiled, more quickly or less; it becomes a distant dream, but the dream becomes a reality which holds the patient enchained wholly or in part, often for the rest of his life. We healthy people, who stand with both feet in reality, see only the ruin of the patient in *this* world, but not the richness of that side of the psyche which is turned away from us.   18:385

If the meaning of a poetic work can be exhausted through the application of a theory of neurosis, then it was nothing but a pathological product in the first place, to which I would never concede the dignity of a work of art. Today, it is true, our taste has become so uncertain that often we no longer know whether a thing is art or a disease.   24*

A person must pay dearly for the divine gift of creative fire. It is as though each of us was born with a limited store of energy. In the artist, the strongest force in his make-up, that is, his creativeness, will seize and all but monopolize this energy, leaving so little over that nothing of value can come of it. The creative impulse can drain him of his humanity to such a degree that the personal ego can exist only on a primitive or inferior level and is driven to develop all sorts of defects—ruthlessness, selfishness ("autoeroticism"), vanity, and other infantile traits. These inferiorities are the only means by which it can maintain its vitality and prevent itself from being wholly depleted.   73:158

The genius, too, has to bear the brunt of an outsize psychic complex; if he can cope with it, he does so with joy, if he can't, he must painfully perform the "symptomatic actions" which his gift lays upon him: he writes, paints, or composes what he suffers.   19:176

Great gifts are the fairest, and often the most dangerous, fruits on the tree of humanity. They hang on the weakest branches, which easily break.   31:244

Problems of Self-Realization

Nothing is so jealous as a truth.   72:190

The investigation of truth must begin afresh with each case, for each "case" is individual and not derivable from any preconceived formula. Each individual is a new experiment of life in her ever-changing moods, and an attempt at a new solution or new adaptation.   4:173

No doubt it is a great nuisance that mankind is not uniform but compounded of individuals whose psychic structure spreads them over a span of at least ten thousand years. Hence there is absolutely no truth that does not spell salvation to one person and damnation to another. All universalisms get stuck in this terrible dilemma.   72:36

In our delusion-ridden world a truth is so precious that nobody wants to let it slip merely for the sake of a few so-called exceptions which refuse to toe the line. And whoever doubts this truth is invariably looked on as a faithless reprobate, so that a note of fanaticism and intolerance everywhere creeps into the discussion. And yet each of us can carry the torch of knowledge but a part of the way, until another takes it from him. If only we could understand all this impersonally—could understand that we are not the personal creators of our truths, but only their exponents, mere mouthpieces of the day's psychic needs, then much venom and bitterness might be spared and we should be able to perceive the profound and supra-personal continuity of the human mind.   63:156f

Conviction easily turns into self-defence and is seduced into rigidity, and this is inimical to life. The test of a firm conviction is its elasticity and flexibility; like every other exalted truth it thrives best on the admission of its errors.

79: 180

Convictions and moral values would have no meaning if they were not believed and did not possess exclusive validity. And yet they are man-made and time-conditioned assertions or explanations which we know very well are capable of all sorts of modifications, as has happened in the past and will happen again in the future.   58: 230

There would appear to be a sort of conscience in mankind which severely punishes every one who does not somehow and at some time, at whatever cost to his virtuous pride, cease to defend and assert himself, and instead confess himself fallible and human. Until he can do this, an impenetrable wall shuts him off from the vital feeling that he is a man among other men.   63: 132

Error is just as important a condition of life's progress as truth.   101: 451

A fact never exists only as it is in itself, but also as we see it.   69: 510

✧

Human reality is made up of a thousand vulgarities.

84: 56*

In this overpoweringly humdrum existence, alas, there is little out of the ordinary that is healthy, and not much room for conspicuous heroism. Not that heroic demands are never put to us: on the contrary—and this is just what is so irritating and irksome—the banal everyday makes banal demands on our patience, our devotion, perseverance, self-sacrifice; and for us to fulfil these demands (as we must) humbly and without courting applause through heroic gestures, a heroism is needed that cannot be seen from the outside. It does not glitter, is not belauded, and it always seeks concealment in everyday attire.   104A: 72

Often it is just as well that we do not know the danger we escape when we rush in where angels fear to tread.

65: 247

Observance of customs and laws can very easily be a cloak for a lie so subtle that our fellow human beings are unable to detect it. It may help us to escape all criticism, we may even be able to deceive ourselves in the belief of our obvious righteousness. But deep down, below the surface of the average man's conscience, he hears a voice whispering, "There is something not right," no matter how much his rightness is supported by public opinion or by the moral code.   109: 80

Be the man through whom you wish to influence others. Mere talk has always been counted hollow, and there is no trick, however artful, by which this simple truth can be evaded in the long run. The fact of being convinced and not the thing we are convinced of—that is what has always, and at all times, worked.   63: 167

For a moral man the ethical problem is a passionate question which has its roots in the deepest instinctual processes as well as in his most idealistic aspirations. The problem for him is devastatingly real. It is not surprising, therefore, that the answer likewise springs from the depths of his nature.   104B: 289

Emotion is not an activity of the individual but something that happens to him.   3: 15

Affects usually occur where adaptation is weakest, and at the same time they reveal the reason for its weakness, namely a certain degree of inferiority and the existence of a lower level of personality. On this lower level with its uncontrolled or scarcely controlled emotions one behaves more or less like a primitive, who is not only the passive victim of his affects but also singularly incapable of moral judgment.   3: 15

It is through the "affect" that the subject becomes involved and so comes to feel the whole weight of reality. The difference amounts roughly to that between a severe illness which one reads about in a text-book and the real illness which one has. In psychology one possesses nothing unless one has experienced it in reality. Hence a purely intellectual insight is not enough, because one knows only the words and not the substance of the thing from inside.

3: 61

Disappointment, always a shock to the feelings, is not only the mother of bitterness but the strongest possible incentive to a differentiation of feeling. The failure of a pet plan, the disappointing behaviour of someone one loves, can supply the impulse either for a more or less brutal outburst of affect or for a modification and adjustment of feeling, and hence for its higher development. This culminates in wisdom if feeling is supplemented by reflection and rational insight. Wisdom is never violent: where wisdom reigns there is no conflict between thinking and feeling.

48: 334

The truth is that we do not enjoy masterless freedom; we are continually threatened by psychic factors which, in the guise of "natural phenomena," may take possession of us at any moment. The withdrawal of metaphysical projections leaves us almost defenceless in the face of this happening, for we immediately identify with every impulse instead of giving it the name of the "other," which would at least hold it at arm's length and prevent it from storming the citadel of the ego.   74:143

Bondage and possession are synonymous. Always, therefore, there is something in the psyche that takes possession and limits or suppresses our moral freedom. In order to hide this undeniable but exceedingly unpleasant fact from ourselves and at the same time pay lip-service to freedom, we have got accustomed to saying apotropaically, "*I have* such and such a desire or habit or feeling of resentment," instead of the more veracious "Such and such a desire or habit or feeling of resentment *has me*." The latter formulation would certainly rob us even of the illusion of freedom. But I ask myself whether this would not be better in the end than fuddling ourselves with words.   74:143

If man were merely a creature that came into being as a result of something already existing unconsciously, he would have no freedom and there would be no point in consciousness. Psychology must reckon with the fact that despite the causal nexus man does enjoy a feeling of freedom, which is identical with autonomy of consciousness. However much the ego can be proved to be dependent and preconditioned, it cannot be convinced that it has no freedom. An absolutely preformed consciousness and a totally dependent ego would be a pointless farce, since everything would proceed just as well or even better unconsciously. The existence of ego consciousness has meaning only if it is free and autonomous. By stating these facts we have, it is true, established an antinomy, but we have at the same time given a picture of things as they are. There are temporal, local, and individual differences in the degree of dependence and freedom. In reality both are always present: the supremacy of the self and the hybris of consciousness.

103:391

Each of us is equipped with a psychic disposition that limits our freedom in high degree and makes it practically illusory. Not only is "freedom of the will" an incalculable problem philosophically, it is also a misnomer in the practical sense, for we seldom find anybody who is not influenced and indeed dominated by desires, habits, impulses, prejudices, resentments, and by every conceivable kind of complex. All these natural facts function exactly like an Olympus full of deities who want to be propitiated, served, feared and worshipped, not only by the individual owner of this assorted pantheon, but by everybody in his vicinity.

74:143

Because we are still such barbarians, any trust in the laws of human nature seems to us a dangerous and unethical naturalism. Why is this? Because under the barbarian's thin veneer of culture the wild beast lurks in readiness, amply justifying his fear. But the beast is not tamed by locking it up in a cage. There is no morality without freedom. When the barbarian lets loose the beast within him, that is not freedom but bondage. Barbarism must first be vanquished before freedom can be won. This happens, in principle, when the basic root and driving force of morality are felt by the individual as constituents of his own nature and not as external restrictions.

69:357

Although contemporary man believes that he can change himself without limit, or be changed through external influences, the astounding, or rather the terrifying, fact remains that despite civilization and Christian education, he is still, morally, as much in bondage to his instincts as an

animal, and can therefore fall victim at any moment to the
beast within.   48: xviii*

✧

Moral law is nothing other than an outward manifestation of man's innate urge to dominate and control himself.
This impulse to domestication and civilization is lost in the
dim, unfathomable depths of man's evolutionary history
and can never be conceived as the consequence of laws
imposed from without. Man himself, obeying his instincts,
created his laws.   101: 486

Morality was not brought down on tables of stone from
Sinai and imposed on the people, but is a function of the
human soul, as old as humanity itself. Morality is not imposed from outside; we have it in ourselves from the start—
not the law, but our moral nature without which the collective life of human society would be impossible. That is
why morality is found at all levels of society. It is the instinctive regulator of action which also governs the collective life of the herd. But moral laws are only valid within
a compact human group. Beyond that, they cease. There the
old truth runs: *Homo homini lupus*. With the growth of
civilization we have succeeded in subjecting ever larger
human groups to the rule of the same morality, without,
however, having yet brought the moral code to prevail beyond the social frontiers, that is, in the free space between
mutually independent societies. There, as of old, reign
lawlessness and licence and mad immorality—though of
course it is only the enemy who dares to say it out loud.

104A: 30

We should never forget that what today seems to us a
moral commandment will tomorrow be cast into the melt-
ing-pot and transformed, so that in the near or distant fu-

ture it may serve as a basis for new ethical formations. This much we ought to have learnt from the history of civilization, that the forms of morality belong to the category of transitory things.   89:667

The only thing that cannot be improved upon is morality, for every alteration of traditional morality is by definition an immorality. This *bon mot* has an edge to it, against which many an innovator has barked his shins.   114:239

Every one of us gladly turns away from his problems; if possible, they must not be mentioned, or, better still, their existence is denied. We wish to make our lives simple, certain, and smooth, and for that reason problems are taboo. We want to have certainties and no doubts—results and no experiments—without even seeing that certainties can arise only through doubt and results only through experiment. The artful denial of a problem will not produce conviction: on the contrary, a wider and higher consciousness is required to give us the certainty and clarity we need.

94:751

Hysterical self-deceivers, and ordinary ones too, have at all times understood the art of misusing everything so as to avoid the demands and duties of life, and above all to shirk the duty of confronting themselves. They pretend to be seekers after God in order not to have to face the truth that they are ordinary egoists.   107:142

Naturally, you can make a wrong use of self-knowledge, just as of any other knowledge.   20:18*

The sense of moral inferiority always indicates that the missing element is something which . . . really ought not be missing, or which could be made conscious if only one took sufficient trouble. The moral inferiority does not come from a collision with the generally accepted and, in a sense, arbitrary moral law, but from the conflict with one's own self which, for reasons of psychic equilibrium, demands that the deficit be redressed. Whenever a sense of moral inferiority appears, it indicates not only a need to assimilate an unconscious component, but also the possibility of such assimilation. In the last resort it is a man's moral qualities which force him, either through direct recognition of the need or indirectly through a painful neurosis, to assimilate his unconscious self and to keep himself fully conscious.

104B: 218

Only through our feebleness and incapacity are we linked up with the unconscious, with the lower world of the instincts and with our fellow beings. Our virtues only enable us to be independent. There we do not need anybody, there we are kings; but in our inferiority we are linked up with mankind.   6: 109*

Wherever an inferiority complex exists, there is a good reason for it. There actually is an inferiority somewhere, though not just where one supposes it is. Modesty and humility are not signs of an inferiority complex. They are highly estimable, indeed admirable virtues and not complexes. They prove that their fortunate possessor is not a presumptuous fool but knows his limitations, and will therefore never stumble beyond the bounds of humanity, dazzled and intoxicated by his imagined greatness.   20: 18*

We psychologists have learned, through long and painful experience, that you deprive a man of his best resource when you help him to get rid of his complexes. You can only help him to become sufficiently aware of them and to start a conscious conflict within himself. In this way the complex becomes a focus of life. Anything that disappears from your psychological inventory is apt to turn up in the guise of a hostile neighbour, who will inevitably arouse your anger and make you aggressive. It is surely better to know that your worst enemy is right there in your own heart.

25:456

We all have complexes; it is a highly banal and uninteresting fact. Even the incest complex which you can find anywhere if you look for it is terribly banal and therefore uninteresting. It is only interesting to know what people *do* with their complexes.

6:94*

The people who fancy they are sure of themselves are the ones who are truly unsure. Our whole life is unsure, so a feeling of unsureness is much nearer to the truth than the illusion and bluff of sureness. In the long run it is the better adapted man who triumphs, not the wrongly self-confident, who is at the mercy of dangers from without and within.

20:18*

It seems to be very hard for people to live with riddles or to let them live, although one would think that life is so full of riddles as it is that a few more things we cannot answer would make no difference. But perhaps it is just this that is so unendurable, that there are irrational things in our own psyche which upset the conscious mind in its illusory certainties by confronting it with the riddle of its existence.

60:307

That the greatest effects come from the smallest causes has become patently clear not only in physics but in the field of psychological research as well. How often in the critical moments of life everything hangs on what appears to be a mere nothing!

59:408

People who strive to be excessively ethical, who always think, feel, and act altruistically and idealistically, avenge themselves for their intolerable ideals by a subtly planned maliciousness, of which they are naturally not conscious as such, but which leads to misunderstandings and unhappy situations. All these difficulties appear to them as "especially unfortunate circumstances," or the fault and the malice of other people, or as tragic complications. Consciously they imagine they are rid of the conflict, but it is still there, unseen, to be stumbled over at every step. 100A:62*

To strive for perfection is a high ideal. But I say: "Fulfil something you are able to fulfil rather than run after what you will never achieve." Nobody is perfect. Remember the saying: "None is good but God alone" [Luke 18:19], and nobody can be. It is an illusion. We can modestly strive to fulfil ourselves and to be as complete human beings as possible, and that will give us trouble enough.

6:149*

If a man is endowed with an ethical sense and is convinced of the sanctity of ethical values, he is on the surest road to a conflict of duty. And although this looks desperately like a moral catastrophe, it alone makes possible a higher differentiation of ethics and a broadening of consciousness. A conflict of duty forces us to examine our conscience and thereby to discover the shadow. 49:17*

The shadow is a moral problem that challenges the whole ego-personality, for no one can become conscious of the shadow without considerable moral effort. To become conscious of it involves recognizing the dark aspects of the personality as present and real. This act is the essential condition for any kind of self-knowledge. 3:14

To confront a person with his shadow is to show him his own light. Once one has experienced a few times what it is like to stand judgingly between the opposites, one begins to understand what is meant by the self. Anyone who perceives his shadow and his light simultaneously sees himself from two sides and thus gets in the middle.   32:872

Filling the conscious mind with ideal conceptions is a characteristic of Western theosophy, but not the confrontation with the shadow and the world of darkness. One does not become enlightened by imagining figures of light, but by making the darkness conscious.   60:335

Only an exceedingly naive and unconscious person could imagine that he is in a position to avoid sin. Psychology can no longer afford childish illusions of this kind; it must ensue the truth and declare that unconsciousness is not only no excuse but is actually one of the most heinous sins. Human law may exempt it from punishment, but Nature avenges herself more mercilessly, for it is nothing to her whether a man is conscious of his sin or not.   26:676

Christ the ideal took upon himself the sins of the world. But if the ideal is wholly outside then the sins of the individual are also outside, and consequently he is more of a fragment than ever, since superficial misunderstanding conveniently enables him, quite literally, to "cast his sins upon Christ" and thus to evade his deepest responsibilities—which is contrary to the spirit of Christianity.   72:9

"Redemption" does not mean that a burden is taken from one's shoulders which one was never meant to bear. Only the "complete" person knows how unbearable man is to himself.   3:125

If only people could realize what an enrichment it is to find one's own guilt, what a sense of honour and spiritual dignity!   1:416

Only the living presence of the eternal images can lend the human psyche a dignity which makes it morally possible for a man to stand by his own soul, and be convinced that it is worth his while to persevere with himself. Only then will he realize that the conflict is *in him*, that the discord and tribulation are his riches, which should not be squandered by attacking others; and that, if fate should exact a debt from him in the form of guilt, it is a debt to himself.   48:511

❖

I cannot love anyone if I hate myself. That is the reason why we feel so extremely uncomfortable in the presence of people who are noted for their special virtuousness, for they radiate an atmosphere of the torture they inflict on themselves. That is not a virtue but a vice. And thus, from so-called goodness, which was once really good, something has arisen which is no longer good; it has become an evasion. Nowadays any coward can make himself respectable by going to church and loving his neighbour. But it is simply an untrue state, an artificial world.   11:88*

The healthy man does not torture others—generally it is the tortured who turn into torturers.   84:56*

To live in perpetual flight from ourselves is a bitter thing, and to live with ourselves demands a number of Christian virtues which we then have to apply to our own case, such as patience, love, faith, hope, and humility. It is all very fine to make our neighbour happy by applying them to him, but the demon of self-admiration so easily claps us on the back and says, "Well done!" And because this is a great psychological truth, it must be stood on its head for an equal number of people so as to give the devil something to carp at. But—does it make *us* happy when we have to apply these virtues to ourselves? when I am the recipient of my own gifts, the least among my brothers whom I must take to my bosom? when I must admit that I need all my patience, my love, my faith, and even my humility, and that I myself am my own devil, the antagonist who always wants the opposite in everything? Can we ever really endure ourselves? "Do unto others . . ."—this is as true of evil as of good.   77:522

Instead of waging war on himself it is surely better for a man to learn to tolerate himself, and to convert his inner difficulties into real experiences instead of expending them in useless fantasies. Then at least he lives, and does not waste his life in fruitless struggles. If people can be educated to see the lowly side of their own natures, it may be hoped that they will also learn to understand and to love their fellow men better. A little less hypocrisy and a little more tolerance towards oneself can only have good results in respect for our neighbour; for we are all too prone to transfer to our fellows the injustice and violence we inflict upon our own natures.   104c:439

We understand another person in the same way as we understand, or seek to understand, ourselves. What we do not understand in ourselves we do not understand in the other person either. So there is plenty to ensure that his image will be for the most part subjective. As we know, even an intimate friendship is no guarantee of objective knowledge.   30:508

If one does not understand a person, one tends to regard him as a fool.   48:147

Certainly strife and misunderstanding will always be among the props of the tragi-comedy of human existence, but it is none the less undeniable that the advance of civilization has led from the law of the jungle to the establishment of courts of justice and standards of right and wrong which are above the contending parties. It is my conviction that a basis for the settlement of conflicting views would be found in the recognition of different types of attitude— a recognition not only of the existence of such types, but also of the fact that every man is so imprisoned in his type that he is simply incapable of fully understanding another standpoint. Failing a recognition of this exacting demand, a violation of the other standpoint is practically inevitable.

69: 847

We still attribute to the other fellow all the evil and inferior qualities that we do not like to recognize in ourselves, and therefore have to criticize and attack him, when all that has happened is that an inferior "soul" has emigrated from one person to another. The world is still full of *bêtes noires* and scapegoats, just as it formerly teemed with witches and werewolves.

9: 130

It is just the beam in one's own eye that enables one to detect the mote in one's brother's eye. The beam in one's own eye does not prove that one's brother has no mote in his. But the impairment of one's own vision might easily give rise to a general theory that all motes are beams. The recognition and taking to heart of the subjective determination of knowledge in general, and of psychological knowledge in particular, are basic conditions for the scientific and impartial evaluation of a psyche different from that of the observing subject. These conditions are fulfilled only when the observer is sufficiently informed about the nature and scope of his own personality. He can, however, be sufficiently informed only when he has in large measure freed himself from the levelling influence of collective opinions and thereby arrived at a clear conception of his own individuality.

69: 10*f*

We always start with the naïve assumption that we are masters in our own house. Hence we must first accustom ourselves to the thought that, in our most intimate psychic life as well, we live in a kind of house which has doors and windows to the world, but that, although the objects or contents of this world act upon us, they do not belong to us. For many people this hypothesis is by no means easy to conceive, just as they do not find it at all easy to understand and to accept the fact that their neighbour's psychology is not necessarily identical with their own.   104B: 329

Everyone who becomes conscious of even a fraction of his unconscious gets outside his own time and social stratum into a kind of solitude.   48: 258

The real existence of an enemy upon whom one can foist off everything evil is an enormous relief to one's conscience. You can then at least say, without hesitation, who the devil is; you are quite certain that the cause of your misfortune is outside, and not in your own attitude.   30: 518

Our unwillingness to see our own faults and the projection of them onto others is the source of most quarrels, and the strongest guarantee that injustice, animosity, and persecution will not easily die out.   20: 15*

A man's hatred is always concentrated on the thing that makes him conscious of his bad qualities.   69: 453

When we allow ourselves to be irritated out of our wits by something, let us not suppose that the cause of our irritation lies simply and solely outside us, in the irritating thing or person. In that way we simply endow them with the power to put us into the state of irritation, and possibly into one of insomnia or indigestion. We then turn around and unhesitatingly condemn the object of offence, while all the time we are raging against an unconscious part of ourselves which is projected into the exasperating object.

30:516

You always become the thing you fight the most.

39c: 119*

Everything that works from the unconscious appears projected on others. Not that these others are wholly without blame, for even the worst projection is at least hung on a hook, perhaps a very small one, but still a hook offered by the other person.

54:99

A man who is unconscious of himself acts in a blind, instinctive way and is in addition fooled by all the illusions that arise when he sees everything that he is not conscious of in himself coming to meet him from outside as projections upon his neighbour.

60:391

Projections change the world into the replica of one's own unknown face.

3:17

❖

The essential thing is that we should be able to stand up to our judgment of ourselves. From outside this attitude looks like self-righteousness, but it is so only if we are incapable of criticizing ourselves. If we can exercise self-criticism, criticism from outside will affect us only on the outside and not pierce to the heart, for we feel that we have a sterner critic within us than any who could judge us from without. And anyway, there are as many opinions as there are heads to think them. We come to realize that our own judgment has as much value as the judgment of others. One cannot please everybody, therefore it is better to be at peace with oneself.

99:911

In each of us there is a pitiless judge who makes us feel guilty even if we are not conscious of having done anything wrong. Although we do not know what it is, it is as though it were known somewhere.   58:164

How can anyone see straight when he does not even see himself and the darkness he unconsciously carries with him into all his dealings?   74:140

Nothing in us ever remains quite uncontradicted, and consciousness can take up no position which will not call up, somewhere in the dark corners of the psyche, a negation or a compensatory effect, approval or resentment. This process of coming to terms with the Other in us is well worth while, because in this way we get to know aspects of our nature which we would not allow anybody else to show us and which we ourselves would never have admitted.
                    48:706

The "other" in us always seems alien and unacceptable; but if we let ourselves be aggrieved the feeling sinks in, and we are the richer for this little bit of self-knowledge
                    99:918

Only a fool is interested in other people's guilt, since he cannot alter it. The wise man learns only from his own guilt. He will ask himself: Who am I that all this should happen to me? To find the answer to this fateful question he will look into his own heart.   72:152

To know where the other person makes a mistake is of little value. It only becomes interesting when you know where *you* make the mistake, for then you can do something about it.   3:424

We are that pair of Dioscuri, one of whom is mortal and the other immortal, and who, though always together, can never be made completely one. The transformation processes strive to approximate them to one another, but our consciousness is aware of resistances, because the other person seems strange and uncanny, and because we cannot get accustomed to the idea that we are not absolute master in our own house. We should prefer to be always "I" and nothing else. But we are confronted with that inner friend or foe, and whether he is our friend or our foe depends on ourselves.   17:235

The "other" may be just as one-sided in one way as the ego is in another. And yet the conflict between them may give rise to truth and meaning—but only if the ego is willing to grant the other its rightful personality.   17:237

One can fall victim to possession if one does not understand betimes why one is possessed. One should ask oneself for once: Why has this idea taken possession of me? What does that mean in regard to myself? A modest doubt like this can save us from falling head first into the idea and vanishing for ever.   37:72

Nowhere are we closer to the sublime secret of all origination than in the recognition of our own selves, whom we always think we know already. Yet we know the immensities of space better than we know our own depths, where —even though we do not understand it—we can listen directly to the throb of creation itself.   5:737

✦

Conscience, and particularly a bad conscience, can be a gift from heaven, a veritable grace if used in the interests of the higher self-criticism. And self-criticism, in the sense of an introspective, discriminating activity, is indispensable in any attempt to understand your own psychology. If you have done something that puzzles you and you ask yourself what could have prompted you to such an action, you need the sting of a bad conscience and its discriminating faculty in order to discover the real motive of your behaviour. It is only then that you can see what motives are governing your actions. The sting of a bad conscience even spurs you on to discover things that were unconscious before, and in this way you may be able to cross the threshold of the unconscious and take cognizance of those impersonal forces which make you an unconscious instrument of the wholesale murderer in man. 74:86

Self-knowledge, in the form of an examination of conscience, is demanded by Christian ethics. They were very pious people who maintained that self-knowledge paves the way to knowledge of God. 7:661

We say that it is egoistic or "morbid" to be preoccupied with oneself; one's own company is the worst, "it makes you melancholy"—such are the glowing testimonials accorded to our human make-up. They are evidently deeply ingrained in our Western minds. Whoever thinks in this way has obviously never asked himself what possible pleasure other people could find in the company of such a miserable coward. 104B:323

Brooding is a sterile activity which runs round in a circle, never reaching a sensible goal. It is not work but a weakness, even a vice. On the other hand, when you've got the blues it is legitimate to make yourself an object of serious study, just as you can earnestly search your conscience without lapsing into moral weakness. Anyone who is in bad odour with himself or feels in need of improvement, anyone who, in brief, wishes to "grow," must take counsel with himself. For unless you change yourself inwardly too, outward changes in the situation are either worthless or actually harmful.   20: 16*f*

Every advance, every conceptual achievement of mankind, has been connected with an advance in self-awareness: man differentiated himself from the object and faced Nature as something distinct from her. Any reorientation of psychological attitude will have to follow the same road.

30: 523

The foremost of all illusions is that anything can ever satisfy anybody. That illusion stands behind all that is unendurable in life and in front of all progress, and it is one of the most difficult things to overcome.   98: 905

It is not enough to jump up, puff yourself out, and shout, "I take the responsibility!" Not only mankind but fate itself would like to know who has promised to take this great step and whether it is someone who *can* take the responsibility. We all know that anyone can *say* so. It is not the position that makes the man, but the man doing his work. Therefore self-searching, with the help of one or more persons, is (or rather should be) the essential condition for taking on a higher responsibility, even if it be only that of realizing the meaning of individual life in the best possible form and to the fullest possible extent. Nature always does that, though without responsibility, for this is the fated and divinely allotted task of man.   20: 17*

The man who promises everything is sure to fulfil nothing, and everyone who promises too much is in danger of using evil means in order to carry out his promises, and is already on the road to perdition.   1: 413

The judgment of others is not in itself a standard of value, it may be no more than a useful piece of information. The individual has a right, indeed it is his duty, to set up and apply his own standard of value. In the last resort ethics are the concern of the individual.   99:912

If ever there was a time when self-reflection was the absolutely necessary and only right thing, it is now, in our present catastrophic epoch. Yet whoever reflects upon himself is bound to strike upon the frontiers of the unconscious, which contains what above all else he needs to know.

104A: 4*

Every individual needs revolution, inner division, overthrow of the existing order, and renewal, but not by forcing these things upon his neighbours under the hypocritical cloak of Christian love or the sense of social responsibility or any of the other beautiful euphemisms for unconscious urges to personal power. Individual self-reflection, return of the individual to the ground of human nature, to his own deepest being with its individual and social destiny— here is the beginning of a cure for that blindness which reigns at the present hour.   104A:5*

I am neither spurred on by excessive optimism nor in love with high ideals, but am merely concerned with the fate of the individual human being—that infinitesimal unit on whom a world depends, and in whom, if we read the meaning of the Christian message aright, even God seeks his goal.   106:588

Between Good and Evil

There are times in the world's history—and our own time may be one of them—when good must stand aside, so that anything destined to be better first appears in evil form. This shows how extremely dangerous it is even to touch these problems, for evil can so easily slip in on the plea that it is, potentially, the better! 21:321

The inner voice makes us conscious of the evil from which the whole community is suffering, whether it be the nation or the whole human race. But it presents this evil in an individual form, so that one might at first suppose it to be only an individual characteristic. 21:319

We are so accustomed to hear that everybody has his "difficulties and problems" that we simply accept it as a banal fact, without considering what these difficulties and problems really mean. Why is one never satisfied with oneself? Why is one unreasonable? Why is one not always good and why must one ever leave a cranny for evil? Why does one do foolish things which could easily be avoided with a little forethought? What is it that is always frustrating us and thwarting our best intentions? Why are there people who never notice these things or cannot even admit their existence? And finally, why do people in the mass beget the historical lunacy of the last thirty years? Why couldn't Pythagoras, twenty-four hundred years ago, have established the rule of wisdom once and for all, or Christianity have set up the kingdom of Heaven upon earth? 77:387

Look at all the incredible savagery going on in our so-called civilized world: it all comes from human beings and the spiritual condition they are in. Look at the devilish

engines of destruction! They are invented by completely
innocuous gentlemen, reasonable, respectable citizens who
are everything we could wish. And when the whole thing
blows up and an indescribable hell of destruction is let
loose, nobody seems to be responsible. It simply happens,
and yet it is all man-made.   74:85

The dammed-up instinctual forces in civilized man are
immensely destructive and far more dangerous than the
instincts of the primitive, who in a modest degree is constantly living out his negative instincts. Consequently no
war of the historical past can rival in grandiose horror the
wars of civilized nations.   69:230

The daemonism of nature, which man had apparently
triumphed over, he has unwittingly swallowed into himself
and so become the devil's marionette. This could happen
only because he believed he had abolished the daemons by
declaring them to be superstition. He overlooked the fact
that they were, at bottom, the products of certain factors in
the human psyche. When these products were dubbed unreal and illusory, their sources were in no way blocked up
or rendered inoperative. On the contrary, after it became
impossible for the daemons to inhabit the rocks, woods,
mountains, and rivers, they used human beings as much
more dangerous dwelling places.   43*

Let man but accumulate sufficient engines of destruction
and the devil within him will soon be unable to resist putting them to their fated use. It is well known that fire-arms
go off of themselves if only enough of them are together.
                                              93:163

Human imperfection is always a discord in the harmony
of our ideals. Unfortunately, no one lives in the world as
we desire it, but in the world of actuality where good and

evil clash and destroy one another, where no creating or building can be done without dirtying one's hands. Whenever things get really bad, there is always some one to assure us amid great applause that nothing has happened and everything is in order. 114:263

The Church has the doctrine of the devil, of an evil principle, whom we like to imagine complete with cloven hoofs, horns, and tail, half man, half beast, a chthonic deity apparently escaped from the rout of Dionysus, the sole surviving champion of the sinful joys of paganism. An excellent picture, and one which exactly describes the grotesque and sinister side of the unconscious; for we have never really come to grips with it and consequently it has remained in its original savage state. Probably no one today would still be rash enough to assert that the European is a lamblike creature and not possessed by a devil. The frightful records of our age are plain for all to see, and they surpass in hideousness everything that any previous age, with its feeble instruments, could have hoped to accomplish.

77:388

Only with Christ did the devil enter the world as the real counterpart of God, and in early Jewish-Christian circles Satan was regarded as Christ's elder brother. 3:113

The splendour of the "light" god has been enhanced beyond measure, but the darkness supposedly represented by the devil has localized itself in man. This strange development was precipitated chiefly by the fact that Christianity, terrified of Manichaean dualism, strove to preserve its monotheism by main force. But since the reality of darkness and evil could not be denied, there was no alternative but to make man responsible for it. Even the devil was largely, if not entirely, abolished, with the result that this metaphysical figure, who at one time was an integral part of the Deity, was introjected into man, who thereupon became the real carrier of the *mysterium iniquitatis*: "omne bonum a Deo, omne malum ab homine." In recent times this development has suffered a diabolical reverse, and the wolf in sheep's clothing now goes about whispering in our ear that evil is really nothing but a misunderstanding of good and an effective instrument of progress. We think that the world of darkness has thus been abolished for good and all, and nobody realizes what a poisoning this is of man's soul. In this way he turns himself into the devil, for the devil is half of the archetype whose irresistible power makes even unbelievers ejaculate "Oh God!" on every suitable and unsuitable occasion.   67:189

Evil needs to be pondered just as much as good, for good and evil are ultimately nothing but ideal extensions and abstractions of doing, and both belong to the chiaroscuro of life. In the last resort there is no good that cannot produce evil and no evil that cannot produce good.   72:36

Good and evil are feeling-values of human provenance, and we cannot extend them beyond the human realm. What happens beyond this is beyond our judgment: God is not to be caught with human attributes. Besides, where would the *fear* of God be if only good—i.e., what seems good to us—were to be expected from him?   65:291

The view that good and evil are spiritual principles outside us, and that man is caught in the conflict between them is more bearable by far than the insight that the opposites are the ineradicable and indispensable preconditions of all psychic life, so much so that life itself is guilt. Even a life dedicated to God is still lived by an ego, which speaks of an ego and asserts an ego in God's despite, which does not instantly merge itself with God but reserves for itself a freedom and a will which it sets up outside God and against him.   48:206

✦

If something which seems to me an error shows itself to be more effective than a truth, then I must first follow up the error, for in it lie power and life which I lose if I hold to what seems to me true. Light has need of darkness —otherwise how could it appear as light?   78:530

We know of course that without sin there is no repentance and without repentance no redeeming grace, also that without original sin the redemption of the world could never have come about; but we assiduously avoid investigating whether in this very power of evil God may not have placed some special purpose which it is most important for us to know. One often feels driven to some such view when, like the psychotherapist, one has to deal with people who are confronted with their blackest shadow.

72:36

Where is a height without depth, and how can there be light that throws no shadow? There is no good that is not opposed by evil. "No man can be redeemed from a sin he has not committed," says Carpocrates; a deep saying for all who wish to understand, and a golden opportunity for all those who prefer to draw false conclusions. What is down below is not just an excuse for more pleasure, but something we fear because it demands to play its part in the life of the more conscious and more complete man.   114:271

Man is constantly inclined to forget that what was once good does not remain good eternally. He follows the old ways that once were good long after they have become bad, and only with the greatest sacrifices and untold suffering can he rid himself of this delusion and see that what was once good is now perhaps grown old and is good no longer. This is so in great things as in small.   69:313

Whatever the metaphysical position of the devil may be, in psychological reality evil is an effective, not to say menacing, limitation of goodness, so that it is no exaggeration to assume that in this world good and evil more or less balance each other, like day and night, and that this is the reason why the victory of the good is always a special act of grace.   65:253

We quite forget that we can be as deplorably overcome by a virtue as by a vice. There is a sort of frenzied, orgiastic virtuousness which is just as infamous as a vice and leads to just as much injustice and violence.   100A:222*

Good does not become better by being exaggerated, but worse, and a small evil becomes a big one through being disregarded and repressed. The shadow is very much a part of human nature, and it is only at night that no shadows exist.   65:286

We all have a great need to be good ourselves, and occasionally we like to show it by the appropriate actions. If good can come of evil self-interest, then the two sides of human nature have co-operated. But when in a fit of enthusiasm we begin with the good, our deep-rooted selfishness remains in the background, unsatisfied and resentful, only waiting for an opportunity to take its revenge in the most atrocious way.   84:56*

✧

Society expects, and indeed must expect, every individual to play the part assigned to him as perfectly as possible, so that a man who is a parson must not only carry out his official functions objectively, but must at all times and in all circumstances play the role of parson in a flawless manner. Society demands this as a kind of surety; each must stand at his post, here a cobbler, there a poet.   104B: 305

The persona is a complicated system of relations between individual consciousness and society, fittingly enough a kind of mask, designed on the one hand to make a definite impression upon others, and, on the other, to conceal the true nature of the individual.   104B: 305

Every calling or profession has its own characteristic persona. It is easy to study these things nowadays, when the photographs of public personalities so frequently appear in the press. A certain kind of behaviour is forced on them by the world, and professional people endeavour to come up to these expectations. Only, the danger is that they become identical with their personas—the professor with his text-book, the tenor with his voice. Then the damage is done; henceforth he lives exclusively against the background of his own biography. . . . The garment of Deianeira has grown fast to his skin, and a desperate decision like that of Heracles is needed if he is to tear this Nessus shirt from his body and step into the consuming fire of the flame of immortality, in order to transform himself into what he really is. One could say, with a little exaggeration, that the persona is that which in reality one is not, but which oneself as well as others think one is.   17: 221

A man cannot get rid of himself in favour of an artificial personality without punishment. Even the attempt to do so brings on, in all ordinary cases, unconscious reactions in the form of bad moods, affects, phobias, compulsive ideas, backslidings, vices, etc. The social "strong man" is in his private life often a mere child where his own states of feeling are concerned; his discipline in public (which he demands quite particularly of others) goes miserably to pieces in private. His "happiness in his work" assumes a woeful countenance at home; his "spotless" public morality looks strange indeed behind the mask—we will not mention deeds, but only fantasies, and the wives of such men would have a pretty tale to tell. As to his selfless altruism, his children have decided views about that.   104B: 307

I once made the acquaintance of a very venerable personage—in fact, one might easily call him a saint. I stalked round him for three whole days, but never a mortal failing did I find in him. My feeling of inferiority grew ominous, and I was beginning to think seriously of how I might better myself. Then, on the fourth day, his wife came to consult me. . . . Well, nothing of the sort has ever happened to me since. But this I did learn: that any man who becomes one with his persona can cheerfully let all disturbances manifest themselves through his wife without her noticing it, though she pays for her self-sacrifice with a bad neurosis.   104B: 306

The meeting with ourselves is one of the more unpleasant things that may be avoided as long as we possess living symbolic figures into which everything unknown in ourselves is projected. The figure of the devil, in particular, is a most valuable possession and a great convenience, for as long as he goes about outside in the form of a roaring lion we know where the evil lurks: in that incarnate Old Harry where it has been in this or that form since primeval times. With the rise of consciousness since the Middle Ages he has been considerably reduced in stature, but in his stead there are human beings to whom we gratefully surrender our shadows. With what pleasure, for instance, we read newspaper reports of crime! A bona fide criminal becomes a popular figure because he unburdens in no small degree the conscience of his fellow men, for now they know once more where the evil is to be found.   10A: 69*f**

It is a fact that cannot be denied: the wickedness of others becomes our own wickedness because it kindles something evil in our own hearts.   1: 408

Whoever looks into the mirror of the water will see first of all his own face. Whoever goes to himself risks a confrontation with himself. The mirror does not flatter, it faithfully shows whatever looks into it; namely, the face we never show to the world because we cover it with the persona, the mask of the actor. But the mirror lies behind the mask and shows the true face.   10: 43

We can certainly hand it to Augustine that all natures are good, yet just not good enough to prevent their badness from being equally obvious.   3: 95

Simple things are always the most difficult. In actual life it requires the greatest art to be simple, and so acceptance of oneself is the essence of the moral problem and the acid test of one's whole outlook on life. That I feed the beggar, that I forgive an insult, that I love my enemy in the name of Christ—all these are undoubtedly great virtues. What I do unto the least of my brethren, that I do unto Christ. But what if I should discover that the least amongst them all, the poorest of all beggars, the most impudent of all offenders, yea the very fiend himself—that these are within me, and that I myself stand in need of the alms of my own kindness, that I myself am the enemy who must be loved—what then? Then, as a rule, the whole truth of Christianity is reversed: there is then no more talk of love and long-suffering; we say to the brother within us "Raca," and condemn and rage against ourselves. We hide him from the world, we deny ever having met this least among the lowly in ourselves, and had it been God himself who drew near to us in this despicable form, we should have denied him a thousand times before a single cock had crowed.　78:520

Unfortunately there can be no doubt that man is, on the whole, less good than he imagines himself or wants to be. Everyone carries a shadow, and the less it is embodied in the individual's conscious life, the blacker and denser it is. If an inferiority is conscious, one always has a chance to correct it. Furthermore, it is constantly in contact with other interests, so that it is continually subjected to modifications. But if it is repressed and isolated from consciousness, it never gets corrected.　74:131

It is a frightening thought that man also has a shadow-side to him, consisting not just of little weaknesses and foibles, but of a positively demonic dynamism. The individual seldom knows anything of this; to him, as an individual, it is incredible that he should ever in any circumstances go beyond himself. But let these harmless creatures form a mass, and there emerges a raging monster; and each individual is only one tiny cell in the monster's body, so that for better or worse he must accompany it on its bloody rampages and even assist it to the utmost. Having a dark suspicion of these grim possibilities, man turns a blind eye to the shadow-side of human nature. Blindly he strives against the salutary dogma of original sin, which is yet so prodigiously true. Yes, he even hesitates to admit the conflict of which he is so painfully aware.　104A:35

The educated man tries to repress the inferior man in himself, not realizing that by so doing he forces the latter into revolt.　74:136

We carry our past with us, to wit, the primitive and inferior man with his desires and emotions, and it is only with an enormous effort that we can detach ourselves from this burden. If it comes to a neurosis, we invariably have to deal with a considerably intensified shadow. And if such a person wants to be cured it is necessary to find a way in which his conscious personality and his shadow can live together. 74:132

As a rule those tendencies that represent the antisocial elements in man's psychic structure—what I call the "statistical criminal" in everybody—are suppressed, that is, they are consciously and deliberately disposed of. But tendencies that are merely repressed are usually of a somewhat doubtful character. They are not so much antisocial as unconventional and socially awkward. The reason why we repress them is equally doubtful. Some people repress them from sheer cowardice, others from conventional morality, and others again for reasons of respectability. Repression is a sort of half-conscious and half-hearted letting go of things, a dropping of hot cakes or a reviling of grapes which hang too high, or a looking the other way in order not to become conscious of one's desires. 74:129

We know that the wildest and most moving dramas are played not in the theatre but in the hearts of ordinary men and women who pass by without exciting attention, and who betray to the world nothing of the conflicts that rage within them except possibly by a nervous breakdown. What is so difficult for the layman to grasp is the fact that in most cases the patients themselves have no suspicion whatever of the internecine war raging in their unconscious. If we remember that there are many people who understand nothing at all about themselves, we shall be less surprised at the realization that there are also people who are utterly unaware of their actual conflicts. 104c:425

To cherish secrets and hold back emotion is a psychic misdemeanour for which nature finally visits us with sickness—that is, when we do these things in private. But when they are done in communion with others they satisfy nature and may even count as useful virtues. It is only restraint practised for oneself alone that is unwholesome. It is as if man had an inalienable right to behold all that is dark, imperfect, stupid, and guilty in his fellow men—for such, of course, are the things we keep secret in order to protect ourselves. It seems to be a sin in the eyes of nature to hide our inferiority—just as much as to live entirely on our inferior side.   63:132

If the repressed tendencies, the shadow as I call them, were obviously evil, there would be no problem whatever. But the shadow is merely somewhat inferior, primitive, unadapted, and awkward; not wholly bad. It even contains childish or primitive qualities which would in a way vitalize and embellish human existence, but—convention forbids.

74:134

In reality, the acceptance of the shadow-side of human nature verges on the impossible. Consider for a moment what it means to grant the right of existence to what is unreasonable, senseless, and evil! Yet it is just this that the modern man insists upon. He wants to live with every side of himself—to know what he is. That is why he casts history aside. He wants to break with tradition so that he can experiment with his life and determine what value and meaning things have in themselves, apart from traditional presuppositions.   78:528

Mere suppression of the shadow is as little of a remedy as beheading would be for headache. To destroy a man's morality does not help either, because it would kill his better self, without which even the shadow makes no sense. The reconciliation of these opposites is a major problem, and even in antiquity it bothered certain minds. 74:133

Taking it in its deepest sense, the shadow is the invisible saurian tail that man still drags behind him. Carefully amputated, it becomes the healing serpent of the mysteries. Only monkeys parade with it. 10A:93*

If you imagine someone who is brave enough to withdraw all his projections, then you get an individual who is conscious of a pretty thick shadow. Such a man has saddled himself with new problems and conflicts. He has become a serious problem to himself, as he is now unable to say that *they* do this or that, *they* are wrong, and *they* must be fought against. He lives in the "House of the Gathering." Such a man knows that whatever is wrong in the world is in himself, and if he only learns to deal with his own shadow he has done something real for the world. He has succeeded in shouldering at least an infinitesimal part of the gigantic, unsolved social problems of our day. 74:140

The shadow is a tight passage, a narrow door, whose painful constriction no one is spared who goes down to the deep well. But one must learn to know oneself in order to know who one is. For what comes after the door is, surprisingly enough, a boundless expanse full of unprecedented uncertainty, with apparently no inside and no outside, no above and no below, no here and no there, no mine and no thine, no good and no bad. It is the world of water, where all life floats in suspension; where the realm of the sympathetic system, the soul of everything living, begins; where I am indivisibly this *and* that; where I experience the other in myself and the other-than-myself experiences me. 10:45

It is of course a fundamental mistake to imagine that when we see the non-value in a value or the untruth in a truth, the value or the truth ceases to exist. It has only become *relative*. Everything human is relative, because everything rests on an inner polarity; for everything is a phenomenon of energy. Energy necessarily depends on a pre-existing polarity, without which there could be no energy. There must always be high and low, hot and cold, etc., so that the equilibrating process—which is energy—can take place. Therefore the tendency to deny all previous values in favour of their opposites is just as much of an exaggeration as the earlier onesidedness. And in so far as it is a question of rejecting universally accepted and indubitable values, the result is a fatal loss. One who acts in this way empties himself out with his values, as Nietzsche has already said.   104A: 115

Nobody can fall so low unless he has a great depth. If such a thing can happen to a man, it challenges his best and highest on the other side; that is to say, this depth corresponds to a potential height, and the blackest darkness to a hidden light.   43*

The difficulty lies in striking the dead centre. For this an awareness of the two sides of man's personality is essential, of their respective aims and origins. These two aspects must never be separated through arrogance or cowardice.

72: 148

The tendency to separate the opposites as much as possible and to strive for singleness of meaning is absolutely necessary for clarity of consciousness, since discrimination is of its essence. But when the separation is carried so far that the complementary opposite is lost sight of, and the blackness of the whiteness, the evil of the good, the depth of the heights, and so on, is no longer seen, the result is one-sidedness, which is then compensated from the unconscious without our help.

48:470

Only unconsciousness makes no difference between good and evil.

3:97

Our knowledge of good and evil has dwindled with our mounting knowledge and experience, and will dwindle still more in the future, without our being able to escape the demands of ethics. In this utmost uncertainty we need the illumination of a holy and whole-making spirit—a spirit that can be anything rather than our reason.

65:267

Even on the highest peak we shall never be "beyond good and evil," and the more we experience of their inextricable entanglement the more uncertain and confused will our moral judgment be. In this conflict, it will not help us in the least to throw the moral criterion on the rubbish heap and to set up new tablets after known patterns; for, as in the past, so in the future the wrong we have done, thought, or intended will wreak its vengeance on our souls, no matter whether we turn the world upside down or not.

65:267

On paper the moral code looks clear and neat enough; but the same document written on the "living tables of the heart" is often a sorry tatter, particularly in the mouths of those who talk the loudest. We are told on every side that evil is evil and that there can be no hesitation in condemning it, but that does not prevent evil from being the most problematical thing in the individual's life and the one which demands the deepest reflection. What above all deserves our keenest attention is the question "Exactly *who* is the doer?" For the answer to this question ultimately decides the value of the deed. It is true that society attaches greater importance at first to what is done, because it is immediately obvious; but in the long run the right deed in the hands of the wrong man will also have a disastrous effect. No one who is far-sighted will allow himself to be hoodwinked by the right deed by the wrong man, any more than by the wrong deed of the right man.   72:36

✧

The primitive form of conscience is paradoxical: to burn a heretic is on the one hand a pious and meritorious act—as John Hus himself ironically recognized when, bound to the stake, he espied an old woman hobbling towards him with a bundle of faggots, and exclaimed, "O sancta simplicitas!"—and on the other hand a brutal manifestation of ruthless and savage lust for revenge.   71:845

Besides the "right" kind of conscience there is a "wrong" one, which exaggerates, perverts, and twists evil into good and good into evil just as our own scruples do; and it does so with the same compulsiveness and with the same emotional consequences as the "right" kind of conscience. Were it not for this paradox the question of conscience would present no problem: we could then rely wholly on its decisions so far as morality is concerned. But since there is great and justified uncertainty in this regard, it needs unusual courage or—what amounts to the same thing—unshakable faith for a person simply to follow the dictates of his own conscience. As a rule one obeys only up to a certain point, which is determined in advance by the moral code. This is where those dreaded conflicts of duty begin. Generally they are answered according to the precepts of the moral code, but only in a very few cases are they really decided by an individual act of judgment. For as soon as the moral code ceases to act as a support, conscience easily succumbs to a fit of weakness.   71:835

"Conscience," in ordinary usage, means the consciousness of a factor which in the case of a "good conscience" affirms that a decision or an act accords with morality and, if it does not, condemns it as "immoral." This view, deriving as it does from the *mores*, from what is customary, can properly be called "moral." Distinct from this is the ethical form of conscience, which appears when two decisions or ways of acting, both affirmed to be moral and therefore regarded as "duties," collide with one another. In these cases, not foreseen by the moral code because they are mostly very individual, a judgment is required which cannot properly be called "moral" or in accord with custom. Here the decision has no custom at its disposal on which it could rely. The deciding factor appears to be something else: it proceeds not from the traditional moral code but from the unconscious foundation of the personality. The decision is drawn from dark and deep waters. It is true these conflicts of duty are solved very often and very conveniently by a decision in accordance with custom, that is, by suppressing one of the opposites. But this is not always so. If one is sufficiently conscientious the conflict is endured to the end, and a creative solution emerges which is produced by the constellated archetype and possesses that compelling authority not unjustly characterized as the voice of God.   71:856

In Christ's sayings there are already indications of ideas which go beyond the traditionally "Christian" morality—for instance the parable of the unjust steward, the moral of which agrees with the logion of the Codex Bezae,* and betrays an ethical standard very different from what is expected. Here the moral criterion is *consciousness*, and not law or convention. One might also mention the strange fact

* An apocryphal insertion at Luke 6:4: "Man, if indeed thou knowest what thou doest, thou art blessed; but if thou knowest not, thou art cursed, and a transgressor of the law."

that it is precisely Peter, who lacks self-control and is fickle in character, whom Christ wishes to make the rock and foundation of his Church. These seem to me to be ideas which point to the inclusion of evil in what I would call a *differential moral valuation*. For instance, it is good if evil is sensibly covered up, but to act unconsciously is evil. One might almost suppose that such views were intended for a time when consideration is given to evil as well as to good, or rather, when it is not suppressed below the threshold in the dubious assumption that we always know exactly what evil is.   7:696

Solicitude for the spiritual welfare of the erring sheep can explain even a Torquemada.   60:391

If, as many are fain to believe, the unconscious were only nefarious, only evil, then the situation would be simple and the path clear: to do good and to eschew evil. But what is "good" and what is "evil"? The unconscious is not just evil by nature, it is also the source of the highest good: not only dark but also light, not only bestial, semi-human and demonic but superhuman, spiritual, and, in the classical sense of the word, "divine."   77:389

Christianity has made the antinomy of good and evil into a world problem and, by formulating the conflict dogmatically, raised it to an absolute principle. Into this as yet unresolved conflict the Christian is cast as a protagonist of good, a fellow player in the world drama. Understood in its deepest sense, being Christ's follower involves a suffering that is unendurable to the great majority of mankind. Consequently the example of Christ is in reality followed either with reservation or not at all, and the pastoral practice of the Church even finds itself obliged to "lighten the yoke of Christ." This means a pretty considerable reduction in the severity and harshness of the conflict and

hence, in practice, a relativism of good and evil. Good is
equivalent to the unconditional imitation of Christ and evil
is its hindrance. Man's moral weakness and sloth are what
chiefly hinder the imitation, and it is to these that probabilism* extends a practical understanding which may sometimes, perhaps, come nearer to Christian tolerance, mild-
ness, and love of one's neighbour than the attitude of those
who see in probabilism a mere laxity.   72:25

"Love thy neighbour" is wonderful, since we then have
nothing to do about ourselves; but when it is a question
of "love thy neighbour as thyself" we are no longer so sure,
for we think it would be egoism to love ourselves. There
was no need to preach "love thyself" to people in olden
times, because they did so as a matter of course. But how is
it nowadays? It would do us good to take this thing somewhat to heart, especially the phrase "as thyself." How can
I love my neighbour if I do not love myself? How can we
be altruistic if we do not treat ourselves decently? But if we
treat ourselves decently, if we love ourselves, we make discoveries, and then we see what we are and what we should
love. There is nothing for it but to put our foot into the
serpent's mouth. He who cannot love can never transform
the serpent, and then nothing is changed.   11:87*

Christ espoused the sinner and did not condemn him.
The true follower of Christ will do the same, and, since one
should do unto others as one would do unto oneself, one
will also take the part of the sinner who is oneself. And as
little as we would accuse Christ of fraternizing with evil,
so little should we reproach ourselves that to love the sinner
who is oneself is to make a pact with the devil. Love makes
a man better, hate makes him worse—even when that man
is oneself.   72:37

* Concerning probabilism, see *Psychology and Alchemy* (1968),
p. 20, n. 10.

The reality of evil and its incompatibility with good cleave the opposites asunder and lead inexorably to the crucifixion and suspension of everything that lives. Since "the soul is by nature Christian" this result is bound to come as infallibly as it did in the life of Jesus: we all have to be "crucified with Christ," i.e., suspended in a moral suffering equivalent to veritable crucifixion. In practice this is only possible up to a point, and apart from that is so unbearable and inimical to life that the ordinary human being can afford to get into such a state only occasionally, in fact as seldom as possible. For how could he remain ordinary in the face of such suffering!

72:24

It is no easy matter to live a life that is modelled on Christ's, but it is unspeakably harder to live one's own life as truly as Christ lived his. Anyone who did this would run counter to the conditions of his own history, and though he might thus be fulfilling them, he would none the less be misjudged, derided, tortured, and crucified.

78:522

Life demands for its completion and fulfilment a balance between joy and sorrow. But because suffering is positively disagreeable, people naturally prefer not to ponder how much fear and sorrow fall to the lot of man. So they speak soothingly about progress and the greatest possible happiness, forgetting that happiness is itself poisoned if the measure of suffering has not been fulfilled.

79:185

Opposites can be united only in the form of compromise, or irrationally, some new thing arising between them which, though different from both, yet has the power to take up their energies in equal measure as an expression of both and of neither. Such an expression cannot be contrived by reason, it can only be created through living.

69:169

What takes place between light and darkness, what unites the opposites, has a share in both sides and can be judged just as well from the left as from the right, without our becoming any the wiser: indeed, we can only open up the opposition again. Here only the symbol helps, for, in accordance with its paradoxical nature, it represents the "tertium" that in logic does not exist, but which in reality is the living truth.   58:199

The symbol is the middle way along which the opposites flow together in a new movement, like a watercourse bringing fertility after a long drought.   69:443

The most intense conflicts, if overcome, leave behind a sense of security and calm which is not easily disturbed, or else a brokenness that can hardly be healed. Conversely, it is just these intense conflicts and their conflagration which are needed in order to produce valuable and lasting results.

54:50

❖

The possession of complexes does not in itself signify neurosis, for complexes are the normal foci of psychic happenings, and the fact that they are painful is no proof of pathological disturbance. Suffering is not an illness; it is the normal counterpole to happiness. A complex becomes pathological only when we think we have not got it.

79:179

Neurosis is always a substitute for legitimate suffering.
74:129

The wounding and painful shafts do not come from outside, through gossip, which only pricks us on the surface, but from the ambush of our own unconscious. It is our own repressed desires that stick like arrows in our flesh.   100:438

Deviation from the truths of the blood begets neurotic restlessness, and we have had about enough of that these days. Restlessness begets meaninglessness, and the lack of meaning in life is a soul-sickness whose full extent and full import our age has not as yet begun to comprehend.

90:815

The Christian doctrine of original sin on the one hand, and of the meaning and value of suffering on the other, is of profound therapeutic significance and is undoubtedly far better suited to Western man than Islamic fatalism. Similarly the belief in immortality gives life that untroubled flow into the future so necessary if stoppages and regressions are to be avoided.   79:186

A psychoneurosis must be understood, ultimately, as the suffering of a soul which has not discovered its meaning. But all creativeness in the realm of the spirit as well as every psychic advance of man arises from the suffering of the soul, and the cause of the suffering is spiritual stagnation, or psychic sterility.   78:497

Suffering that is not understood is hard to bear, while on the other hand it is often astounding to see how much a person can endure when he understands the why and the wherefore. A philosophical or religious view of the world enables him to do this, and such views prove to be, at the very least, psychic methods of healing if not of salvation.

51:692*

To be adapted is certainly an ideal, but adaptation is not always possible. There are situations in which the only adaptation is patient endurance.   69:427

Man is never helped in his suffering by what he thinks of for himself; only suprahuman, revealed truth lifts him out of his distress. 78: 531

It is well to remind ourselves of St. Paul and his split consciousness: on one side he felt he was the apostle directly called and enlightened by God, and, on the other hand, a sinful man who could not pluck out the "thorn in the flesh" and rid himself of the Satanic angel who plagued him. That is to say, even the most enlightened person remains what he is, and is never more than his own limited ego before the One who dwells within him, whose form has no knowable boundaries, who encompasses him on all sides, fathomless as the abysms of the earth and vast as the sky. 7: 758

The Life of the Spirit

For a long time the spirit, and the sufferings of the spirit, were positive values and the things most worth striving for in our peculiar Christian culture. Only in the course of the nineteenth century, when spirit began to degenerate into intellect, did a reaction set in against the unbearable dominance of intellectualism, and this led to the unpardonable mistake of confusing intellect with spirit and blaming the latter for the misdeeds of the former. The intellect does indeed do harm to the soul when it dares to possess itself of the heritage of the spirit. It is in no way fitted to do this, for spirit is something higher than intellect since it embraces the latter and includes the feelings as well. It is a guiding principle of life that strives towards superhuman, shining heights.   112:7

Our intellect has achieved the most tremendous things, but in the meantime our spiritual dwelling has fallen into disrepair. We are absolutely convinced that even with the aid of the latest and largest reflecting telescope, now being built in America, men will discover behind the farthest nebulae no fiery empyrean; and we know that our eyes will wander despairingly through the dead emptiness of interstellar space. Nor is it any better when mathematical physics reveals to us the world of the infinitely small. In the end we dig up the wisdom of all ages and peoples, only to find that everything most dear and precious to us has already been said in the most superb language. Like greedy children we stretch out our hands and think that, if only we could grasp it, we would possess it too. But what we possess is no longer valid, and our hands grow weary from the grasping, for riches lie everywhere, as far as the eye can reach. All these possessions turn to water, and more than one sorcerer's apprentice has been drowned in the waters called up by himself—if he did not first succumb to the saving delusion that *this* wisdom was good and *that* was bad. It is from these adepts that there come those terrifying invalids who think they have a prophetic mission. For the artificial sundering of true and false wisdom creates a tension in the psyche, and from this there arises a loneliness and a craving like that of the morphine addict, who always hopes to find companions in his vice.   10:31

When our natural inheritance has been dissipated, then the spirit too, as Heraclitus says, has descended from its fiery heights. But when spirit becomes heavy it turns to water, and with Luciferian presumption the intellect usurps the seat where once the spirit was enthroned. The spirit may legitimately claim the *patria potestas* over the soul; not so the earth-born intellect, which is man's sword or hammer, and not a creator of spiritual worlds, a father of the soul.   10:32

The intellect may be the devil, but the devil is the "strange son of chaos" who can most readily be trusted to deal effectively with his mother. The Dionysian experience will give this devil plenty to do should he be looking for work, since the resultant settlement with the unconscious far outweighs the labours of Hercules. In my opinion it presents a whole world of problems which the intellect could not settle even in a hundred years—the very reason why it has so often gone off on a holiday to recuperate on lighter tasks. And this is also the reason why the psyche is forgotten so often and so long, and why the intellect makes such frequent use of magical, apotropaic words like "occult" and "mystic," in the hope that even intelligent people will think these mutterings really mean something.   72:119

Rational truths are not the last word, there are also irrational ones. In human affairs, what appears impossible by way of the intellect has often become true by way of the irrational. Indeed, all the greatest changes that have ever affected mankind have come not by way of intellectual calculation, but by ways which contemporary minds either ignored or rejected as absurd, and which were recognized only long afterwards because of their intrinsic necessity. More often than not they are never recognized at all, for the all-important laws of mental development are still a book with seven seals. 69:135

The irrationality of events is shown by what we call chance, which we are obviously compelled to deny because we cannot in principle think of any process that is not causal and necessary, whence it follows that it cannot happen by chance. In practice, however, chance reigns everywhere, and so obtrusively that we might as well put our causal philosophy in our pocket. The plenitude of life is governed by law and yet not governed by law, rational and yet irrational. Hence reason and the will that is grounded in reason are valid only up to a point. The further we go in the direction selected by reason, the surer we may be that we are excluding the irrational possibilities of life which have just as much right to be lived. It was indeed highly expedient for man to become somewhat more capable of directing his life. It may justly be maintained that the acquisition of reason is the greatest achievement of humanity; but that is not to say that things must or will always continue in that direction. 104A:72

Old Heraclitus, who was indeed a very great sage, discovered the most marvellous of all psychological laws: the regulative function of opposites. He called it *enantiodromia,* a running contrariwise, by which he meant that sooner or later everything runs into its opposite. . . . Thus the rational attitude of culture necessarily runs into its opposite, namely the irrational devastation of culture. We should never identify ourselves with reason, for man is not and never will be a creature of reason alone, a fact to be noted by all pedantic culture-mongers. The irrational cannot be and must not be extirpated. The gods cannot and must not die. 104A: 111

I am far from wishing to belittle the divine gift of reason, man's highest faculty. But in the role of absolute tyrant it has no meaning—no more than light would have in a world where its counterpart, darkness, was absent. Man would do well to heed the wise counsel of the mother and obey the inexorable law of nature which sets limits to every being. He ought never to forget that the world exists only because opposing forces are held in equilibrium. So, too, the rational is counterbalanced by the irrational, and what is planned and purposed by what *is*. 67: 174

Reason can give a man equilibrium only if his reason is already an equilibrating organ. But for how many individuals and at what periods in history has it been that? As a rule, a man needs the opposite of his actual situation to force him to find his place in the middle. For the sake of mere reason he can never forgo life's riches and the sensuous appeal of the immediate situation. Against the power and delight of the temporal he must set the joy of the eternal, and against the passion of the sensual the ecstasy of the spiritual. The undeniable reality of the one must be matched by the compelling power of the other. 69: 386

It is just the most unexpected, the most terrifyingly chaotic things which reveal a deeper meaning. . . . Gradually breakwaters are built against the surging of chaos, and the meaningful divides itself from the meaningless. When sense and nonsense are no longer identical, the force of

chaos is weakened by their subtraction; sense is then en-
dued with the force of meaning, and nonsense with the force
of meaninglessness. In this way a new cosmos arises.

10:64

✧

The ancient world contained a large slice of nature and
a number of questionable things which Christianity was
bound to overlook if the security of a spiritual standpoint
was not to be hopelessly compromised. No penal code and
no moral code, not even the sublimest casuistry, will ever be
able to codify and pronounce just judgment upon the confusions, the conflicts of duty, and the invisible tragedies of
the natural man in collision with the exigencies of culture.
"Spirit" is one aspect, "Nature" another. "You may pitch
Nature out with a fork, yet she'll always come back again,"
says the poet.* Nature *must not* win the game, but she *cannot* lose. And whenever the conscious mind clings to hard
and fast concepts and gets caught in its own rules and reg-
ulations—as is unavoidable and of the essence of civilized
consciousness—nature pops up with her inescapable demands. Nature is not matter only, she is also spirit. Were
that not so, the only source of spirit would be human
reason.   58:229

We should not pretend to understand the world only by
the intellect; we apprehend it just as much by feeling.
Therefore the judgment of the intellect is, at best, only a
half-truth, and must, if it be honest, also admit its
inadequacy.   69:856

There are, besides the gifts of the head, also those of the
heart, which are no whit less important, although they may
easily be overlooked because in such cases the head is often

* Horace, *Epistola*, I, x, 24.

the weaker organ. And yet people of this kind sometimes contribute more to the well-being of society, and are more valuable, than those with other talents.   31:242

One can, it is true, understand many things with the heart, but then the head often finds it difficult to follow up with an intellectual formulation that gives suitable expression to what has been understood. There is also an understanding with the head, particularly of the scientific kind, where there is sometimes too little room for the heart.

75:934

The utterances of the heart—unlike those of the discriminating intellect—always relate to the whole. The heartstrings sing like an Aeolian harp only to the gentle breath of a premonitory mood, which does not drown the song but listens. What the heart hears are the great things that span our whole lives, the experiences which we do nothing to arrange but which we ourselves suffer.   87:9*

I believe only what I *know*. Everything else is hypothesis and beyond that I can leave a lot of things to the Unknown. They do not bother me. But they would begin to bother me, I am sure, if I felt that I *ought* to know about them.   74:79

Paradox . . . does more justice to the *unknowable* than clarity can do, for uniformity of meaning robs the mystery of its darkness and sets it up as something that is *known*. That is a usurpation, and it leads the human intellect into hybris by pretending that it, the intellect, has got hold of the transcendent mystery by a cognitive act and "grasped" it. The paradox therefore reflects a higher level of intellect and, by not forcibly representing the unknowable as known, gives a more faithful picture of the real state of affairs.   103:417

The final appeal to reason would be very fine if man were by nature a rational animal, but he is not; on the contrary, he is quite as much irrational. Hence reason is often not sufficient to modify the instinct and make it conform to the rational order.	79:178

There are of course forced answers and solutions, but in principle and in the long run they are neither desirable nor satisfying. No Gordian knot can be permanently cut; it has the awkward property of always tying itself again.

79:178

✧

The wheel of history cannot be put back; we can only strive towards an attitude that will allow us to live out our fate as undisturbedly as the primitive pagan in us really wants. Only on this condition can we be sure of not perverting spirituality into sensuality, and vice versa; for both must live, each drawing life from the other.	44:336

Nothing is more repulsive than a furtively prurient spirituality; it is just as unsavoury as gross sensuality.	44:336

If certain South American Indians really and truly call themselves red cockatoos and expressly repudiate a figurative interpretation of this fact, this has absolutely nothing to do with any sexual repression on "moral" grounds, but is due to the law of independence inherent in the thinking function and to its emancipation from the concretism of sensuous perceptions. We must assign a separate principle to the thinking function, a principle which coincides with the beginnings of sexuality only in the polyvalent germinal disposition of the very young child. To reduce the origins of thinking to mere sexuality is an undertaking that runs counter to the basic facts of human psychology.	64:79

I am convinced that a truly scientific attitude in psychology must lead to the conclusion that the dynamic processes of the psyche cannot be reduced to this or that concrete instinct—we should merely find ourselves back at the stage of the phlogiston theory. We shall be obliged to take the instincts as constituent parts of the psyche, and then abstract our principle of explanation from their mutual relationship. I have therefore pointed out that we would do well to posit a hypothetical quantity, an "energy," as a psychological explanatory principle, and to call it "libido" in the classical sense of the word, without harbouring any prejudice with regard to its substantiality. With the help of such a quantity, the psychodynamic processes could be explained in an unobjectionable manner, without that unavoidable distortion which a concrete ground of explanation necessarily entails. 85:7

Man finds himself simultaneously driven to act and free to reflect. This contrariety in his nature has no moral significance, for instinct is not in itself bad any more than spirit is good. Both can be both. Negative electricity is as good as positive electricity: first and foremost it is electricity. 53:406

Instinct is not an isolated thing, nor can it be isolated in practice. It always brings in its train archetypal cont ts of a spiritual nature, which are at once its foundation and its limitation. In other words, an instinct is always and inevitably coupled with something like a philosophy of life, however archaic, unclear, and hazy this may be. Instinct stimulates thought, and if a man does not think of his own free will, then you get compulsive thinking, for the two pol s of the psyche, the physiological and the mental, are indissolubly connected. For this reason instinct cannot be freed without freeing the mind, just as mind divorced from instinct is condemned to futility. 79:185

What would the spirit be if it had no peer among the instincts to oppose it? It would be nothing but an empty form.   54:107

We could call sexuality the spokesman of the instincts, which is why from the spiritual standpoint sex is the chief antagonist, not because sexual indulgence is in itself more immoral than excessive eating and drinking, avarice, tyranny, and other extravagances, but because the spirit senses in sexuality a counterpart equal and indeed akin to itself. For just as the spirit would press sexuality, like every other instinct, into its service, so sexuality has an ancient claim upon the spirit, which it once—in procreation, pregnancy, birth, and childhood—contained within itself, and whose passion the spirit can never dispense with in its creations.   54:107

The spiritual principle does not, strictly speaking, conflict with instinct as such but only with blind instinctuality, which really amounts to an unjustified preponderance of the instinctual nature over the spiritual. The spiritual appears in the psyche also as an instinct, indeed as a real passion, a "consuming fire," as Nietzsche once expressed it. It is not derived from any other instinct, as the psychologists of instinct would have us believe, but is a principle *sui generis*, a specific and necessary form of instinctual power.

54:108

Man living in the state of nature is in no sense merely "natural" like an animal, but sees, believes, fears, worships things whose meaning is not at all discoverable from the conditions of his natural environment. Their underlying meaning leads us in fact far away from all that is natural, obvious, and easily intelligible, and quite often contrasts most sharply with the natural instincts. We have only to think of all those gruesome rites and customs against which every natural feeling rises in revolt, or of all those beliefs and ideas which stand in insuperable contradiction to the evidence of the facts. All this drives us to the assumption that the spiritual principle (whatever that may be) asserts itself against the merely natural conditions with incredible strength. One can say that this too is "natural," and that both have their origin in one and the same "nature." I do not in the least doubt this origin, but must point out that this "natural" something consists of a conflict between two principles, to which you can give this or that name according to taste, and that this opposition is the expression, and perhaps also the basis, of the tension we call psychic energy.   54:98

The fact that all immediate experience is psychic and that immediate reality can only be psychic explains why it is that primitive man puts spirits and magical influences on the same plane as physical events. He has not yet torn his original experience into antithetical parts. In his world, spirit and matter still interpenetrate each other, and his gods still wander through forest and field. He is like a child, only half born, still enclosed in his own psyche as in a dream, in a world not yet distorted by the difficulties of understanding that beset a dawning intelligence. When this aboriginal world fell apart into spirit and nature, the West rescued nature for itself. It was prone by temperament to a belief in nature, and only became the more entangled in it with every painful effort to make itself spiritual. The East, on the other hand, took spirit for its own, and by explaining away matter as mere illusion—Maya—continued to dream in Asiatic filth and misery. But since there is only *one* earth and *one* mankind, East and West cannot rend humanity into two different halves. Psychic reality still exists in its original oneness, and awaits man's advance to a level of consciousness where he no longer believes in the one part and denies the other, but recognizes both as constituent elements of one psyche.   12:682

Through scientific understanding, our world has become dehumanized. Man feels himself isolated in the cosmos. He is no longer involved in nature and has lost his emotional participation in natural events, which hitherto had a symbolic meaning for him. Thunder is no longer the voice of a god, nor is lightning his avenging missile. No river contains a spirit, no tree means a man's life, no snake is the embodiment of wisdom, and no mountain still harbours a great demon. Neither do things speak to him nor can he speak to things, like stones, springs, plants, and animals. He no longer has a bush-soul identifying him with a wild animal. His immediate communication with nature is gone for ever.   8:95*

The conflict between nature and spirit is itself a reflection of the paradox of psychic life. This reveals a physical and a spiritual aspect which appear a contradiction because, ultimately, we do not understand the nature of psychic life itself. Whenever, with our human understanding, we want to make a statement about something which in the last analysis we have not grasped and cannot grasp, then we must, if we are honest, be willing to contradict ourselves, we must pull this something into its antithetical parts in order to be able to deal with it at all. The conflict between the physical and the spiritual aspects only shows that psychic life is in the last analysis an incomprehensible "something."   12:680

We have stripped all things of their mystery and numinosity: nothing is holy any longer.   8:94*

All through our lives we possess, side by side with our newly acquired directed and adapted thinking, a fantasy-thinking which corresponds to the antique state of mind. Just as our bodies still retain vestiges of obsolete functions and conditions in many of their organs, so our minds, which have apparently outgrown those archaic impulses, still bear the marks of the evolutionary stages we have traversed, and re-echo the dim bygone in dreams and fantasies.   100: 36

There is not a single important idea or view that does not possess historical antecedents. Ultimately they are all founded on primordial archetypal forms whose concreteness dates from a time when consciousness did not *think*, but only *perceived*. "Thoughts" were objects of inner perception, not thought at all, but sensed as external phenomena—seen or heard, so to speak. Thought was essentially revelation, not invented but forced upon us or bringing conviction through its immediacy and actuality.

10: 69

The religions should constantly recall to us the origin and original character of the spirit, lest man should forget what he is drawing into himself and with what he is filling his consciousness. He himself did not create the spirit, rather the spirit makes *him* creative, always spurring him on, giving him lucky ideas, staying power, "enthusiasm" and "inspiration."   59: 393

The limitations of knowledge which leave so many incomprehensible and wonderful things unexplained do not, however, exempt us from the task of trying to understand the revelations of the spirit that are embodied in dogma, otherwise there is a danger that the treasures of supreme knowledge which lie hidden in it will evaporate into nothing and become a bloodless phantom, an easy prey for all shallow rationalists. It would be a great step forward, in my opinion, if at least it were recognized how far the truth of dogma is rooted in the human psyche, which is not the work of human hands. 48:489

Progress and development are ideals not lightly to be rejected, but they lose all meaning if man only arrives at his new state as a fragment of himself, having left his essential hinterland behind him in the shadow of the unconscious, in a state of primitivity or, indeed, barbarism. The conscious mind, split off from its origins, incapable of realizing the meaning of the new state, then relapses all too easily into a situation far worse than the one from which the innovation was intended to free it—*exempla sunt odiosa!*

76:293

It would be a ridiculous and unwarranted assumption on our part if we imagined that we were more energetic or more intelligent than the men of the past. Our material knowledge has increased, but not our intelligence. This means that we are just as bigoted in regard to new ideas, and just as impervious to them, as people were in the darkest days of antiquity. We have become rich in knowledge, but poor in wisdom. 100:23

Nothing is less effective than an intellectual idea. But when an idea is a psychic fact that crops up in two such totally different fields as psychology and physics, apparently without historical connection, then we must give it our closest attention. For ideas of this kind represent forces which are logically and morally unassailable; they are always stronger than man and his brain. He fancies that he makes these ideas, but in reality they make him—and make him their unwitting mouthpiece. 63:147

There is a temperament which regards ideas as real entities and not merely as *nomina*. It so happens—by the merest accident, one might say—that for the past two hundred years we have been living in an age in which it has become unpopular or even unintelligible to suppose that ideas could be anything but *nomina*. Anyone who continues to think as Plato did must pay for his anachronism by seeing the "supracelestial," i.e., metaphysical, essence of the Idea relegated to the unverifiable realm of faith and superstition, or charitably left to the poet. Once again, in the age-old controversy over universals, the nominalistic standpoint has triumphed over the realistic, and the Idea has evaporated into a mere *flatus vocis*. This change was accompanied—and, indeed, to a considerable degree caused —by the marked rise of empiricism, the advantages of which were only too obvious to the intellect. Since that time the Idea is no longer something *a priori,* but is secondary and derived. 67:149

Widely accepted ideas are never the personal property of their so-called author; on the contrary, he is the bondservant of his ideas. Impressive ideas which are hailed as truths have something peculiar about them. Although they come into being at a definite time, they are and have always been timeless; they arise from that realm of creative psychic life out of which the ephemeral mind of the single human being grows like a plant that blossoms, bears fruit and seed, and then withers and dies. Ideas spring from something greater than the personal human being. Man does not make his ideas; we could say that man's ideas make him. 28:769

The Platonic freedom of the spirit does not make a whole judgment possible: it wrenches the light half of the picture away from the dark half. This freedom is to a large extent a phenomenon of civilization, the lofty preoccupation of that fortunate Athenian whose lot it was not to be born a slave. We can only rise above nature if somebody else carries the weight of the earth for us. What sort of phi-

losophy would Plato have produced had he been his own
house-slave? What would the Rabbi Jesus have taught if
he had had to support a wife and children? If he had had
to till the soil in which the bread he broke had grown, and
weed the vineyard in which the wine he dispensed had
ripened? The dark weight of the earth must enter into the
picture of the whole.   65:264

Anyone who is conscious of his guiding principle knows
with what indisputable authority it rules his life. But generally consciousness is too preoccupied with the attainment
of some beckoning goal to consider the nature of the spirit
that determines its course.   91:642

There are many spirits, both light and dark. We should,
therefore, be prepared to accept the view that spirit is not
absolute, but something relative that needs completing and
perfecting through life.   91:645

For the Chinese, "spirit" does not signify order, meaning,
and everything that is good: on the contrary, it is a fiery
and sometimes dangerous power.   41:939

Just as there is a passion that strives for blind unrestricted
life, so there is a passion that would like to sacrifice all life
to the spirit because of its superior creative power. This
passion turns the spirit into a malignant growth that senselessly destroys human life.   91:646

Man conquers not only nature, but spirit also, without
realizing what he is doing. To the man of enlightened intellect it seems like the correction of a fallacy when he recognizes that what he took to be spirits is simply the human
spirit and ultimately his own spirit. All the superhuman
things, whether good or bad, that former ages predicated
of the *daimonia*, are reduced to "reasonable" proportions

as though they were pure exaggeration, and everything seems to be in the best possible order. But were the unanimous convictions of the past really and truly only exaggerations? If they were not, then the integration of the spirit means nothing less than its demonization, since the superhuman spiritual agencies that were formerly tied up in nature are introjected into human nature, thus endowing it with a power which extends the bounds of the personality *ad infinitum*, in the most perilous way.   59:454

After the last World War we hoped for reason: we go on hoping. But already we are fascinated by the possibilities of atomic fission and promise ourselves a Golden Age— the surest guarantee that the abomination of desolation will grow to limitless dimensions. And who or what is it that causes all this? It is none other than that harmless (!), ingenious, inventive, and sweetly reasonable human spirit who unfortunately is abysmally unconscious of the demonism that still clings to him. Worse, this spirit does everything to avoid looking himself in the face, and we all help him like mad. Only, heaven preserve us from psychology —*that* depravity might lead to self-knowledge! Rather let us have wars, for which somebody else is always to blame, nobody seeing that all the world is driven to do just what all the world flees from in terror.   59:454

Myths are miracle tales and treat of all those things which, very often, are also objects of belief. In the everyday world of consciousness such things hardly exist; that is to say, until 1933 only lunatics would have been found in possession of living fragments of mythology. After this date the world of heroes and monsters spread like a devastating fire over whole nations, proving that the strange world of myth had suffered no loss of vitality during the centuries of reason and enlightenment. If metaphysical ideas no longer have such a fascinating effect as before, this is certainly not due to any lack of primitivity in the European psyche, but simply and solely to the fact that the erstwhile symbols no longer express what is now welling up from the unconscious as the end-result of the development of Christian consciousness through the centuries. This end-result is a true *antimimon pneuma*, a false spirit of arrogance, hysteria, woolly-mindedness, criminal amorality, and doctrinaire fanaticism, a purveyor of shoddy spiritual goods, spurious art, philosophical stutterings, and Utopian humbug, fit only to be fed wholesale to the mass man of to-day. That is what the post-Christian spirit looks like.

3:66*f*

✧

Life is a touchstone for the truth of the spirit. Spirit that drags a man away from life, seeking fulfilment only in itself, is a false spirit—though the man too is to blame, since he can choose whether he will give himself up to this spirit or not. Life and spirit are two powers or necessities between which man is placed. Spirit gives meaning to his life, and the possibility of its greatest development. But life is essential to spirit, since its truth is nothing if it cannot live.

91:647*f*

Without soul, spirit is as dead as matter, because both are artificial abstractions; whereas man originally regarded spirit as a volatile body, and matter as not lacking in soul.

112:76*n*

The gulf that Christianity opened out between nature and spirit enabled the human mind to think not only beyond nature but in opposition to it, thus demonstrating its divine freedom. 65:261

Faith is a charisma not granted to all; instead, man has the gift of thought, which can strive after the highest things. 65:170

Only a life lived in a certain spirit is worth living. It is a remarkable fact that a life lived entirely from the ego is dull not only for the person himself but for all concerned.

91:645

To find happiness in the spirit one must be possessed of a "spirit" to find happiness in. A life of ease and security has convinced everyone of all the material joys, and has even compelled the spirit to devise new and better ways to material welfare, but it has never *produced* spirit. Probably only suffering, disillusion, and self-denial do that. 84:6*

The manifestations of the spirit are truly wondrous, and as varied as Creation itself. The living spirit grows and even outgrows its earlier forms of expression; it freely chooses the men who proclaim it and in whom it lives. This living spirit is eternally renewed and pursues its goal in manifold and inconceivable ways throughout the history of mankind. Measured against it, the names and forms which men have given it mean very little; they are only the changing leaves and blossoms on the stem of the eternal tree.

78:537f

ON ULTIMATE THINGS

Western and Eastern Points of View

Consciousness determines *Weltanschauung*. All conscious awareness of motives and intentions is a *Weltanschauung* in the bud; every increase in experience and knowledge is a step in the development of a *Weltanschauung*. And with the picture that the thinking man fashions of the world he also changes himself. The man whose sun still moves round the earth is essentially different from the man whose earth is a satellite of the sun. Giordano Bruno's reflections on infinity were not in vain: they represent one of the most important beginnings of modern consciousness. The man whose cosmos hangs in the empyrean is different from one whose mind is illuminated by Kepler's vision. The man who is still dubious about the sum of twice two is different from the thinker for whom nothing is less doubtful than the *a priori* truths of mathematics. In short, it is not a matter of indifference what sort of *Weltanschauung* we possess, since not only do we create a picture of the world, but this picture retroactively changes us.   5:696

A science can never be a *Weltanschauung* but merely the tool with which to make one. Whether we take this tool in hand or not depends on the sort of *Weltanschauung* we already have. For no one is without a *Weltanschauung* of some sort. Even in an extreme case, he will at least have the *Weltanschauung* that education and environment have forced on him. If this tells him, to quote Goethe, that "the highest joy of man should be the growth of personality," he will unhesitatingly seize upon science and its conclusions, and with this as a tool will build himself a *Weltanschauung*—to his own edification. But if his hereditary convictions tell him that science is not a tool but an end in itself, he will follow the watchword that has become more and more prevalent during the last one hundred and fifty years and has proved to be the decisive one in practice. Here and there single individuals have desperately resisted it, for to their way of thinking the meaning of life culminates in the perfection of the human personality and not in the differentiation of techniques, which inevitably leads to an extremely one-sided development of a single instinct, for instance the instinct for knowledge. If science is an end in itself, man's *raison d'être* lies in being a mere intellect. If art is an end in itself, then his sole value lies in the imaginative faculty, and the intellect is consigned to the lumber-room. If making money is an end in itself, both science and art can quietly shut up shop. No one can deny that our modern consciousness, in pursuing these mutually exclusive ends, has become hopelessly fragmented. The consequence is that people are trained to develop one quality only; they become tools themselves.   5:731

The totality of the psyche can never be grasped by intellect alone. Whether we will or no, philosophy keeps breaking through, because the psyche seeks an expression that will embrace its total nature.   104A:201

The intellect is only one among several fundamental psychic functions and therefore does not suffice to give a complete picture of the world. For this another function—feeling—is needed too. Feeling often arrives at convictions that are different from those of the intellect, and we cannot always prove that the convictions of feeling are necessarily inferior.   68:600

We can understand at once the fear that the child and the primitive have of the great unknown. We have the same childish fear of our inner side, where we likewise touch upon a great unknown world. All we have is the affect, the fear, without knowing that this is a world-fear—for the world of affects is invisible. We have either purely theoretical prejudices against it, or superstitious ideas. One cannot even talk about the unconscious before many educated people without being accused of mysticism. The fear is legitimate in so far as our rational *Weltanschauung* with its scientific and moral certitudes—so hotly believed in because so deeply questionable—is shattered by the facts of the other side.   104B : 324

Freud was a great destroyer, but the turn of the century offered so many opportunities for debunking that even Nietzsche was not enough. Freud completed the task, very thoroughly indeed. He aroused a wholesome mistrust in people and thereby sharpened their sense of real values. All that gush about man's innate goodness, which had addled so many brains after the dogma of original sin was no longer understood, was blown to the winds by Freud, and the little that remains will, let us hope, be driven out for good and all by the barbarism of the twentieth century.   37 : 69

In the last one hundred and fifty years we have witnessed a plethora of *Weltanschauungen*—a proof that the whole idea of a *Weltanschauung* has been discredited, for the more difficult an illness is to treat, the more the remedies multiply, and the more remedies there are, the more disreputable each one becomes.   5 : 732

The nineteenth century has left us such a legacy of dubious propositions that doubt is not only possible but altogether justified, indeed meritorious. The gold will not prove its worth save in the fire.   37 : 69

The fatal error of every *Weltanschauung* so far has been that it claims to be an objectively valid truth, and ultimately a kind of scientific evidence of this truth. This would lead to the insufferable conclusion that, for instance, the same

God must help the Germans, the French, the English, the
Turks, and the heathen—in short, everybody against everybody else.   5:734

If the picture we create of the world did not have a retro-
active effect on us, we could be content with any sort of
beautiful or diverting sham. But self-deception recoils on
us, making us unreal, foolish, and ineffectual. Because we
are tilting at a false picture of the world, we are overcome
by the superior power of reality.   5:699

If we have a disagreeable view of a situation or thing,
our pleasure in it is spoiled, and then it does in fact usually
disagree with us. And, conversely, how many things become bearable and even acceptable if we can give up certain
prejudices and change our point of view.   80:218

To have a *Weltanschauung* means to create a picture of
the world and of oneself, to know what the world is and
who I am. Taken literally, this would be too much. No
one can know what the world is, just as little as can he know
himself. But, *cum grano salis*, it means the best possible
knowledge—a knowledge that esteems wisdom and abhors
unfounded assumptions, arbitrary assertions, and didactic
opinions. Such knowledge seeks the well-founded hypothesis, without forgetting that all knowledge is limited and
subject to error.   5:698

The world changes its face—*tempora mutantur et nos
mutamur in illis*—for we can grasp the world only as a
psychic image in ourselves, and it is not always easy to decide, when the image changes, whether the world or ourselves have changed, or both. The picture of the world can
change at any time, just as our conception of ourselves
changes. Every new discovery, every new thought, can put

a new face on the world. We must be prepared for this, else we suddenly find ourselves in an antiquated world, itself a relic of lower levels of consciousness. We shall all be as good as dead one day, but in the interests of life we should postpone this moment as long as possible, and this we can only do by never allowing our picture of the world to become rigid.

5: 700

If we do not fashion for ourselves a picture of the world, we do not see ourselves either, who are the faithful reflections of that world. Only when mirrored in our picture of the world can we see ourselves in the round. Only in our creative acts do we step forth into the light and see ourselves whole and complete. Never shall we put any face on the world other than our own, and we have to do this precisely in order to find ourselves. For higher than science or art as an end in itself stands man, the creator of his instruments.

5: 737

The world exists not merely in itself but also as it appears to me. Indeed, at bottom, we have absolutely no criterion that could help us to form a judgment of a world which was unassimilable by the subject. If we were to ignore the subjective factor, it would be a complete denial of the great doubt as to the possibility of absolute cognition. And this would mean a relapse into the stale and hollow positivism that marred the turn of the century—an attitude of intellectual arrogance accompanied by crudeness of feeling, a violation of life stupid as it is presumptuous. By overvaluing our capacity for objective cognition we repress the importance of the subjective factor, which simply means a denial of the subject. But what is the subject? The subject is man himself—we are the subject. Only a sick mind could forget that cognition must have a subject, and that there is no knowledge whatever and no world at all unless "I "know" has been said, though with this statement one has already expressed the subjective limitation of all knowledge.

69 : 621

If we were conscious of the spirit of the age, we should know why we are so inclined to account for everything on physical grounds; we should know that it is because, up till now, too much was accounted for in terms of spirit. This realization would at once make us critical of our bias. We would say: most likely we are now making exactly the same mistake on the other side. We delude ourselves with the thought that we know much more about matter than about a "metaphysical" mind or spirit, and so we over-estimate material causation and believe that it alone affords us a true explanation of life. But matter is just as inscrutable as mind. As to the ultimate things we can know nothing, and only when we admit this do we return to a state of equilibrium.

12 : 657

I know nothing of a "super-reality." Reality contains everything I can know, for everything that acts upon me is real and actual. If it does not act upon me, then I notice nothing and can, therefore, know nothing about it. Hence I can make statements only about real things, but not about things that are unreal, or surreal, or subreal. Unless, of course, it should occur to someone to limit the concept of reality in such a way that the attribute "real" applied only to a particular segment of the world's reality. This restriction to the so-called material or concrete reality of objects perceived by the senses is a product of a particular way of thinking—the thinking that underlies "sound common sense" and our ordinary use of language. It operates on the celebrated principle "Nihil est in intellectu quod non antea fuerit in sensu," regardless of the fact that there are very many things in the mind which did not derive from the data of the senses. According to this view, everything is "real" which comes, or seems to come, directly or indirectly from the world revealed by the senses. This limited picture of the world is a reflection of the one-sidedness of Western man.

81:742f

Has mankind ever really got away from myths? Everyone who has his eyes and wits about him can see that the world is dead, cold, and unending. Never yet has he beheld a God, or been compelled to require the existence of such a God from the evidence of his senses. On the contrary, it needed the strongest inner compulsion, which can only be explained by the irrational force of instinct, for man to invent those religious beliefs whose absurdity was long since pointed out by Tertullian. In the same way one can withhold the material content of primitive myths from a child but not take from him the need for mythology, and still less his ability to manufacture it for himself. One could almost say that if all the world's traditions were cut off at a single blow, the whole of mythology and the whole history of religion would start all over again with the next generation.

100:30

Man is not a machine that can be remodelled for quite other purposes as occasion demands, in the hope that it will go on functioning as regularly as before but in a quite different way. He carries his whole history with him; in his very structure is written the history of mankind. The historical element in man represents a vital need to which a wise psychic economy must respond. Somehow the past must come alive and participate in the present. Total assimilation to the object will always arouse the protest of the suppressed minority of those elements that belong to the past and have existed from the very beginning.

69:570

How totally different did the world appear to medieval man! For him the earth was eternally fixed and at rest in the centre of the universe, circled by a sun that solicitously bestowed its warmth. Men were all children of God under the loving care of the Most High, who prepared them for eternal blessedness; and all knew exactly what they should do and how they should conduct themselves in order to rise from a corruptible world to an incorruptible and joyous existence. Such a life no longer seems real to us, even in our dreams. Science has long ago torn this lovely veil to shreds. That age lies as far behind as childhood, when one's own father was unquestionably the handsomest and strongest man on earth.   93:162

Is a thing beautiful because I attribute beauty to it? Or is it the objective beauty of the thing that compels me to acknowledge it? As we know, great minds have wrestled with the problem whether it is the glorious sun that illuminates the world, or the sunlike human eye. Archaic man believes it to be the sun, and civilized man believes it to be the eye—so far, at any rate, as he reflects at all and does not suffer from the disease of the poets. He must de-psychize nature in order to dominate her; and in order to see his world objectively he must take back all his archaic projections.   9:135

Primitive man, being closer to his instincts, like the animal, is characterized by fear of novelty and adherence to tradition. To our way of thinking he is painfully backward, whereas we exalt progress. But our progressiveness, though it may result in a great many delightful wish-fulfillments, piles up an equally gigantic Promethean debt, which has to be paid off from time to time in the form of hideous catastrophes. For ages man has dreamed of flying, and all we have got for it is saturation bombing! We smile today at the Christian hope of a life beyond the grave, and yet we often fall into chiliasms a hundred times more ridiculous than the notion of a happy Hereafter.   76:276

✧

A man is only half understood when we know how everything in him came into being. If that were all, he could just as well have been dead years ago. As a living being he is not understood, for life does not have only a yesterday, nor is it explained by reducing today to yesterday. Life has also a tomorrow, and today is understood only when we can add to our knowledge of what was yesterday the beginnings of tomorrow. This is true of all life's psychological expressions, even of pathological symptoms.

104A:67

Psychology teaches us that, in a certain sense, there is nothing in the psyche that is old; nothing that can really, finally die away. Even Paul was left with a thorn in the flesh. Whoever protects himself against what is new and strange and regresses to the past falls into the same neurotic condition as the man who identifies himself with the new and runs away from the past. The only difference is that the one has estranged himself from the past and the other from the future. In principle both are doing the same thing: they are reinforcing their narrow range of consciousness instead of shattering it in the tension of opposites and building up a state of wider and higher consciousness.

94:767

The conscious mind must have reason, firstly to discover some order in the chaos of disorderly individual events occurring in the world, and secondly to create order, at least in human affairs. We are moved by the laudable and useful ambition to extirpate the chaos of the irrational both within and without to the best of our ability. Apparently the process has gone pretty far. As a mental patient once told me: "Doctor, last night I disinfected the whole heavens with bichloride of mercury, but I found no God." Something of the sort has happened to us as well.   104A: 110

And what kind of an answer did the next generation give to the individualism of Nietzsche's superman? It answered with a collectivism, a mass organization, a herding together of the mob, *tam ethice quam physice*, that made everything that went before look like a bad joke. Suffocation of the personality and an impotent Christianity that may well have received its death-wound—such is the unadorned balance-sheet of our time.   72:559

When something happens to a man and he supposes it to be personal only to himself, whereas in reality it is a quite universal experience, then his attitude is obviously wrong, that is, too personal, and it tends to exclude him from human society. By the same token we need to have not only a personal, contemporary consciousness, but also a suprapersonal consciousness with a sense of historical continuity.

2:99

We are now reaping the fruit of nineteenth-century education. Throughout that period the Church preached to young people the merit of blind faith, while the universities inculcated an intellectual rationalism, with the result that today we plead in vain whether for faith or reason. Tired of this warfare of opinions, the modern man wishes to find out for himself how things are. And though this desire opens the door to the most dangerous possibilities, we cannot help seeing it as a courageous enterprise and giving it some measure of sympathy. It is no reckless adventure, but an effort inspired by deep spiritual distress to bring meaning once more into life on the basis of fresh and unprejudiced experience.   78:529

Life is crazy and meaningful at once. And when we do not laugh over the one aspect and speculate about the other, life is exceedingly drab, and everything is reduced to the littlest scale. There is then little sense and little non-sense either. When you come to think about it, nothing has any meaning, for when there was nobody to think, there was nobody to interpret what happened. Interpretations are only for those who don't understand; it is only the things we don't understand that have any meaning. Man woke up in a world he did not understand, and that is why he tries to interpret it.   10:65

The least of things with a meaning is always worth more in life than the greatest of things without it.   2:96

In all chaos there is a cosmos, in all disorder a secret order.   10:66

❖

The East teaches us another, broader, more profound, and higher understanding—understanding through life. We know this only by hearsay, as a shadowy sentiment expressing a vague religiosity, and we are fond of putting "Oriental wisdom" in quotation marks and banishing it to the dim region of faith and superstition. But that is wholly to misunderstand the realism of the East. Texts of this kind do not consist of the sentimental, overwrought mystical intuitions of pathological cranks and recluses, but are based on the practical insights of highly evolved Chinese minds, which we have not the slightest justification for undervaluing.   112:2

Everything requires for its existence its own opposite, or else it fades into nothingness. The ego needs the self and vice versa. The changing relations between these two entities constitute a field of experience which Eastern introspection has exploited to a degree almost unattainable to Western man. The philosophy of the East, although so vastly different from ours, could be an inestimable treasure for us too; but, in order to possess it, we must first earn it.

36:961

Western man is held in thrall by the "ten thousand things"; he sees only particulars, he is ego-bound and thing-bound, and unaware of the deep root of all being. Eastern man, on the other hand, experiences the world of particulars, and even his own ego, like a dream; he is rooted essentially in the "Ground," which attracts him so powerfully that his relations with the world are relativized to a degree that is often incomprehensible to us.

72:8

While the Western mind carefully sifts, weighs, selects, classifies, isolates, the Chinese picture of the moment encompasses everything down to the minutest nonsensical detail, because all of the ingredients make up the observed moment.

111:969

Whatever happens in a given moment has inevitably the quality of that moment.

111:970

The West is always seeking uplift, but the East seeks a sinking or deepening. Outer reality, with its bodiliness and weight, appears to make a much stronger and sharper impression on the European than it does on the Indian. The European seeks to raise himself above this world, while the Indian likes to turn back into the maternal depths of Nature.

75:936

In general, meditation and contemplation have a bad reputation in the West. They are regarded as a particularly reprehensible form of idleness or as pathological narcissism. No one has time for self-knowledge or believes that it could serve any sensible purpose. Also, one knows in advance that it is not worth the trouble to know oneself, for any fool can know what he is. We believe exclusively in doing and do not ask about the doer, who is judged only by achievements that have collective value. The general public seems to have taken cognizance of the existence of the unconscious psyche more than the so-called experts, but still nobody has drawn any conclusions from the fact that Western man confronts himself as a stranger and that self-knowledge is one of the most difficult and exacting of the arts.   48:709

The Christian during contemplation would never say "*I* am Christ," but will confess with Paul: "Not I, but Christ liveth in me" (Gal. 2:20). Our sutra however, says: "Thou wilt know that *thou* art the Buddha." At bottom the two confessions are identical, in that the Buddhist only attains this knowledge when he is *anātman*, 'without self.' But there is an immeasurable difference in the formulation. The Christian attains his end *in Christ,* the Buddhist knows *he* is the Buddha. The Christian gets *out* of the transitory and ego-bound world of consciousness, but the Buddhist *still* reposes on the eternal ground of his inner nature, whose oneness with Deity, or with universal Being, is confirmed in other Indian testimonies.   75:949

The Christian West considers man to be wholly dependent upon the grace of God, or at least upon the Church as the exclusive and divinely sanctioned earthly instrument of man's redemption. The East, however, insists that man is the sole cause of his higher development, for it believes in "self-liberation."   23:770

If the supreme value (Christ) and the supreme negation (sin) are outside, then the soul is void: its highest and lowest are missing. The Eastern attitude (more particularly the Indian) is the other way about: everything, highest and lowest, is in the (transcendental) Subject. Accordingly the significance of the Atman, the Self, is heightened beyond all bounds. But with Western man the value of the self sinks to zero. 72:9

There is no conflict between religion and science in the East, as no science is there based upon a passion for facts, and no religion upon faith; there is religious cognition and cognitive religion. 23:768

Great as is the value of Zen Buddhism for understanding the religious transformation process, its use among Western people is very problematical. The mental education necessary for Zen is lacking in the West. Who among us would place such implicit trust in a superior Master and his incomprehensible ways? This respect for the greater human personality is found only in the East. Could any of us boast that he believes in the possibility of a boundlessly paradoxical transformation experience, to the extent, moreover, of sacrificing many years of his life to the wearisome pursuit of such a goal? And finally, who would dare to take upon himself the authority for such an unorthodox transformation experience—except a man who was little to be trusted, one who, maybe for pathological reasons, has too much to say for himself? Just such a person would have no cause to complain of any lack of following among us. But let a "Master" set us a hard task, which requires more than mere parrot-talk, and the European begins to have doubts, for the steep path of self-development is to him as mournful and gloomy as the path to hell. 98:902

Western consciousness is by no means the only kind of consciousness there is; it is historically conditioned and geographically limited, and representative of only one part of mankind. The widening of our consciousness ought not to proceed at the expense of other kinds of consciousness; it should come about through the development of those elements of our psyche which are analogous to those of the alien psyche, just as the East cannot do without our technology, science, and industry. The European invasion of the East was an act of violence on a grand scale, and it has left us with the duty—*noblesse oblige*—of understanding the mind of the East. This is perhaps more necessary than we realize at present. 112:84

Because the European does not know his own unconscious, he does not understand the East and projects into it everything he fears and despises in himself. 34:8*

I have no wish to depreciate the tremendous differentiation of the Western intellect; compared with it the Eastern intellect must be described as childish. (Naturally this has nothing to do with intelligence.) If we should succeed in elevating another, and possibly even a third psychic function to the dignified position accorded to the intellect, then the West might expect to surpass the East by a very great margin. 112:8

The usual mistake of Western man when faced with this problem of grasping the ideas of the East is like that of the student in *Faust*. Misled by the devil, he contemptuously turns his back on science and, carried away by Eastern occultism, takes over yoga practices word for word and becomes a pitiable imitator. (Theosophy is our best example of this.) Thus he abandons the one sure foundation of the Western mind and loses himself in a mist of words and ideas that could never have originated in European brains and can never be profitably grafted upon them. 112:3

There could be no greater mistake than for a Westerner to take up the direct practice of Chinese yoga, for that would merely strengthen his will and consciousness against the unconscious and bring about the very effect to be avoided. The neurosis would then simply be intensified. It cannot be emphasized enough that we are not Orientals, and that we have an entirely different point of departure in these matters. 112:16

Yoga in Mayfair or Fifth Avenue, or in any other place which is on the telephone, is a spiritual fake. 23:802

Sometimes, when we look back at history, it seems as though the present time had analogies with certain periods in the past, when great empires and civilizations had passed their zenith and were hastening irresistibly towards decay. But these analogies are deceptive, for there are always renaissances. What *does* move more clearly into the foreground is Europe's position midway between the Asiatic East and the Anglo-Saxon—or shall we say American?—West. Europe now stands between two colossi, both uncouth in their form but implacably opposed to one another in their nature. They are profoundly different not only racially but in their ideals. In the West there is the maximum political freedom with the minimum personal freedom; in the East it is just the opposite. We see in the West a tremendous development of Europe's technological and scientific tendencies, and in the Far East an awakening of all those spiritual forces which, in Europe, these tendencies hold in check. The power of the West is material, that of the East ideal. 114:237

Western man has no need of more superiority over nature, whether outside or inside. He has both in almost devilish perfection. What he lacks is conscious recognition of his inferiority to the nature around and within him. He must learn that he may not do exactly as he wills. If he does not learn this, his own nature will destroy him. 116:870

The Indian can forget neither the body nor the mind, while the European is always forgetting either the one or the other. With this capacity to forget he has, for the time being, conquered the world. Not so the Indian. He not only knows his own nature, but he also knows how much he himself is nature. The European, on the other hand, has a science of nature and knows astonishingly little of his own nature, the nature within him. For the Indian, it comes as a blessing to know of a method which helps him to control the supreme power of nature within and without. For the European, it is sheer poison to suppress his nature, which is warped enough as it is, and to make out of it a willing robot.   116:867

The extraverted tendency of the West and the introverted tendency of the East have one important purpose in common: both make desperate efforts to conquer the mere naturalness of life. It is the assertion of mind over matter, the *opus contra naturam*, a symptom of the youthfulness of man, still delighting in the use of the most powerful weapon ever devised by nature: the conscious mind. The afternoon of humanity, in a distant future, may yet evolve a different ideal. In time, even conquest will cease to be the dream.   23:787

The breathless drive for power and aggrandizement in the political, social, and intellectual sphere, gnawing at the soul of the Westerner with apparently insatiable greed, is spreading irresistibly in the East and threatens to have incalculable consequences. Not only in India but in China, too, much has already perished where once the soul lived and throve. The externalization of culture may do away with a great many evils whose removal seems most desirable and beneficial, yet this step forward, as experience shows, is all too dearly paid for with a loss of spiritual culture.   36:962

The wisdom and mysticism of the East have very much to say to us, even when they speak their own inimitable language. They serve to remind us that we in our culture possess something similar, which we have already forgotten, and to direct our attention to the fate of the inner man.

36:963

In the East, the inner man has always had such a firm hold on the outer man that the world had no chance of tearing him away from his inner roots; in the West, the outer man gained the ascendancy to such an extent that he was alienated from his innermost being.   23:785

A growing familiarity with the spirit of the East should be taken merely as a sign that we are beginning to relate to the alien elements within ourselves. Denial of our historical foundations would be sheer folly and would be the best way to bring about another uprooting of consciousness. Only by standing firmly on our own soil can we assimilate the spirit of the East.   112:72

Instead of learning the spiritual techniques of the East by heart and imitating them in a thoroughly Christian way—*imitatio Christi!*—with a correspondingly forced attitude, it would be far more to the point to find out whether there exists in the unconscious an introverted tendency similar to that which has become the guiding spiritual principle of the East. We should then be in a position to build on our own ground with our own methods. If we snatch these things directly from the East, we have merely indulged our Western acquisitiveness, confirming yet again that "everything good is outside," whence it has to be fetched and pumped into our barren souls. It seems to me that we have really learned something from the East when we understand that the psyche contains riches enough without having to be primed from outside, and when we feel capable of evolving out of ourselves with or without divine grace. 23:773

If you want to learn the greatest lesson India can teach you, wrap yourself in the cloak of your moral superiority, go to the Black Pagoda of Konarak, sit down in the shadow of the mighty ruin that is still covered with the most amazing collection of obscenities, read Murray's cunning old *Handbook for India*, which tells you how to be properly shocked by this lamentable state of affairs, and how you should go into the temples in the evening, because in the lamplight they look if possible "more (and how beautifully!) wicked"; and then analyse carefully and with the utmost honesty all your reactions, feelings, and thoughts. It will take you quite a while, but in the end, if you have done good work, you will have learned something about yourself, and about the white man in general, which you have probably never heard from anyone else. 108:1013

❖

The spirit of the age will not let itself be trifled with. It is a religion, or, better, a creed which has absolutely no connection with reason, but whose significance lies in the unpleasant fact that it is taken as the absolute measure of all truth and is supposed always to have common sense upon its side. 12:652

The tasks of every age differ, and it is only in retrospect that we can discern with certainty what had to be and what should not have been. In the momentary present the conflict of opinions will always rage, for "war is the father of all." History alone decides the issue. Truth is not eternal —it is a programme to be fulfilled. The more "eternal" a truth, the more lifeless it is and worthless; it says nothing more to us because it is self-evident. 69:87

Anything new should always be questioned and tested with caution, for it may very easily turn out to be only a new disease. That is why true progress is impossible without mature judgment. But a well-balanced judgment requires a firm standpoint, and this in turn can only rest on a sound knowledge of what has been. The man who is unconscious of the historical context and lets slip his link with the past is in constant danger of succumbing to the crazes and delusions engendered by all novelties. 31:251

Knowledge of the universal origins builds the bridge between the lost and abandoned world of the past and the still largely inconceivable world of the future. How should we lay hold of the future, how should we assimilate it, unless we are in possession of the human experience which the past has bequeathed to us? Dispossessed of this, we are without root and without perspective, defenceless dupes of whatever novelties the future may bring. 31:250

The man of the present must work for the future and leave others to conserve the past. He is therefore not only a builder but also a destroyer. He and his world have both become questionable and ambiguous. The ways that the past shows him and the answers it gives to his questions are insufficient for the needs of the present. All the old, comfortable ways are blocked, new paths have been opened up, and new dangers have arisen of which the past knew nothing. It is proverbial that one never learns anything from history, and in regard to present-day problems it usually teaches us nothing. The new path has to be made through untrodden regions, without presuppositions and often, unfortunately, without piety. 114:239

It is the duty of one who goes his own way to inform society of what he finds on his voyage of discovery, be it cooling water for the thirsty or the sandy wastes of unfruitful error. The one helps, the other warns. Not the criticism of individual contemporaries will decide the truth or falsity of his discoveries, but future generations. There are things that are not yet true today, perhaps we dare not find them true, but tomorrow they may be. So every man whose fate it is to go his individual way must proceed with hopefulness and watchfulness, ever conscious of his loneliness and its dangers.

104A:201

New ideas, if they are not just a flash in the pan, generally require at least a generation to take root. Psychological innovations probably take much longer, since in this field more than in any other practically everybody sets himself up as an authority.

104A:8*

One's contemporaries are always dense and never understand that what appears to them unseemly ebullience comes less from personal temperament than from the still unknown wellsprings of a new age. How people looked askance at Nietzsche's volcanic emotion, and how long he will be spoken of in times to come! Even Paracelsus has now been gratefully disinterred after four hundred years in an attempt to resuscitate him in modern dress.   86:4*

To think otherwise than as our contemporaries think is somehow illegitimate and disturbing; it is even indecent, morbid or blasphemous, and therefore socially dangerous for the individual. He is stupidly swimming against the social current.

12:653

Our modern attitude looks back arrogantly upon the mists of superstition and of medieval or primitive credulity, entirely forgetting that we carry the whole living past in the lower storeys of the skyscraper of rational consciousness. Without the lower storeys our mind is suspended in mid air. No wonder it gets nervous. The true history of the mind is not preserved in learned volumes but in the living psychic organism of every individual. 74:56

Great innovations never come from above; they come invariably from below, just as trees never grow from the sky downward, but upward from the earth. The upheaval of our world and the upheaval of our consciousness are one and the same. Everything has become relative and therefore doubtful. And while man, hesitant and questioning, contemplates a world that is distracted with treaties of peace and pacts of friendship, with democracy and dictatorship, capitalism and Bolshevism, his spirit yearns for an answer that will allay the turmoil of doubt and uncertainty. And it is just the people from the obscurer levels who follow the unconscious drive of the psyche; it is the much-derided, silent folk of the land, who are less infected with academic prejudices than the shining celebrities are wont to be. 93:177

The "present" is a thin surface stratum that is laid down in the great centres of civilization. If it is very thin, as in Tsarist Russia, it has no meaning, as events have shown. But once it has attained a certain strength, we can speak of civilization and progress, and then problems arise that are characteristic of an epoch. 114:239

What is a problem of the present day? If we speak of a general problem nowadays, it is because it exists in the heads of many people. These individuals are somehow chosen by fate and destined by their own natures to suffer under a collectively unsatisfactory condition and to make it a problem. Therefore it is always single individuals who are moved by the collective problem and who are called upon to respond and contribute to its solution by tackling it in their own lives and not running away from it. 11:86*

Who has fully realized that history is not contained in thick books but lives in our very blood? 114:266

The time is as great as one thinks it, and man grows to the stature of the time. 41:945

Life is a flux, a flowing into the future, and not a stoppage or a backwash. It is therefore not surprising that so many of the mythological saviours are child gods.

76:278

It was of profound psychological significance when Christianity first proclaimed that the orientation to the future was the redeeming principle for mankind. In the past nothing can be altered, and in the present little, but the future is ours and capable of raising life's intensity to the highest pitch. A little span of youth belongs to us, all the rest belongs to our children. 89:668

The Development of the Personality

The best cannot be told, anyhow, and the second best does not strike home. One must be able to let things happen. I have learned from the East what is meant by *wu-wei*: "not-doing," "letting be," which is quite different from doing nothing. Some Occidentals, also, have known what this not-doing means; for instance, Meister Eckhart, who speaks of *sich lassen*, "letting go." The region of darkness into which one falls is not empty; it is the "lavishing mother" of Lao-tzu, the "images" and the "seed." When the surface has been cleared, things can grow out of the depths. People always suppose that they have lost their way when they come up against these depths of experience. But if they do not know how to go on, the only answer, the only advice that makes any sense is "Wait for what the unconscious has to say about the situation." A way is only *the* way when one finds it and follows it oneself. There is no general prescription for "how to do it."

97A: 31f*

We must be able to let things happen in the psyche. For us, this is an art of which most people know nothing. Consciousness is forever interfering, helping, correcting, and negating, never leaving the psychic processes to grow in peace. It would be simple enough, if only simplicity were not the most difficult of all things.

112: 20

The fundamental error persists in the public that there are definite answers, "solutions," or views which need only be uttered in order to spread the necessary light. But the most beautiful truth—as history has shown a thousand times over—is no use at all unless it has become the innermost experience and possession of the individual. Every unequivocal, so-called "clear" answer always remains stuck in the head, but only very rarely does it penetrate to the heart. The needful thing is not to *know* the truth but to *experience* it. Not to have an intellectual conception of things, but to find our way to the inner, and perhaps wordless, irrational experience—that is the great problem. Nothing is more fruitless than talking of how things must or should be, and nothing is more important than finding the way to these far-off goals.

40:7*

We must never forget that the world is, in the first place, a subjective phenomenon. The impressions we receive from these accidental happenings are also our own doing. It is not true that the impressions are forced on us unconditionally; our own predisposition conditions the impression. A man whose libido is blocked will have, as a rule, quite different and very much more vivid impressions than one whose libido is organized in a wealth of activities. A person who is sensitive in one way or another will receive a deep impression from an event which would leave a less sensitive person cold.

101:400

Faced with the bewildering profusion of animated objects, we create an abstraction, an abstract universal image which conjures the welter of impressions into a fixed form. This image has the magical significance of a defence against the chaotic flux of experience. The abstracting type becomes so lost and submerged in this image that finally its abstract truth is set above the reality of life; and because life might disturb the enjoyment of abstract beauty, it gets completely suppressed. He turns himself into an abstraction, he identifies with the eternal validity of the image and petrifies in it, because for him it has become a redeeming formula. He divests himself of his real self and puts his whole life into his abstraction, in which he is, so to speak, crystallized. The empathetic type suffers a similar fate. Since his activity, his life is empathized into the object, he himself gets into the object because the empathized content is an essential part of himself. He becomes the object, he identifies with it and in this way gets outside himself. By turning himself into an object he desubjectifies himself.

69 : 499*f*

Is not every experience, even in the best of circumstances, at least fifty-per-cent subjective interpretation? On the other hand, the subject is also an objective fact, a piece of the world; and what comes from him comes, ultimately, from the stuff of the world itself, just as the rarest and strangest organism is none the less supported and nourished by the earth which is common to all. It is precisely the most subjective ideas which, being closest to nature and to our own essence, deserve to be called the truest. But: "What is truth?"   28 : 770

There are experiences which one must go through and for which reason is no substitute. Such experiences are often of inestimable value to the patient.   101 : 446

Experiences cannot be *made*. They happen—yet fortunately their independence of man's activity is not absolute but relative. We can draw closer to them—that much lies within our human reach. There are ways which bring us nearer to living experience, yet we should beware of calling these ways "methods." The very word has a deadening effect. The way to experience, moreover, is anything but a clever trick; it is rather a venture which requires us to commit ourselves with our whole being.   78 : 501

Caution has its place, no doubt, but we cannot refuse our support to a serious venture which challenges the whole of the personality. If we oppose it, we are trying to suppress what is best in man—his daring and his aspirations. And should we succeed, we should only have stood in the way of that invaluable experience which might have given a meaning to life. What would have happened if Paul had allowed himself to be talked out of his journey to Damascus? 78:529

❖

The man whose interests are all outside is never satisfied with what is necessary, but is perpetually hankering after something more and better which, true to his bias, he always seeks outside himself. He forgets completely that, for all his outward successes, he himself remains the same inwardly, and he therefore laments his poverty if he possesses only one automobile when the majority have two. Obviously the outward lives of men could do with a lot more bettering and beautifying, but these things lose their meaning when the inner man does not keep pace with them. To be satiated with "necessities" is no doubt an inestimable source of happiness, yet the inner man continues to raise his claim, and this can be satisfied by no outward possessions. And the less this voice is heard in the chase after the brilliant things of this world, the more the inner man becomes the source of inexplicable misfortune and uncomprehended unhappiness in the midst of living conditions whose outcome was expected to be entirely different. The externalization of life turns to incurable suffering, because no one can understand why he should suffer from himself. No one wonders at his insatiability, but regards it as his lawful right, never thinking that the one-sidedness of this psychic diet leads in the end to the gravest disturbances of equilibrium. That is the sickness of Western man, and he will not rest until he has infected the whole world with his own greedy restlessness. 36:962

Too many still look outwards, some believing in the illusion of victory and of victorious power, others in treaties and laws, and others again in the overthrow of the existing order. But still too few look inwards, to their own selves, and still too few ask themselves whether the ends of human society might not best be served if each man tried to abolish the old order in himself, and to practise in his own person and in his own inward state those precepts and victories which he preaches at every street-corner, instead of always expecting these things of his fellow men.   104A: 5*

Doubtless there are exceptional people who are able to sacrifice their entire life to a particular formula; but for most of us such exclusiveness is impossible in the long run.
69: 587

From a consideration of the claims of the inner and outer worlds, or rather, from the conflict between them, the possible and the necessary follows. Unfortunately our Western mind, lacking all culture in this respect, has never yet devised a concept, nor even a name, for the *union of opposites through the middle path*, that most fundamental item of inward experience, which could respectably be set against the Chinese concept of Tao. It is at once the most individual fact and the most universal, the most legitimate fulfilment of the meaning of the individual's life.

104B: 327

The tragic counterplay between inside and outside (depicted in Job and *Faust* as the wager with God) represents, at bottom, the energetics of the life process, the polar tension that is necessary for self-regulation. However different, to all intents and purposes, these opposing forces may be, their fundamental meaning and desire is the life of the individual: they always fluctuate round this centre of balance. Just because they are inseparably related through opposition, they also unite in a mediatory meaning, which, willingly or unwillingly, is born out of the individual and is therefore divined by him. He has a strong feeling of

what should be and what could be. To depart from this
divination means error, aberration, illness.   104B: 311

The man who is only wise and only holy interests me
about as much as the skeleton of a rare saurian, which
would not move me to tears. The insane contradiction, on
the other hand, between existence beyond Māyā in the cosmic Self, and that amiable human weakness which fruit-
fully sinks many roots into the black earth, repeating for
all eternity the weaving and rending of the veil as the ageless melody of India—this contradiction fascinates me; for
how else can one perceive the light without the shadow,
hear the silence without the noise, attain wisdom without
foolishness?   36: 953

It requires no art to become stupid; the whole art lies in
extracting wisdom from stupidity. Stupidity is the mother
of the wise, but cleverness never.   58: 222

✦

The myth of the hero . . . is first and foremost a self-
representation of the longing of the unconscious, of its un-
quenched and unquenchable desire for the light of consciousness. But consciousness, continually in danger of being
led astray by its own light and of becoming a rootless will o'
the wisp, longs for the healing power of nature, for the
deep wells of being and for unconscious communion with
life in all its countless forms.   100: 299

Just as the unconscious world of mythological images
speaks indirectly, through the experience of external things,
to the man who surrenders himself wholly to the outer
world, so the real world and its demands find their way indirectly to the man who has surrendered himself wholly to
the soul; for no man can escape both realities. If he is in-

tent only on the outer reality, he must live his myth; if he is turned only towards the inner reality, he must dream his outer, so-called real life. 69:280

We know that there is no human foresight or wisdom that can prescribe direction to our life, except for small stretches of the way. This is of course true only of the "ordinary" type of life, not of the "heroic" type. The latter kind also exists, though it is much rarer. Here we are certainly not entitled to say that no marked direction can be given to life, or only for short distances. The heroic style of life is absolute—that is, it is oriented by fateful decisions, and the decision to go in a certain direction holds, sometimes, to the bitter end. 104A:72

Man needs difficulties; they are necessary for health.
102:143

All the greatest and most important problems of life are fundamentally insoluble. They must be so, for they express the necessary polarity inherent in every self-regulating system. They can never be solved, but only outgrown.
112:18

This "outgrowing" proved on further investigation to be a new level of consciousness. Some higher or wider interest appeared on the patient's horizon, and through this broadening of his outlook the insoluble problem lost its urgency. It was not solved logically in its own terms, but faded out when confronted with a new and stronger life urge. It was not repressed and made unconscious, but merely appeared in a different light, and so really did become different. What, on a lower level, had led to the wildest conflicts and to panicky outbursts of emotion, from the higher level of personality now looked like a storm in the valley seen from the mountain top. This does not mean that the storm is robbed of its reality, but instead of being in it one is above it.   112:17

The serious problems in life are never fully solved. If ever they should appear to be so it is a sure sign that something has been lost. The meaning and purpose of a problem seem to lie not in its solution but in our working at it incessantly. This alone preserves us from stultification and petrifaction.

94:771

The goal is important only as an idea; the essential thing is the *opus* which leads to the goal: *that* is the goal of a lifetime.   77:400

❖

The urge and compulsion to self-realization is a law of nature and thus of invincible power, even though its effect, at the outset, is insignificant and improbable.   76:289

Nature is aristocratic, but not in the sense of having reserved the possibility of differentiation exclusively for species high in the scale. So too with the possibility of psychic development: it is not reserved for specially gifted individuals. In other words, in order to undergo a far-reaching psychological development, neither outstanding intelligence nor any other talent is necessary, since in this development moral qualities can make up for intellectual shortcomings.

104A:198

To become a personality is not the absolute prerogative of the genius, for a man may be a genius without being a personality. In so far as every individual has the law of his life inborn in him, it is theoretically possible for any man to follow this law and so become a personality, that is, to achieve wholeness. But since life only exists in the form of living units, i.e., individuals, the law of life always tends towards a life individually lived.   21:307

Behind a man's actions there stands neither public opinion nor the moral code, but the personality of which he is still unconscious. Just as a man still is what he always was, so he already is what he will become. The conscious mind does not embrace the totality of a man, for this totality consists only partly of his conscious contents, and for the other and far greater part, of his unconscious, which is of indefinite extent with no assignable limits. In this totality the conscious mind is contained like a smaller circle within a larger one.   103:390

The ego-conscious personality is only a part of the whole man, and its life does not yet represent his total life. The more he is merely "I," the more he splits himself off from the collective man, of whom he is also a part, and may even find himself in opposition to him. But since everything living strives for wholeness, the inevitable one-sidedness of our conscious life is continually being corrected and compensated by the universal human being in us, whose goal is the ultimate integration of conscious and unconscious, or better, the assimilation of the ego to a wider personality.   52:557

Just as a lapis Philosophorum, with its miraculous powers, was never produced, so psychic wholeness will never be attained empirically, as consciousness is too narrow and too one-sided to comprehend the full inventory of the psyche. Always we shall have to begin again from the beginning. From ancient times the adept knew that he was concerned with the "res simplex," and the modern man too will find by experience that the work does not prosper without the greatest simplicity.   48:759

We know that the first impressions of childhood accompany us inalienably throughout life, and that, just as indestructibly, certain educational influences can keep people all their lives within those limits. In these circumstances it is not surprising that conflicts break out between the personality moulded by educational and other influences of the infantile milieu and one's own individual style of life. It is a conflict which all those must face who are called upon to live a life that is independent and creative.   101: 310

One could hardly expect the educated public, which has only just begun to hear about the obscure world of the psyche, to form any adequate conception of the spiritual state of a man caught in the toils of the individuation process—which is my term for "becoming whole." People then drag out the vocabulary of pathology and console themselves with the terminology of neurosis and psychosis, or else they whisper about the "creative secret." But what can a man "create" if he doesn't happen to be a poet? This misunderstanding has caused not a few persons in recent times to call themselves—by their own grace—"artists," just as if art had nothing to do with ability. But if you have nothing at all to create, then perhaps you create yourself.

98: 906

Exceptional human beings, carefully hedged about and secluded, are invariably a gift of nature, enriching and widening the scope of our consciousness—but only if our capacity for reflection does not suffer shipwreck. Enthusiasm can be a veritable gift of the gods or a monster from hell. With the hybris which attends it, corruption sets in, even if the resultant clouding of consciousness seems to put the attainment of the highest goals almost within one's grasp. The only true and lasting gain is heightened and broadened reflection.   36: 960

Life that just happens in and for itself is not real life; it is real only when it is *known*. Only a unified personality can experience life, not that personality which is split up into partial aspects, that bundle of odds and ends which also calls itself "man."   72:105

Self-reflection or—what comes to the same thing—the urge to individuation gathers together what is scattered and multifarious, and exalts it to the original form of the One, the Primordial Man. In this way our existence as separate beings, our former ego nature, is abolished, the circle of consciousness is widened, and because the paradoxes have been made conscious the sources of conflict are dried up.

103:401

Man started from an unconscious state and has ever striven for greater consciousness. The development of consciousness is the burden, the suffering, and the blessing of mankind.   39F:A*

✧

Complete human beings are exceptions. It is true that an overwhelming majority of educated people are fragmentary personalities and have a lot of substitutes instead of the genuine goods.   74:75

The individual may strive after perfection but must suffer from the opposite of his intentions for the sake of his completeness.   3:123

The development of personality from the germ-state to full consciousness is at once a charisma and a curse, because its first fruit is the conscious and unavoidable segregation of the single individual from the undifferentiated and unconscious herd. This means isolation, and there is no more comforting word for it. Neither family nor society nor position can save him from this fate, nor yet the most successful adaptation to his environment, however smoothly he fits in. The development of personality is a favour that must be paid for dearly.   21:294

No one develops his personality because somebody tells him that it would be useful or advisable to do so. Nature has never yet been taken in by well-meaning advice. The only thing that moves nature is causal necessity, and that goes for human nature too. Without necessity nothing budges, the human personality least of all. It is tremendously conservative, not to say torpid. Only acute necessity is able to rouse it. The developing personality obeys no caprice, no command, no insight, only brute necessity; it needs the motivating force of inner or outer fatalities. Any other development would be no better than individualism. That is why the cry of "individualism" is a cheap insult when flung at the natural development of personality.

21:293

The personality is seldom, in the beginning, what it will be later on. For this reason the possibility of enlarging it exists, at least during the first half of life. The enlargement may be effected through an accretion from without, by new vital contents finding their way into the personality from outside and being assimilated. In this way a considerable increase of personality may be experienced. We therefore tend to assume that this increase comes *only* from without, thus justifying the prejudice that one becomes a personality by stuffing into oneself as much as possible from outside. But the more assiduously we follow this recipe, and the more stubbornly we believe that all increase has to come from without, the greater becomes our inner poverty. Therefore, if some great idea takes hold of us from outside, we must understand that it takes hold of us only because something in us responds to it and goes out to meet it. Richness of mind consists in mental receptivity, not in the accumulation of possessions. What comes to us from outside, and, for that matter, everything that rises up from within, can only be made our own if we are capable of an inner amplitude equal to that of the incoming content. Real increase of personality means consciousness of an enlargement that flows from inner sources. Without psychic depth we can never be adequately related to the magnitude of our object. It has therefore been said quite truly that a man grows with the greatness of his task. But he must have within himself the capacity to grow; otherwise even the most difficult task is of no benefit to him. More likely he will be shattered by it.   17:215

All beginnings are small. Therefore we must not mind doing tedious but conscientious work on obscure individuals, even though the goal towards which we strive seems unattainably far off. But one goal we can attain, and that is to develop and bring to maturity individual personalities. And inasmuch as we are convinced that the individual is the carrier of life, we have served life's purpose if one tree at least succeeds in bearing fruit, though a thousand others remain barren. Anyone who proposed to bring all growing things to the highest pitch of luxuriance would soon find the weeds—those hardiest of perennials—waving above his head. I therefore consider it the prime task of psychotherapy today to pursue with singleness of purpose the goal of individual development. So doing, our efforts will follow nature's own striving to bring life to the fullest possible fruition in each individual, for only in the individual can life fulfil its meaning—not in the bird that sits in a gilded cage.   80:229

When we say "the animal in man," this always strikes us as something horrible. But this animal in man is not horrible, no more than animals are horrible, for they fulfil God's will most faithfully; they live to fulfil their Creator's purpose. We do not do this. We meddle with the work of the Creator, for we always want to be something different from what we are. Our ambition is not to be the whole of ourselves, for that would be unpleasant. But the animals are themselves and they fulfil the will of God that is within them in a true and faithful manner.   11:87*

One cannot live from anything except what one is.

48:310

Consciousness hedged about by psychic powers, sustained or threatened or deluded by them, is the age-old experience of mankind. This experience has projected itself into the archetype of the child, which expresses man's wholeness. The "child" is all that is abandoned and exposed and at the same time divinely powerful; the insignificant, dubious beginning, and the triumphal end. The "eternal child" in man is an indescribable experience, an incongruity, a handicap, and a divine prerogative; an imponderable that determines the ultimate worth or worthlessness of a personality.   76:300

Personality is a seed that can only develop by slow stages throughout life. There is no personality without definiteness, wholeness, and ripeness. These three qualities cannot and should not be expected of the child, as they would rob it of childhood.   21:288

In every adult there lurks a child—an eternal child, something that is always becoming, is never completed, and calls for unceasing care, attention, and education. That is the part of the human personality which wants to develop and become whole. But the man of today is far indeed from this wholeness.   21:286

When a summit of life is reached, when the bud unfolds and from the lesser the greater emerges, then, as Nietzsche says, "One becomes Two," and the greater figure, which one always was but which remained invisible, appears to the lesser personality with the force of a revelation. He who is truly and hopelessly little will always drag the revelation of the greater down to the level of his littleness, and will never understand that the day of judgment for his littleness has dawned. But the man who is inwardly great will know that the long expected friend of his soul, the immortal one, has now really come, "to lead captivity captive" [Ephesians 4:8]; that is, to seize hold of him by whom this immortal had always been confined and held prisoner, and to make his life flow into that greater life—a moment of deadliest peril!   17:217

❖

Only the man who can consciously assent to the power of the inner voice becomes a personality; but if he succumbs to it he will be swept away by the blind flux of psychic events and destroyed. That is the great and liberating thing about any genuine personality: he voluntarily sacrifices himself to his vocation, and consciously translates into his own individual reality what would only lead to ruin if it were lived unconsciously by the group.   21:308

The demand made by the *imitatio Christi*—that we should follow the ideal and seek to become like it—ought logically to have the result of developing and exalting the inner man. In actual fact, however, the ideal has been turned by superficial and formalistically-minded believers into an external object of worship, and it is precisely this veneration for the object that prevents it from reaching down into the depths of the psyche and giving the latter a wholeness in keeping with the ideal. Accordingly the divine mediator stands outside as an image, while man remains fragmentary and untouched in the deepest part of him. Christ can indeed be imitated even to the point of stigmatization without the imitator coming anywhere near the ideal or its meaning. For it is not a question of an imitation that leaves a man unchanged and makes him into a mere artifact, but of realizing the ideal on one's own account— *Deo concedente*—in one's own individual life.   72:7

Everything good is costly, and the development of personality is one of the most costly of all things. It is a matter of saying yea to oneself, of taking oneself as the most serious of tasks, of being conscious of everything one does, and keeping it constantly before one's eyes in all its dubious aspects—truly a task that taxes us to the utmost.   112:24

Personality can never develop unless the individual chooses his own way, consciously and with moral deliberation. Not only the causal motive—necessity—but conscious moral decision must lend its strength to the process of building the personality. If the first is lacking, then the alleged development is a mere acrobatics of the will; if the second, it will get stuck in unconscious automatism. But a man can make a moral decision to go his own way only if he holds that way to be the best. If any other way were held to be better, then he would live and develop that other personality instead of his own. The other ways are conventionalities of a moral, social, political, philosophical, or religious nature. The fact that the conventions always flourish in one form or another only proves that the vast majority of mankind do not choose their own way, but convention, and consequently develop not themselves but a method and a collective mode of life at the cost of their own wholeness.   21:296

Personality is the supreme realization of the innate idiosyncrasy of a living being. It is an act of high courage flung in the face of life, the absolute affirmation of all that constitutes the individual, the most successful adaptation to the universal conditions of existence coupled with the greatest possible freedom for self-determination.   21:289

To the extent that a man is untrue to the law of his being and does not rise to personality, he has failed to realize his life's meaning. Fortunately, in her kindness and patience, Nature never puts the fatal question as to the meaning of their lives into the mouths of most people. And where no one asks, no one need answer.   21:314

So often among so-called "primitives" one comes across spiritual personalities who immediately inspire respect, as though they were the fully matured products of an undisturbed fate.   44:336

Personality consists of two things: first, consciousness and whatever this covers, and second, an indefinitely large hinterland of unconscious psyche. So far as the former is concerned, it can be more or less clearly defined and delimited; but as for the sum total of human personality, one has to admit the impossibility of a complete description or definition. In other words, there is bound to be an illimitable and indefinable addition to every personality, because the latter consists of a conscious and observable part which does not contain certain factors whose existence, however, we are forced to assume in order to explain certain observable facts. The unknown factors form what we call the unconscious part of the personality.   74:66

The intrinsically goal-like quality of the self and the urge to realize this goal are not dependent on the participation of consciousness. They cannot be denied any more than one can deny one's ego-consciousness. It, too, puts forward its claims peremptorily, and very often in overt or covert opposition to the needs of the evolving self. In reality, i.e., with few exceptions, the entelechy of the self consists in a succession of endless compromises, ego and self laboriously keeping the scales balanced if all is to go well. Too great a swing to one side or the other is often no more than an example of how not to set about it. This certainly does not mean that extremes, when they occur in a natural way, are in themselves evil. We make the right use of them when we examine their meaning, and they give us ample opportunity to do this in a manner deserving our gratitude.

36 : 960

✧

What does "wholeness" mean? I feel that there is every reason here for some anxiety, since man as a whole being casts a shadow. The fourth was not separated from the three and banished to the kingdom of everlasting fire for nothing. Does not an uncanonical saying of our Lord declare, "Whoso is near unto me is near unto the fire"? Such dire ambiguities are not meant for grown-up children—which is why Heraclitus of old was named "the dark," because he spoke too plainly and called life itself an "everliving fire." And that is why there are uncanonical sayings for those that have ears to hear.

72 : 297

There is no light without shadow and no psychic wholeness without imperfection. To round itself out, life calls not for perfection but for completeness; and for this the "thorn in the flesh" is needed, the suffering of defects without which there is no progress and no ascent.

72 : 208

It is only the intervention of time and space here and now that makes reality. Wholeness is realized for a moment only—the moment that Faust was seeking all his life.

72 : 321

Every life is the realization of a whole, that is, of a self, for which reason this realization can also be called "individuation." All life is bound to individual carriers who realize it, and it is simply inconceivable without them. But every carrier is charged with an individual destiny and destination, and the realization of these alone makes sense of life. True, the "sense" is often something that could just as well be called "nonsense," for there is a certain incommensurability between the mystery of existence and human understanding. "Sense" and "nonsense" are merely man-made labels which serve to give us a reasonably valid sense of direction.

72:330

The difference between the "natural" individuation process, which runs its course unconsciously, and the one which is consciously realized, is tremendous. In the first case consciousness nowhere intervenes; the end remains as dark as the beginning. In the second case so much darkness comes to light that the personality is permeated with light, and consciousness necessarily gains in scope and insight. The encounter between conscious and unconscious has to ensure that the light which shines in the darkness is not only comprehended by the darkness, but comprehends it.

7:756

In so far as the individuation process runs its course unconsciously as it has from time immemorial, it means no more than that the acorn becomes an oak, the calf a cow, and the child an adult. But if the individuation process is made conscious, consciousness must confront the unconscious and a balance between the opposites must be found. As this is not possible through logic, one is dependent on symbols which make the irrational union of opposites possible. They are produced spontaneously by the unconscious and are amplified by the conscious mind.

7:755

It is the task of the conscious mind to understand these hints. If this does not happen, the process of individuation will nevertheless continue. The only difference is that we become its victims and are dragged along by fate towards that inescapable goal which we might have reached walking upright, if only we had taken the trouble and been patient enough to understand the meaning of the numina that cross our path.   7 : 746

Individuation does not shut one out from the world, but gathers the world to oneself.   53 : 432

Fate, Death, and Renewal

What is it, in the end, that induces a man to go his own way and to rise out of unconscious identity with the mass as out of a swathing mist? Not necessity, for necessity comes to many, and they all take refuge in convention. Not moral decision, for nine times out of ten we decide for convention likewise. What is it, then, that inexorably tips the scales in favour of the *extra-ordinary*? It is what is commonly called *vocation*: an irrational factor that destines a man to emancipate himself from the herd and from its well-worn paths. True personality is always a vocation and puts its trust in it as in God, despite its being, as the ordinary man would say, only a personal feeling. But vocation acts like a law of God from which there is no escape. The fact that many a man who goes his own way ends in ruin means nothing to one who has a vocation. He *must* obey his own law, as if it were a daemon whispering to him of new and wonderful paths. Anyone with a vocation hears the voice of the inner man: he is *called*. 21:299*f*

Much indeed can be attained by the will, but, in view of the fate of certain markedly strong-willed personalities, it is a fundamental error to try to subject our own fate at all costs to our will. Our will is a function regulated by reflection; hence it is dependent on the quality of that reflection. This, if it really is reflection, is supposed to be rational, i.e., in accord with reason. But has it ever been shown, or will it ever be, that life and fate are in accord with reason, that they too are rational? We have on the contrary good grounds for supposing that they are irrational, or rather that in the last resort they are grounded beyond human reason. 104A:72

We cannot rate reason highly enough, but there are times when we must ask ourselves: do we really know enough about the destinies of individuals to entitle us to give good advice under *all* circumstances? Certainly we must act according to our best convictions, but are we so sure that our convictions are for the best as regards the other person? Very often we do not know what is best for ourselves, and in later years we may occasionally thank God from the bottom of our hearts that his kindly hand has preserved us from the "reasonableness" of our former plans. It is easy for the critic to say after the event, "Ah, but then it wasn't the right sort of reason!" Who can know with unassailable certainty when he has the right sort? Moreover, is it not essential to the true art of living, sometimes, in defiance of all reason and fitness, to include the unreasonable and the unfitting within the ambiance of the possible?

77:462

Reason must always seek the solution in some rational, consistent, logical way, which is certainly justifiable enough in all normal situations but is entirely inadequate when it comes to the really great and decisive questions. It is incapable of creating the symbol because the symbol is irrational. When the rational way proves to be a *cul de sac*—as it always does after a time—the solution comes from the side it was least expected. 69:438

We distinctly resent the idea of invisible and arbitrary forces, for it is not so long ago that we made our escape from that frightening world of dreams and superstitions, and constructed for ourselves a picture of the cosmos worthy of our rational consciousness—that latest and greatest achievement of man. We are now surrounded by a world that is obedient to rational laws. It is true that we do not know the causes of everything, but in time they will be discovered, and these discoveries will accord with our

reasoned expectations. There are, to be sure, also chance occurrences, but they are merely accidental, and we do not
doubt that they have a causality of their own. Chance happenings are repellent to the mind that loves order. They
disturb the regular, predictable course of events in the most
absurd and irritating way. We resent them as much as we
resent invisible, arbitrary forces, for they remind us too
much of Satanic imps or of the caprice of a *deus ex
machina*. They are the worst enemies of our careful calculations and a continual threat to all our undertakings. Being admittedly contrary to reason, they deserve all our
abuse, and yet we should not fail to give them their due.

9: 113

What if there were a living agency beyond our everyday human world—something even more purposeful than
electrons? Do we delude ourselves in thinking that we possess and control our own psyches, and is what science calls
the "psyche" not just a question-mark arbitrarily confined
within the skull, but rather a door that opens upon the human world from a world beyond, allowing unknown and
mysterious powers to act upon man and carry him on the
wings of the night to a more than personal destiny?

73: 148

"The stars of thine own fate lie in thy breast," says Seni
to Wallenstein—a dictum that should satisfy all astrologers
if we knew even a little about the secrets of the heart. But
for this, so far, men have had little understanding. Nor
would I dare to assert that things are any better today.

10: 9

Whether primitive or not, mankind always stands on the
brink of actions it performs itself but does not control. The
whole world wants peace and the whole world prepares
for war, to take but one example. Mankind is powerless

against mankind, and the gods, as ever, show it the ways of fate. Today we call the gods "factors," which comes from *facere*, 'to make.' The makers stand behind the wings of the world-theatre. It is so in great things as in small. In the realm of consciousness we are our own masters; we seem to be the "factors" themselves. But if we step through the door of the shadow we discover with terror that we are the objects of unseen factors. 10:49

It is dangerous to avow spiritual poverty, for the poor man has desires, and whoever has desires calls down some fatality on himself. A Swiss proverb puts it drastically: "Behind every rich man stands a devil, and behind every poor man two." 10:28

In our strength we are independent and isolated, and are masters of our own fate; in our weakness we are dependent and bound, and become unwilling instruments of fate, for here it is not the individual will that counts but the will of the species. 114:261

Without wishing it, we human beings are placed in situations in which the great "principles" entangle us in something, and God leaves it to us to find a way out.

32:869

People often behave as if they did not rightly understand what constitutes the destructive character of the creative force. A woman who gives herself up to passion, particularly under present-day civilized conditions, experiences this all too soon. We must think a little beyond the framework of purely bourgeois moral conditions to understand the feeling of boundless uncertainty which befalls the man who gives himself over unconditionally to fate. Even to be fruitful is to destroy oneself, for with the creation of a new generation the previous generation has passed beyond its climax. Our offspring thus become our most dangerous enemies, with whom we cannot get even, for they will survive us and so inevitably will take the power out of our weakening hands. Fear of our erotic fate is quite understandable, for there is something unpredictable about it.

100A: 101*f**

It is not I who create myself, rather I happen to myself.

103: 391

What happens to a person is characteristic of him. He represents a pattern and all the pieces fit. One by one, as his life proceeds, they fall into place according to some predestined design.

39F: B

The reality of good and evil consists in things and situations that just happen to you, that are too big for you, where you are always facing death. Anything that comes upon me with this intensity I experience as numinous, no matter whether I call it divine or devilish or just "fate."

32: 871

The great decisions in human life usually have far more to do with the instincts and other mysterious unconscious factors than with conscious will and well-meaning reasonableness. The shoe that fits one person pinches another; there is no universal recipe for living. Each of us carries his own life-form within him—an irrational form which no other can outbid.

2: 81

Fear of fate is a very understandable phenomenon, for it is incalculable, immeasurable, full of unknown dangers. The perpetual hesitation of the neurotic to launch out into life is readily explained by his desire to stand aside so as not to get involved in the dangerous struggle for existence. But anyone who refuses to experience life must stifle his desire to live—in other words, he must commit partial suicide.   100:165

In the domain of pathology I believe I have observed cases where the tendency of the unconscious would have to be regarded, by all human standards, as essentially destructive. But it may not be out of place to reflect that the self-destruction of what is hopelessly inefficient or evil can be understood in a higher sense as another attempt at compensation. There are murderers who feel that their execution is condign punishment, and suicides who go to their death in triumph.   48:149

Grounds for an unusually intense fear of death are nowadays not far to seek: they are obvious enough, the more so as all life that is senselessly wasted and misdirected means death too. This may account for the unnatural intensification of the fear of death in our time, when life has lost its deeper meaning for so many people, forcing them to exchange the life-preserving rhythm of the aeons for the dread ticking of the clock.   26:696

❖

In the secret hour of life's midday the parabola is reversed, death is born. The second half of life does not signify ascent, unfolding, increase, exuberance, but death, since the end is its goal. The negation of life's fulfilment is synonymous with the refusal to accept its ending. Both mean not wanting to live, and not wanting to live is identical with not wanting to die. Waxing and waning make one curve.   90:800

Like a projectile flying to its goal, life ends in death. Even its ascent and its zenith are only steps and means to this goal.   90:803

Death is psychologically as important as birth and, like it, is an integral part of life.   112:68

The birth of a human being is pregnant with meaning, why not death? For twenty years and more the growing man is being prepared for the complete unfolding of his individual nature, why should not the older man prepare himself twenty years and more for his death?   90:803

As a doctor I am convinced that it is hygienic—if I may use the word—to discover in death a goal towards which one can strive, and that shrinking away from it is something unhealthy and abnormal which robs the second half of life of its purpose.   94:792

We know of course that when for one reason or another we feel out of sorts, we are liable to commit not only the minor follies, but something really dangerous which, given the right psychological moment, may well put an end to our lives. The popular saying, "Old so-and-so chose the right time to die," comes from a sure sense of the secret psychological cause.   104A:194

That the highest summit of life can be expressed through the symbolism of death is a well-known fact, for any growing beyond oneself means death.   100:432

The psyche pre-existent to consciousness (e.g., in the child) participates in the maternal psyche on the one hand, while on the other it reaches across to the daughter psyche. We could therefore say that every mother contains her daughter in herself and every daughter her mother, and that every woman extends backwards into her mother and forwards into her daughter. This participation and inter-mingling give rise to that peculiar uncertainty as regards *time*: a woman lives earlier as a mother, later as a daughter. The conscious experience of these ties produces the feeling that her life is spread out over generations—the first step towards the immediate experience and conviction of being outside time, which brings with it a feeling of *immortality*. The individual's life is elevated into a type, indeed it becomes the archetype of woman's fate in general. This leads to a restoration or *apocatastasis* of the lives of her ancestors, who now, through the bridge of the momentary individual, pass down into the generations of the future. An experience of this kind gives the individual a place and a meaning in the life of the generations, so that all unnecessary obstacles are cleared out of the way of the lifestream that is to flow through her. At the same time the individual is rescued from her isolation and restored to wholeness.   66: 316

Our life is indeed the same as it ever was. At all events, in our sense of the word it is not transitory; for the same physiological and psychological processes that have been man's for hundreds of thousands of years still endure, instilling into our inmost hearts this profound intuition of the "eternal" continuity of the living. But the self, as an inclusive term that embraces our whole living organism, not only contains the deposit and totality of all past life, but is also a point of departure, the fertile soil from which all future life will spring. This premonition of futurity is as clearly impressed upon our innermost feelings as is the historical aspect. The idea of immortality follows legitimately from these psychological premises.   104B: 303

For the man of today the expansion of life and its culmination are plausible goals, but the idea of life after death seems to him questionable or beyond belief. Life's cessation, that is, death, can only be accepted as a reasonable goal either when existence is so wretched that we are only too glad for it to end, or when we are convinced that the sun strives to its setting "to illuminate distant races" with the same logical consistency it showed in rising to the zenith. But to believe has become such a difficult art today that it is beyond the capacity of most people, particularly the educated part of humanity. They have become too accustomed to the thought that, with regard to immortality and such questions, there are innumerable contradictory opinions and no convincing proofs. And since "science" is the catchword that seems to carry the weight of absolute conviction in the temporary world, we ask for "scientific" proofs. But educated people who can think know very well that proof of this kind is a philosophical impossibility. We simply cannot know anything whatever about such things.

94 : 790

One should not be deterred by the rather silly objection that nobody knows whether these old universal ideas—God, immortality, freedom of the will, and so on—are "true" or not. Truth is the wrong criterion here. One can only ask whether they are helpful or not, whether man is better off and feels his life more complete, more meaningful and more satisfactory with or without them.   39B : 147*

It would all be so much simpler if only we could deny the existence of the psyche. But here we are with our immediate experiences of something that *is*—something that has taken root in the midst of our measurable, ponderable, three-dimensional reality, that differs mysteriously from this in every respect and in all its parts, and yet reflects it. The psyche could be regarded as a mathematical point and at the same time as a universe of fixed stars. It is small wonder, then, if, to the unsophisticated mind, such a paradoxical being borders on the divine. If it occupies no space, it has no body. Bodies die, but can something invisible and incorporeal disappear? What is more, life and psyche existed for me before I could say "I," and when this "I" disappears, as in sleep or unconsciousness, life and psyche still go on, as our observation of other people and our own dreams inform us. Why should the simple mind deny, in the face of such experiences, that the "soul" lives in a realm beyond the body?   12:671

Everything psychic is pregnant with the future.   48:53

The cult of the dead is rationally based on the belief in the supra-temporality of the soul, but its irrational basis is to be found in the psychological need of the living to do something for the departed. This is an elementary need which forces itself upon even the most "enlightened" individuals when faced by the death of relatives and friends. That is why, enlightenment or no enlightenment, we still have all manner of ceremonies for the dead. If Lenin had to submit to being embalmed and put on show in a sumptuous mausoleum like an Egyptian pharaoh, we may be quite sure it was not because his followers believed in the resurrection of the body. Apart, however, from the Masses said for the soul in the Catholic Church, the provisions we make for the dead are rudimentary and on the lowest level, not because we cannot convince ourselves of the soul's immortality, but because we have rationalized the above-mentioned psychological need out of existence. We behave as if we did not have this need, and because we cannot believe in a life after death we prefer to do nothing about it. Simpler-minded people follow their own feelings, and, as in Italy, build themselves funeral monuments of gruesome beauty. The Catholic Masses for the soul are on a level considerably above this, because they are expressly intended for the psychic welfare of the deceased and are not a mere gratification of lachrymose sentiments.   22:855

Flight from life does not exempt us from the laws of old age and death. The neurotic who tries to wriggle out of the necessity of living wins nothing and only burdens himself with a constant foretaste of aging and dying, which must appear especially cruel on account of the total emptiness and meaninglessness of his life. If it is not possible for the libido to strive forwards, to lead a life that willingly accepts all dangers and ultimate decay, then it strikes back along the other road and sinks into its own depths, working down to the old intimation of the immortality of all that lives, to the old longing for rebirth.   100:617

The sun, rising triumphant, tears himself from the enveloping womb of the sea, and leaving behind him the noonday zenith and all its glorious works, sinks down again into the maternal depths, into all-enfolding and all-regenerating night. This image is undoubtedly a primordial one, and there was profound justification for its becoming a symbolical expression of human fate: in the morning of life the son tears himself loose from the mother, from the domestic hearth, to rise through battle to his destined heights. Always he imagines his worst enemy in front of him, yet he carries the enemy within himself—a deadly longing for the abyss, a longing to drown in his own source, to be sucked down to the realm of the Mothers. His life is a constant struggle against extinction, a violent yet fleeting deliverance from ever-lurking night. This death is no external enemy, it is his own inner longing for the stillness and profound peace of all-knowing non-existence, for all-seeing sleep in the ocean of coming-to-be and passing away. Even in his highest strivings for harmony and balance, for the profundities of philosophy and the raptures of the artist, he seeks death, immobility, satiety, rest. If, like Peirithous, he tarries too long in this abode of rest and peace, he is overcome by apathy, and the poison of the serpent paralyses him for all time. If he is to live, he must fight and sacrifice his longing for the past in order to rise to his own heights. And having reached the noonday heights, he must sacrifice his love for his own achievement, for he may not loiter. The sun, too, sacrifices its greatest strength in order to hasten onward to the fruits of autumn, which are the seeds of rebirth.   100:553

Only that which can destroy itself is truly alive.   72:93

✧

The highest value, which gives life and meaning, has got lost. This is a typical experience that has been repeated many times, and its expression therefore occupies a central place in the Christian mystery. The death or loss must always repeat itself: Christ always dies, and always he is born: for the psychic life of the archetype is timeless in comparison with our individual time-boundness. According to what laws now one and now another aspect of the archetype enters into active manifestation, I do not know. I only know—and here I am expressing what countless other people know—that the present is a time of God's death and disappearance. The myth says he was not to be found where his body was laid. "Body" means the outward, visible form, the erstwhile but ephemeral setting for the highest value. The myth further says that the value rose again in a miraculous manner, transformed.   74:149

The three days' descent into hell during death describes the sinking of the vanished value into the unconscious, where, by conquering the power of darkness, it establishes a new order, and then rises up to heaven again, that is, attains supreme clarity of consciousness. The fact that only a few people see the Risen One means that no small difficulties stand in the way of finding and recognizing the transformed value.   74:149

When the libido leaves the bright upper world, whether from choice, or from inertia, or from fate, it sinks back into its own depths, into the source from which it originally flowed, and returns to the point of cleavage, the navel, where it first entered the body. This point of cleavage is called the mother, because from her the current of life reached us. Whenever some great work is to be accomplished, before which a man recoils, doubtful of his strength, his libido streams back to the fountainhead—and that is the dangerous moment when the issue hangs between annihilation and new life. For if the libido gets stuck in the wonderland of this inner world, then for the upper world man is nothing but a shadow, he is already moribund or at least seriously ill. But if the libido manages to tear itself loose and force its way up again, something like a miracle happens: the journey to the underworld was a plunge into the fountain of youth, and the libido, apparently dead, wakes to renewed fruitfulness.   100:449

The birth of a saviour is equivalent to a great catastrophe, because a new and powerful life springs up just where there had seemed to be no life and no power and no possibility of further development. It comes streaming out of the unconscious, from that unknown part of the psyche which is treated as nothing by all rationalists. From this discredited and rejected region comes the new afflux of energy, the renewal of life. But what is this discredited and rejected source of vitality? It consists of all those psychic contents that were repressed because of their incompatibility with conscious values—everything hateful, immoral, wrong, unsuitable, useless, etc., which means everything that at one time or another appeared so to the individual concerned. The danger is that when these things reappear in a new and wonderful guise, they may make such an impact on him that he will forget or repudiate all his former values. What he once despised now becomes the supreme principle, and what was once truth now becomes error. This reversal of values amounts to the destruction of the old ones and is similar to the devastation of a country by floods.   69:449

If the old were not ripe for death, nothing new would appear; and if the old were not blocking the way for the new, it could not and need not be rooted out.   69:446

Everything old in our unconscious hints at something coming.   69:630

The mere fact that people talk about rebirth, and that there is such a concept at all, means that a store of psychic experiences designated by that term must actually exist. What these experiences are like we can only infer from the statements that have been made about them. So, if we want to find out what rebirth really is, we must turn to history in order to ascertain what "rebirth" has been understood to mean.   17:206

Rebirth is an affirmation that must be counted among the primordial affirmations of mankind.   17:207

In the initiation of the living, "Beyond" is not a world beyond death, but a reversal of the mind's intentions and outlook, a psychological "Beyond" or, in Christian terms, a "redemption" from the trammels of the world and of sin. Redemption is a separation and deliverance from an earlier condition of darkness and unconsciousness, and leads to a condition of illumination and releasedness, to victory and transcendence over everything "given."   22:841

We are so hemmed in by things which jostle and oppress that we never get a chance, in the midst of all these "given" things, to wonder by whom they are "given."   22:841

A great reversal of standpoint, calling for much sacrifice, is needed before we can see the world as "given" by the very nature of the psyche. It is so much more straightforward, more dramatic, impressive, and therefore more convincing, to see all the things that happen to me than to observe how I make them happen. Indeed, the animal nature of man makes him resist seeing himself as the maker of his circumstances.   22 : 841

If I know and admit that I am giving myself, forgoing myself, and do not want to be repaid for it, then I have sacrificed my claim, and thus a part of myself. Consequently, all absolute giving, a giving which is a total loss from the start, is a self-sacrifice. Ordinary giving for which no return is received is felt as a loss; but a sacrifice is meant to be like a loss, so that one may be sure that the egoistic claim no longer exists. Therefore the gift should be given as if it were being destroyed. But since the gift represents myself, I have in that case destroyed myself, given myself away without expectation of return. Yet, looked at in another way, this intentional loss is also a gain, for if you can give yourself it proves that you possess yourself. Nobody can give what he has not got.   103 : 390

From that sacrifice we gain ourselves—our "self"—for we have only what we give.   103 : 398

Fear of self-sacrifice lurks deep in every ego, and this fear is often only the precariously controlled demand of the unconscious forces to burst out in full strength. No one who strives for selfhood (individuation) is spared this dangerous passage, for that which is feared also belongs to the wholeness of the self—the sub-human, or supra-human, world of psychic "dominants" from which the ego originally emancipated itself with enormous effort, and then only partially, for the sake of a more or less illusory freedom. This liberation is certainly a very necessary and very heroic undertaking, but it represents nothing final: it is merely the creation of a *subject*, who, in order to find fulfilment, has still to be confronted by an *object*. This, at first sight, would appear to be the world, which is swelled out with projections for that very purpose. Here we seek and find our difficulties, here we seek and find our enemy, here we seek and find what is dear and precious to us; and it is comforting to know that all evil and all good is to be found out there, in the visible object, where it can be conquered, punished, destroyed, or enjoyed. But nature herself does not allow this paradisal state of innocence to continue for ever. There are, and always have been, those who cannot help but see that the world and its experiences are in the nature of a symbol, and that it really reflects something that lies hidden in the subject himself, in his own transsubjective reality.

22:849

The effect of the unconscious images has something fateful about it. Perhaps—who knows—these eternal images are what men mean by fate.

104A:183

If the demand for self-knowledge is willed by fate and is refused, this negative attitude may end in real death. The demand would not have come to this person had he still been able to strike out on some promising by-path. But he is caught in a blind alley from which only self-knowledge can extricate him. If he refuses this then no other way is open to him. Usually he is not conscious of his situation, either, and the more unconscious he is the more he is at the mercy of unforeseen dangers: he cannot get out of the way of a car quickly enough, in climbing a mountain he misses his foothold somewhere, out skiing he thinks he can negotiate a tricky slope, and in an illness he suddenly loses the courage to live. The unconscious has a thousand

ways of snuffing out a meaningless existence with surprising swiftness.   48:675

Consciousness is always only a part of the psyche and
therefore never capable of psychic wholeness: for that the
indefinite extension of the unconscious is needed. But the
unconscious can neither be caught with clever formulas nor
exorcized by means of scientific dogmas, for something
of destiny clings to it—indeed, it is sometimes destiny
itself.   98:906

The new thing prepared by fate seldom or never comes
up to conscious expectations. And still more remarkable,
though the new thing goes against deeply rooted instincts
as we have known them, it is a strangely appropriate expression of the total personality, an expression which one
could not imagine in a more complete form.   112:19

If you sum up what people tell you about their experiences, you can formulate it this way: They came to themselves, they could accept themselves, they were able to become reconciled to themselves, and thus were reconciled to
adverse circumstances and events. This is almost like what
used to be expressed by saying: He has made his peace with
God, he has sacrificed his own will, he has submitted himself to the will of God.   74:138

When I examined the course of development in patients
who quietly, and as if unconsciously, outgrew themselves,
I saw that their fates had something in common. The new
thing came to them from obscure possibilities either outside
or inside themselves; they accepted it and grew with its
help. It seemed to me typical that some took the new thing
from outside themselves, others from inside; or rather, that
it grew into some persons from without, and into others
from within. But the new thing never came exclusively

either from within or from without. If it came from outside, it became a profound inner experience; if it came from inside, it became an outer happening. In no case was it conjured into existence intentionally or by conscious willing, but rather seemed to be borne along on the stream of time.

112: 18

The Way to God

For thousands of years the mind of man has worried about the sick soul, perhaps even earlier than it did about the sick body. The propitiation of gods, the perils of the soul and its salvation, these are not yesterday's problems. Religions are psychotherapeutic systems in the truest sense of the word, and on the grandest scale. They express the whole range of the psychic problem in mighty images; they are the avowal and recognition of the soul, and at the same time the revelation of the soul's nature. From this universal foundation no human soul is cut off; only the individual consciousness that has lost its connection with the psychic totality remains caught in the illusion that the soul is a small circumscribed area, a fit subject for "scientific" theorizing. The loss of this great relationship is the prime evil of neurosis.

95:367

The very absurdity and impossibility of [religious] statements . . . [are] the real ground for belief, as was formulated most brilliantly in Tertullian's "prorsus credible, quia ineptum."* (The audacity of Tertullian's argument is undeniable, and so is its danger, but that does not detract from its psychological truth.) An improbable opinion has to submit sooner or later to correction. But the statements of religion are the most improbable of all and yet they persist for thousands of years. Their wholly unexpected vitality proves the existence of a sufficient cause which has so far eluded scientific investigation.

103:379

The ways and customs of childhood, once so sublimely good, can hardly be laid aside even when their harmful-

---

* "Et mortuus est Dei filius, prorsus credible est, quia ineptum est. Et sepultus resurrexit; certum est, quia impossible est" (And the Son of God is dead, which is to be believed because it is absurd. And buried He rose again, which is certain because it is impossible).

ness has long since been proved. The same, only on a gigantic scale, is true of historical changes of attitude. A collective attitude is equivalent to a religion, and changes of religion constitute one of the most painful chapters in the world's history. In this respect our age is afflicted with a blindness that has no parallel. We think we have only to declare an accepted article of faith incorrect and invalid, and we shall be psychologically rid of all the traditional effects of Christianity or Judaism. We believe in enlightenment, as if an intellectual change of front somehow had a profounder influence on the emotional processes or even on the unconscious. We entirely forget that the religion of the last two thousand years is a psychological attitude, a definite form and manner of adaptation to the world without and within, that lays down a definite cultural pattern and creates an atmosphere which remains wholly uninfluenced by any intellectual denials.   69:313

Everything to do with religion, everything it is and asserts, touches the human soul so closely that psychology least of all can afford to overlook it.   65:172

If Christian doctrine is able to assimilate the fateful impact of psychology, that is a sign of vitality, for life is assimilation. Anything that ceases to assimilate dies.

48:455*n*

It would be a regrettable mistake if anybody should take my observations as a kind of proof of the existence of God. They prove only the existence of an archetypal God-image, which to my mind is the most we can assert about God psychologically.   74:102

The competence of psychology as an empirical science only goes so far as to establish, on the basis of comparative research, whether for instance the imprint found in the psyche can or cannot reasonably be termed a "God-image." Nothing positive or negative has thereby been asserted about the possible existence of God, any more than the archetype of the "hero" proves the actual existence of a hero.

72:15

It is, in fact, impossible to demonstrate God's reality to oneself except by using images which have arisen spontaneously or are sanctified by tradition, and whose psychic nature and effects the naive-minded person has never separated from their unknowable metaphysical background. He instantly equates the effective image with the transcendental x to which it points. The seeming justification for this procedure appears self-evident and is not considered a problem so long as the statements of religion are not seriously questioned. But if there is occasion for criticism, then it must be remembered that the image and the statement are psychic processes which are different from their transcendental object: they do not posit it, they merely point to it.

7:558

If, for instance, we say "God," we give expression to an image or verbal concept that has undergone many changes in the course of time. We are, however, unable to say with any degree of certainty—unless it be by faith—whether these changes affect only the images and concepts, or the Unspeakable itself.

7:555

In religious matters it is a well-known fact that we cannot understand a thing until we have experienced it inwardly.

72:15

It is in the inward experience that the connection between the psyche and the outward image or creed is first revealed as a relationship or correspondence like that of *sponsus* and *sponsa*. Accordingly when I say as a psychologist that God

is an archetype, I mean by that the "type" in the psyche.
The word "type" is, as we know, derived from the Greek
τύπος, "blow" or "imprint"; thus an "archetype" presupposes an imprinter. 72:15

The ideas of the moral order and of God belong to the
ineradicable substrate of the human soul. That is why any
honest psychology, which is not blinded by the garish con-
ceits of enlightenment, must come to terms with these facts.
They cannot be explained away and killed with irony. In
physics we can do without a God-image, but in psychology it is a definite fact that has got to be reckoned with,
just as we have to reckon with "affect," "instinct," "mother,"
etc. It is the fault of the everlasting contamination of object and image that people can make no conceptual distinction between "God" and "God-image," and therefore think
that when one speaks of the "God-image" one is speaking
of God and offering "theological" explanations. It is not for
psychology, as a science, to demand a hypostatization of
the God-image. But the facts being what they are, it does
have to reckon with the existence of a God-image. 30:528

The idea of God is an absolutely necessary psychological
function of an irrational nature, which has nothing whatever to do with the question of God's existence. The human intellect can never answer this question, still less give
any proof of God. Moreover such proof is superfluous,
for the idea of an all-powerful divine Being is present
everywhere, unconsciously if not consciously, because it is
an archetype. 104A:110

If we consider the fact that the idea of God is an "unscientific" hypothesis, we can easily explain why people
have forgotten to think along such lines. And even if they
do cherish a certain belief in God they would be deterred
from the idea of a God within by their religious education,

which has always depreciated this idea as "mystical." Yet it is precisely this "mystical" idea which is forced upon the conscious mind by dreams and visions.   74:101

The creative mystic was ever a cross for the Church, but it is to him that we owe what is best in humanity.

48:531

The materialistic error was probably unavoidable at first. Since the throne of God could not be discovered among the galactic systems, the inference was that God had never existed. The second unavoidable error is psychologism: if God is anything, he must be an illusion derived from certain motives—from will to power, for instance, or from repressed sexuality. These arguments are not new. Much the same thing was said by the Christian missionaries who overthrew the idols of heathen gods. But whereas the early missionaries were conscious of serving a new God by combatting the old ones, modern iconoclasts are unconscious of the one in whose name they are destroying old values.

74:142

I have been asked so often whether I believe in the existence of God that I am somewhat concerned lest I be taken for an adherent of "psychologism" far more commonly than I suspect. What most people overlook or seem unable to understand is the fact that I regard the psyche as *real*. They believe only in physical facts, and must consequently come to the conclusion that either the uranium itself or the laboratory equipment created the atom bomb. That is no less absurd than the assumption that a nonreal psyche is responsible for it. God is an obvious psychic and nonphysical fact, i.e., a fact that can be established psychically but not physically.   7:751

Owing to the undervaluation of the psyche that everywhere prevails, every attempt at psychological understanding is immediately suspected of psychologism. . . . If, in physics, one seeks to explain the nature of light, nobody expects that as a result there will be no light. But in the case of psychology everybody believes that what is explained is explained away. 7:749*n*

At a time when all available energy is spent in the investigation of nature, very little attention is paid to the essence of man, which is his psyche, although many researches are made into its conscious functions. But the really unknown part, which produces symbols, is still virtually unexplored. We receive signals from it every night, yet deciphering these communications seems to be such an odious task that very few people in the whole civilized world can be bothered with it. Man's greatest instrument, his psyche, is little thought of, if not actually mistrusted and despised. "It's only psychological" too often means: it is nothing. 8:102*

We always think that Christianity consists in a particular confession of faith and in belonging to a Church. No, Christianity is our world. Everything we think is the fruit of the Middle Ages and indeed of the Christian Middle Ages. Our whole science, everything that passes through our head, has inevitably gone through this history. It lives in us and has left its stamp upon us for all time and will always form a vital layer of our psyche, just like the phylogenetic traces in our body. The whole character of our mentality, the way we look at things, is also the result of the Christian Middle Ages; whether we know it or not is quite immaterial. The age of rational enlightenment has eradicated nothing. Even our method of rational enlightenment is Christian. The Christian *Weltanschauung* is therefore a psychological fact

that does not allow of any further rationalization; it is
something that has happened, that is present. We are inevitably stamped as Christians, but we are also stamped by
what existed before Christianity.   11:84*

All of us who have had a religious education are deeply
impressed by the idea that Christianity entered into history
without an historical past, like a stroke of lightning out of
a clear sky. This attitude was necessary, but I am convinced
it is not true. Everything has its history, everything has
"grown," and Christianity, which is supposed to have appeared suddenly as a unique revelation from heaven, undoubtedly also has its history. Moreover, how it began is as
clear as daylight. I need not speak of the rites of the Mass
and certain peculiarities of the priests' clothing which are
borrowed from pagan times, for the fundamental ideas of
the Christian Church also have their predecessors. But a
break in continuity has occurred because we are all overcome by the impression of the uniqueness of Christianity.
It is exactly as if we had built a cathedral over a pagan tem-
ple and no longer knew that it is still there underneath. The
result is that the inner correspondence with the outer
God-image is undeveloped through lack of psychic culture
and has remained stuck in paganism.   11:84*

The great events of our world as planned and executed
by man do not breathe the spirit of Christianity but rather
of unadorned paganism. These things originate in a psychic
condition that has remained archaic and has not been even
remotely touched by Christianity. The Church assumes,
not altogether without reason, that the fact of *semel
credidisse* (having once believed) leaves certain traces behind it; but of these traces nothing is to be seen in the broad
march of events. Christian civilization has proved hollow to
a terrifying degree: it is all veneer, but the inner man has
remained untouched and therefore unchanged. His soul is

out of key with his external beliefs; in his soul the Christian has not kept pace with external developments. Yes, everything is to be found outside—in image and in word, in Church and Bible—but never inside. Inside reign the archaic gods, supreme as of old. 72:12

To the degree that the modern mind is passionately concerned with anything and everything rather than religion, religion and its prime object—original sin—have mostly vanished into the unconscious. That is why, today, nobody believes in either. People accuse psychology of dealing in squalid fantasies, and yet even a cursory glance at ancient religions and the history of morals should be sufficient to convince them of the demons hidden in the human soul. This disbelief in the devilishness of human nature goes hand in hand with a blank incomprehension of religion and its meaning. 100:106

Between the religion of a people and its actual mode of life there is always a compensatory relation, otherwise religion would have no practical significance at all. Beginning with the highly moral religion of the Persians and the notorious dubiousness—even in antiquity—of Persian habits of life, right down to our "Christian" epoch, when the religion of love assisted at the greatest blood-bath in the world's history—wherever we turn this rule holds true.

69:229

In the same measure as the conscious attitude may pride itself on a certain godlikeness by reason of its lofty and absolute standpoint, an unconscious attitude develops with a godlikeness oriented downwards to an archaic god whose nature is sensual and brutal. The enantiodromia of Heraclitus ensures that the time will come when this *deus absconditus* shall rise to the surface and press the God of our ideals to the wall. 69:150

The pagan religions met this danger by giving drunken ecstasy a place within their cult. Heraclitus doubtless saw what was at the back of it when he said, "But Hades is that same Dionysos in whose honour they go mad and keep the feast of the wine-vat." For this very reason orgies were granted religious licence, so as to exorcise the danger that threatened from Hades. Our solution, however, has served to throw the gates of hell wide open.   72:182

At a time when a large part of mankind is beginning to discard Christianity, it may be worth our while to try to understand why it was accepted in the first place. It was accepted as a means of escape from the brutality and unconsciousness of the ancient world. As soon as we discard it, the old brutality returns in force, as has been made overwhelmingly clear by contemporary events.... We have had bitter experience of what happens when a whole nation finds the moral mask too stupid to keep up. The beast breaks loose, and a frenzy of demoralization sweeps over the civilized world.   100:341

The tremendous compulsion towards goodness and the immense moral force of Christianity are not merely an argument in the latter's favour, they are also a proof of the strength of its suppressed and repressed counterpart—the antichristian, barbarian element. The existence within us of something that can turn against us, that can become a serious matter for us, I regard not merely as a dangerous peculiarity, but as a valuable and congenial asset as well. It is a still untouched fortune, an uncorrupted treasure, a sign of youthfulness, an earnest of rebirth.   85:20

The Church represents a higher spiritual substitute for the purely natural, or "carnal," tie to the parents. Consequently it frees the individual from an unconscious natural relationship which, strictly speaking, is not a relationship at all but simply a condition of inchoate, unconscious identity. This, just because it is unconscious, possesses a tremendous inertia and offers the utmost resistance to any kind of spiritual development. It would be hard to say what the essential difference is between this state and the soul of an animal. Now, it is by no means the special prerogative of the Christian Church to try to make it possible for the individual to detach himself from his original, animal-like condition; the Church is simply the latest, and specifically Western, form of an instinctive striving that is probably as old as mankind itself.   104A: 172

When, therefore, I am treating practising Catholics, and am faced with the transference problem, I can, by virtue of my office as a doctor, step aside and lead the problem over to the Church. But if I am treating a non-Catholic, that way out is debarred, and by virtue of my office as a doctor I cannot step aside, for there is as a rule nobody there, nothing towards which I could suitably lead the father-imago. I can, of course, get the patient to recognize with his reason that I am not the father. But by that very act I become the reasonable father and remain despite everything the father. Not only nature, but the patient too, abhors a vacuum. He has an instinctive horror of allowing the parental imagos and his childhood psyche to fall into nothingness, into a hopeless past that has no future. His instinct tells him that, for the sake of his own wholeness, these things must be kept alive in one form or another. He knows that a complete withdrawal of the projection will be followed by an apparently endless isolation within the ego, which is all the more burdensome because he has so little love for it. He found it unbearable enough before, and he is unlikely to bear it now simply out of sweet reasonableness. Therefore at this juncture the Catholic who has been freed from an excessively personal tie to his parents can return fairly easily to the mysteries of the Church, which he is now in a position to understand better and more deeply. There are also Protestants who can discover in one of the newer variants of Protestantism a meaning which appeals to them, and so regain a genuine religious attitude.   80:218

With the methods employed hitherto we have not succeeded in Christianizing the soul to the point where even the most elementary demands of Christian ethics can exert any decisive influence on the main concerns of the Christian European. The Christian missionary may preach the gospel to the poor naked heathen, but the spiritual heathen who populate Europe have as yet heard nothing of Christianity.   72:13

Christian education has done all that is humanly possible; but it has not been enough. Too few people have experienced the divine image as the innermost possession of their own souls.   72:12

No one can know what the ultimate things are. We must therefore take them as we experience them. And if such experience helps to make life healthier, more beautiful, more complete, and more satisfactory to yourself and to those you love, you may safely say: "This was the grace of God." No transcendental truth is thereby demonstrated, and we must confess in all humility that religious experience is *extra ecclesiam*, subjective, and liable to boundless error.   74:167*f*

Religious symbols are phenomena of life, plain facts and not intellectual opinions. If the Church clung for so long to the idea that the sun rotates round the earth, and then abandoned this contention in the nineteenth century, she can always appeal to the psychological truth that for mil-

lions of people the sun did revolve round the earth and that
it was only in the nineteenth century that any major portion
of mankind became sufficiently sure of the intellectual function to grasp the proof of the earth's planetary nature. Unfortunately there is no "truth" unless there are people to
understand it.   72:166

The history of Protestantism has been one of chronic
iconoclasm. One wall after another fell. And the work of
destruction was not too difficult once the authority of the
Church had been shattered. We all know how, in large
things as in small, in general as well as in particular, piece
after piece collapsed, and how the alarming poverty of symbols that is now the condition of our life came about. With
that the power of the Church has vanished too—a fortress
robbed of its bastions and casemates, a house whose walls
have been plucked away, exposed to all the winds of the
world and to all dangers. Although this is, properly speaking, a lamentable collapse that offends our sense of history,
the disintegration of Protestantism into nearly four hundred denominations is yet a sure sign that the restlessness
continues. The Protestant is cast out into a state of defence-
lessness that might well make the natural man shudder.
His enlightened consciousness, of course, refuses to take
cognizance of this fact, and is quietly looking elsewhere
for what has been lost to Europe. We seek the effective
images, the thought-forms that satisfy the restlessness of
heart and mind, and we find the treasures of the East.

                                                          10:23f

I am convinced that the growing impoverishment of symbols has a meaning. It is a development that has an inner
consistency. Everything that we have not thought about,
and that has therefore been deprived of a meaningful connection with our developing consciousness, has got lost. If
we now try to cover our nakedness with the gorgeous

trappings of the East, as the theosophists do, we would be playing our own history false. A man does not sink down to beggary only to pose afterwards as an Indian potentate. It seems to me that it would be far better stoutly to avow our spiritual poverty, our symbol-lessness, instead of feigning a legacy to which we are not the legitimate heirs at all. We are, surely, the rightful heirs of Christian symbolism, but somehow we have squandered this heritage. We have let the house our fathers built fall into decay, and now we try to break into Oriental palaces that our fathers never knew.   10:28

The fact is that archetypal images are so packed with meaning in themselves that people never think of asking what they really do mean. That the gods die from time to time is due to man's sudden discovery that they do not mean anything, that they are made by human hands, useless idols of wood and stone. In reality, however, he has merely discovered that up till then he has never thought about his images at all.   10:22

Religious sentimentality instead of the *numinosum* of divine experience: this is the well-known characteristic of a religion that has lost its living mystery. It is readily understandable that such a religion is incapable of giving help or having any other moral effect.   74:52

This whole development is fate. I would not lay the blame either on Protestantism or on the Renaissance. But one thing is certain—that modern man, Protestant or otherwise, has lost the protection of the ecclesiastical walls erected and reinforced so carefully since Roman days, and because of this loss has approached the zone of world-destroying and world-creating fire. Life has become quickened and intensified. Our world is shot through with waves of uneasiness and fear.   74:84

Thus, the sickness of dissociation in our world is at the same time a process of recovery, or rather, the climax of a period of pregnancy which heralds the throes of birth. A time of dissociation such as prevailed during the Roman Empire is simultaneously an age of rebirth. Not without reason do we date our era from the age of Augustus, for that epoch saw the birth of the symbolical figure of Christ, who was invoked by the early Christians as the Fish, the Ruler of the aeon of Pisces which had just begun. He became the ruling spirit of the next two thousand years. Like the teacher of wisdom in Babylonian legend, Oannes, he rose up from the sea, from the primeval darkness, and brought a world-period to an end. It is true that he said, "I am come not to bring peace but a sword." But that which brings division ultimately creates union. Therefore his teaching was one of all-uniting love.

45:293

❖

"God" is a primordial experience of man, and from the remotest times humanity has taken inconceivable pains either to portray this baffling experience, to assimilate it by means of interpretation, speculation, and dogma, or else to deny it. And again and again it has happened, and still happens, that one hears too much about the "good" God and knows him too well, so that one confuses him with one's own ideas and regards them as sacred because they can be traced back a couple of thousand years. This is a superstition and an idolatry every bit as bad as the Bolshevist delusion that "God" can be educated out of existence.

13:480

The primitive mentality does not *invent* myths, it *experiences* them. Myths are original revelations of the preconscious psyche, involuntary statements about unconscious psychic happenings, and anything but allegories of physical processes. Such allegories would be an idle amusement for an unscientific intellect. Myths, on the contrary, have a vital meaning. Not merely do they represent, they *are* the mental life of the primitive tribe, which immediately falls to pieces and decays when it loses its mythological heritage, like a man who has lost his soul. A tribe's mythology is its living religion, whose loss is always and everywhere, even among the civilized, a moral catastrophe. But religion is a vital link with psychic processes independent of and beyond consciousness, in the dark hinterland of the psyche.

76:261

What is the use of a religion without a mythos, since religion means, if anything at all, precisely that function which links us back to the eternal myth?   7:647

Religious experience is absolute; it cannot be disputed. You can only say that you have never had such an experience, whereupon your opponent will reply: "Sorry, I have." And there your discussion will come to an end.   74:167

No matter what the world thinks about religious experience, the one who has it possesses a great treasure, a thing that has become for him a source of life, meaning, and beauty, and that has given a new splendour to the world and to mankind. He has *pistis* and peace. Where is the criterion by which you could say that such a life is not legitimate, that such an experience is not valid, and that such *pistis* is mere illusion? Is there, as a matter of fact, any better truth about the ultimate things than the one that helps you to live?   74:167

Belief is no adequate substitute for inner experience, and where this is absent even a strong faith which came miraculously as a gift of grace may depart equally miraculously.

People call faith the true religious experience, but they do not stop to consider that actually it is a secondary phenomenon arising from the fact that something happened to us in the first place which instilled *pistis* into us—that is, trust and loyalty.   106:521

Religion means dependence on and submission to the irrational facts of experience.   106:505

So long as religion is only faith and outward form, and the religious function is not experienced in our own souls, nothing of any importance has happened. It has yet to be understood that the *mysterium magnum* is not only an actuality but is first and foremost rooted in the human psyche. The man who does not know this from his own experience may be a most learned theologian, but he has no idea of religion and still less of education.   72:13

Theology does not help those who are looking for the key, because theology demands faith, and faith cannot be made: it is in the truest sense a gift of grace. We moderns are faced with the necessity of rediscovering the life of the spirit; we must experience it anew for ourselves. It is the only way in which to break the spell that binds us to the cycle of biological events.   28:780

The world is not a garden of God the Father, it is a place of horror. Not only is heaven no father and earth no mother and men not brothers, but they represent so many hostile destructive forces to which we are the more surely delivered over the more confidently and thoughtlessly we entrust ourselves to the so-called fatherly hand of God.

100A:224*

But God himself cannot flourish if man's soul is starved.

114:275

The more highly developed men of our time do not want to be guided by a creed or a dogma; they want to understand. So it is not surprising if they throw aside everything they do not understand; and religious symbols, being the least intelligible of all, are generally the first to go overboard. The sacrifice of the intellect demanded by a positive belief is a violation against which the conscience of the more highly developed individual rebels.   101:434

The bridge from dogma to the inner experience of the individual has broken down. Instead, dogma is "believed"; it is hypostatized, as the Protestants hypostatize the Bible, illegitimately making it the supreme authority, regardless of its contradictions and controversial interpretations. (As we know, anything can be authorized out of the Bible.) Dogma no longer formulates anything, no longer expresses anything; it has become a tenet to be accepted in and for itself, with no basis in any experience that would demonstrate its truth. Indeed, faith has itself become that experience.   3:276

The word "belief" is a difficult thing for me. I don't *believe*. I must have a reason for a certain hypothesis. Either I *know* a thing, and then I know it—I don't need to believe it.   39D:51

What is needed are a few illuminating truths, but not articles of faith. Where an intelligible truth works, it finds in faith a willing ally; for faith has always helped when thinking and understanding could not quite make the grade. Understanding is never the handmaiden of faith— on the contrary, faith completes understanding. To educate men to a faith they do not understand is certainly a well-meant undertaking, but one runs the risk of creating an attitude that believes everything it does not understand.

43*

Dogmas fall on deaf ears, because nothing in our known world responds to such assertions. But if we understand these things for what they are, as symbols, then we can only marvel at the unfathomable wisdom that is in them and be grateful to the institution which has not only conserved them, but developed them dogmatically. The man of today lacks the very understanding that would help him to believe.

65:293

It is not ethical principles, however lofty, or creeds, however orthodox, that lay the foundations for the freedom and autonomy of the individual, but simply and solely the empirical awareness, the incontrovertible experience of an intensely personal, reciprocal relationship between man and an extramundane authority which acts as a counterpoise to the "world" and its "reason."

106:509

✧

The individual's decision not to belong to a Church does not necessarily denote an anti-Christian attitude; it may mean exactly the reverse: a reconsidering of the kingdom of God in the human heart where, in the words of St. Augustine, the *mysterium paschale* is accomplished "in its inward and higher meanings." The ancient and long obsolete idea of man as a microcosm contains a supreme psychological truth that has yet to be discovered. In former times this truth was projected upon the body, just as alchemy projected the unconscious psyche upon chemical substances. But it is altogether different when the microcosm is understood as the interior world whose inward nature is fleetingly glimpsed in the unconscious.

77:397

The more unconscious we are of the religious problem in the future, the greater the danger of our putting the divine germ within us to some ridiculous or demoniacal use, puffing ourselves up with it instead of remaining conscious that we are no more than the stable in which the Lord is born.   65:267

Being "very man" means being at an extreme remove and utterly different from God. "De profundis clamavi ad te, Domine"—this cry demonstrates both, the remoteness and the nearness, the outermost darkness and the dazzling spark of the Divine. God in his humanity is presumably so far from himself that he has to seek himself through absolute self-surrender. And where would God's wholeness be if he could not be the "wholly other"?   103:380

People who merely believe and don't think always forget that they continually expose themselves to their own worst enemy: doubt. Wherever belief reigns, doubt lurks in the background. But thinking people welcome doubt: it serves them as a valuable stepping-stone to better knowledge. People who can believe should be a little more tolerant with those of their fellows who are only capable of thinking. Belief has already conquered the summit which thinking tries to win by toilsome climbing. The believer ought not to project his habitual enemy, doubt, upon the thinker, thereby suspecting him of destructive designs.   65:170

Although the actual moment of conversion often seems quite sudden and unexpected, we know from experience that such a fundamental upheaval always requires a long period of incubation. It is only when this preparation is complete, that is to say when the individual is ripe for conversion, that the new insight breaks through with violent emotion. Saul, as he was then called, had unconsciously been a Christian for a long time, and this would explain his fanatical hatred of the Christians, because fanaticism is always found in those who have to stifle a secret doubt. That is why converts are always the worst fanatics.

68:582

A Christian of today no longer ought to cling obstinately to a one-sided credo, but should face the fact that Christianity has been in a state of schism for four hundred years, with the result that every single Christian has a split in his psyche. Naturally this lesion cannot be treated or healed if everyone insists on his own standpoint. Behind those barriers he can rejoice in his absolute and consistent convictions and deem himself above the conflict, but outside them he keeps the conflict alive by his intransigence and continues to deplore the pig-headedness and stiff-neckedness of everybody else. It seems as if Christianity had been from the outset the religion of chronic squabblers, and even now it does everything in its power never to let the squabbles rest. Remarkably enough, it never stops preaching the gospel of neighbourly love.

48:257

One cannot and may not think about an object held to be indisputable. One can only assert it, and for this reason there can be no reconciliation between the divergent assertions. Thus Christianity, the religion of brotherly love, offers the lamentable spectacle of one great and many small schisms, each faction helplessly caught in the toils of its own unique rightness.

48:786

The physical world and the perceptual world are two very different things. Knowing this we have no encouragement whatever to think that our metaphysical picture of the world corresponds to the transcendental reality. Moreover, the statements made about the latter are so boundlessly varied that with the best of intentions we cannot know who is right. The denominational religions recognized this long ago and in consequence each of them claims that it is the only true one and, on top of this, that it is not merely a human truth but the truth directly inspired and revealed by God. Every theologian speaks simply of "God," by which he intends it to be understood that his "god" is *the* God. But one speaks of the paradoxical God of the Old Testament, another of the incarnate God of Love, a third of the God who has a heavenly bride, and so on, and each criticizes the other but never himself.   48:781

This objectivity is just what my psychology is most blamed for: it is said not to decide in favour of this or that religious doctrine. Without prejudice to my own subjective convictions I should like to raise the question: Is it not thinkable that when one refrains from setting oneself up as an *arbiter mundi* and, deliberately renouncing all subjectivism, cherishes on the contrary the belief, for instance, that God has expressed himself in many languages and appeared in divers forms and that all these statements are *true*—is it not thinkable, I say, that this too is a decision? The objection raised, more particularly by Christians, that it is impossible for contradictory statements to be true, must permit itself to be politely asked: Does one equal three? How can three be one? Can a mother be a virgin? And so on. Has it not yet been observed that all religious statements contain logical contradictions and assertions that are impossible in principle, that this is in fact the essence of religious assertion?   72:18

When psychology speaks of the motif of the virgin birth, it is only concerned with the fact that there is such an idea, but it is not concerned with the question whether such an idea is true or false in any other sense. The idea is psychologically true inasmuch as it exists.   74:4

Religious statements without exception have to do with the reality of the *psyche* and not with the reality of *physis*.   7:752

❖

Oddly enough the paradox is one of our most valuable spiritual possessions, while uniformity of meaning is a

sign of weakness. Hence a religion becomes inwardly im-
poverished when it loses or waters down its paradoxes; but
their multiplication enriches because only the paradox
comes anywhere near to comprehending the fullness of
life. Non-ambiguity and non-contradiction are one-sided
and thus unsuited to express the incomprehensible.   72:18

Unequivocal statements can be made only in regard to
immanent objects; transcendental ones can be expressed
only by paradox.   48:715

The mystery of the Virgin Birth, or the homoousia of the
Son with the Father, or the Trinity which is nevertheless
not a triad—these no longer lend wings to any philosophical fancy. They have stiffened into mere objects of belief. So it is not surprising if the religious need, the believing mind, and the philosophical speculations of the educated
European are attracted by the symbols of the East—those
grandiose conceptions of divinity in India and the abysms
of Taoist philosophy in China—just as once before the
heart and mind of the men of antiquity were gripped by
Christian ideas. There are many Europeans who began by
surrendering completely to the influence of the Christian
symbol until they landed themselves in a Kierkegaardian
neurosis, or whose relation to God, owing to the progressive impoverishment of symbolism, developed into an un-
bearably sophisticated I-You relationship—only to fall victims in their turn to the magic and novelty of Eastern symbols. This surrender is not necessarily a defeat; rather it
proves the receptiveness and vitality of the religious sense.
We can observe much the same thing in the educated
Oriental, who not infrequently feels drawn to the Christian symbol or to the science that is so unsuited to the
Oriental mind, and even develops an enviable understanding of them. That people should succumb to these eternal
images is entirely normal, in fact it is what these images are

for. They are meant to attract, to convince, to fascinate, and to overpower. They are created out of the primal stuff of revelation and reflect the ever-unique experience of divinity.

10: 11

Agnosticism maintains that it does not possess any knowledge of God or of anything metaphysical, overlooking the fact that one never *possesses* a metaphysical belief but is *possessed* by it.

7: 735

Since the only salutary powers visible in the world today are the great psychotherapeutic systems which we call the religions, and from which we expect the soul's salvation, it is quite natural that many people should make the justifiable and often successful attempt to find a niche for themselves in one of the existing creeds and to acquire a deeper insight into the meaning of the traditional saving verities. This solution is normal and satisfying in that the dogmatically formulated truths of the Christian Church express, almost perfectly, the nature of psychic experience. They are the repositories of the secrets of the soul, and this matchless knowledge is set forth in grand symbolical images. The unconscious thus possesses a natural affinity with the spiritual values of the Church, particularly in their dogmatic form, which owes its special character to centuries of theological controversy—absurd as this seemed in the eyes of later generations—and to the passionate efforts of many great men.

77: 390*f*

Dogmas are spiritual structures of supreme beauty, and they possess a wonderful meaning which I have sought to fathom in my fashion. Compared with them our scientific endeavours to devise models of the objective psyche are unsightly in the extreme. They are bound to earth and reality, full of contradictions, logically and aesthetically unsatisfying.

83: 663*

The beauty of the ritual action is one of its essential properties, for man has not served God rightly unless he has also served him in beauty. 103:379

If the spiritual adventure of our time is the exposure of human consciousness to the undefined and indefinable, there would seem to be good reasons for thinking that even the Boundless is pervaded by psychic laws, which no man invented, but of which he has "gnosis" in the symbolism of Christian dogma. Only heedless fools will wish to destroy this; the lover of the soul, never. 74:168

If the theologian really believes in the almighty power of God on the one hand and in the validity of dogma on the other, why then does he not trust God to speak in the soul? Why this fear of psychology? Or is, in complete contradiction to dogma, the soul itself a hell from which only demons gibber? Even if this were really so it would not be any the less convincing; for as we all know the horrified perception of the reality of evil has led to at least as many conversions as the experience of good. 72:19

If I have ventured to submit old dogmas, now grown stale, to psychological scrutiny, I have certainly not done so in the priggish conceit that I knew better than others, but in the sincere conviction that a dogma which has been such a bone of contention for so many centuries cannot possibly be an empty fantasy. I felt it was too much in line with the *consensus omnium*, with the archetype, for that. It was only when I realized this that I was able to establish any relationship with the dogma at all. As a metaphysical "truth" it remained wholly inaccessible to me, and I suspect that I am by no means the only one to find himself in that position. A knowledge of the universal archetypal background was, in itself, sufficient to give me the courage to treat "that which is believed always, everywhere, by everybody" as a *psychological fact* which extends far beyond the confines of Christianity, and to approach it as an object of scientific study, as a *phenomenon* pure and simple, regardless of the "metaphysical" significance that may have been attached to it.   65:294

That a psychological approach to these matters draws man more into the centre of the picture as the measure of all things cannot be denied. But this gives him a significance which is not without justification. The two great world religions, Buddhism and Christianity, have, each in its own way, accorded man a central place, and Christianity has stressed this tendency still further by the dogma that God became very man. No psychology in the world could vie with the dignity that God himself has accorded to him.

48:789

There can be no doubt that man's importance is enormously enhanced if God himself deigns to become one.

7:650

✧

For thousands of years, rites of initiation have been teaching rebirth from the spirit; yet, strangely enough, man forgets again and again the meaning of divine procreation. Though this may be poor testimony to the strength of the spirit, the penalty for misunderstanding is neurotic decay, embitterment, atrophy, and sterility. It is easy enough to drive the spirit out of the door, but when we have done so the meal has lost its savour—the salt of the earth. Fortunately, we have proof that the spirit always renews its strength in the fact that the essential teaching of the initiations is handed on from generation to generation. Ever and again there are human beings who understand what it means that God is their father. The equal balance of the flesh and the spirit is not lost to the world.   28:783

The fact that the life of Christ is largely myth does absolutely nothing to disprove its factual truth—quite the contrary. I would even go so far as to say that the mythical character of a life is just what expresses its universal human validity. It is perfectly possible, psychologically, for the unconscious or an archetype to take complete possession of a man and to determine his fate down to the smallest detail. At the same time objective, nonpsychic parallel phenomena can occur which also represent the archetype. It not only seems so, it simply is so, that the archetype fulfils itself not only psychically in the individual, but objectively outside the individual. My own conjecture is that Christ was such a personality. The life of Christ is just what it had to be if it is the life of a god and a man at the same time. It is a *symbolum*, a bringing together of heterogeneous natures, rather as if Job and Yahweh were combined in a single personality. Yahweh's intention to become man, which resulted from his collision with Job, is fulfilled in Christ's life and suffering. 7:648

Although it is generally assumed that Christ's unique sacrifice broke the curse of original sin and finally placated God, Christ nevertheless seems to have had certain misgivings in this respect. What will happen to man, and especially to his own followers, when the sheep have lost their shepherd, and when they miss the one who interceded for them with the father? He assures his disciples that he will always be with them, nay more, that he himself abides within them. Nevertheless this does not seem to satisfy him completely, for in addition he promises to send them from the father another *paracletos* (advocate, "Counsellor") in his stead, who will assist them by word and deed and remain with them forever. 7:691

Despite the fact that he is potentially redeemed, the Christian is given over to moral suffering, and in his suffering he needs the Comforter, the Paraclete. He cannot overcome the conflict on his own resources; after all, he didn't invent it. He has to rely on divine comfort and mediation, that is to say on the spontaneous revelation of the spirit, which does not obey man's will but comes and goes as *it* wills. This spirit is an autonomous psychic happening, a hush that follows the storm, a reconciling light in the darknesses of man's mind, secretly bringing order into the chaos of his soul. The Holy Ghost is a comforter like the Father, a mute, eternal, unfathomable One in whom God's love and God's terribleness come together in wordless union. And through this union the original meaning of the still-unconscious Father-world is restored and brought within the scope of human experience and reflection. Looked at from a quaternary standpoint, the Holy Ghost is a reconciliation of opposites and hence the answer to the suffering in the God-head which Christ personifies.

65:260

The sending of the Paraclete has still another aspect. This Spirit of Truth and Wisdom is the Holy Ghost by whom Christ was begotten. He is the spirit of physical and spiritual procreation who from now on shall make his abode in creaturely man. Since he is the Third Person of the Deity, this is as much as to say that God will be begotten in creaturely man.

7:692

For that purpose he has chosen, through the Holy Ghost, the creaturely man filled with darkness—the natural man who is tainted with original sin and who learnt the divine arts and sciences from the fallen angels. The guilty man is eminently suitable and is therefore chosen to become the vessel for the continuing incarnation, not the guiltless one who holds aloof from the world and refuses to pay his tribute to life, for in him the dark God would find no room.

7:746

God has a terrible double aspect: a sea of grace is met by a seething lake of fire, and the light of love glows with a fierce dark heat of which it is said "ardet non lucet"—it burns but gives no light. That is the eternal, as distinct from the temporal, gospel: one can love God but must fear him.

7:733

Since the Apocalypse we now know again that God is not only to be loved, but also to be feared. He fills us with evil as well as with good, otherwise he would not need to be feared; and because he wants to become man, the uniting of his antinomy must take place in man. This involves man in a new responsibility. He can no longer wriggle out of it on the plea of his littleness and nothingness, for the dark God has slipped the atom bomb and chemical weapons into his hands and given him the power to empty out the apocalyptic vials of wrath on his fellow creatures. Since he has been granted an almost godlike power, he can no longer remain blind and unconscious. He must know something of God's nature and of metaphysical processes if he is to understand himself and thereby achieve gnosis of the Divine.

7:747

The fact that Christian ethics leads to collisions of duty speaks in its favour. By engendering insoluble conflicts and consequently an *afflictio animae*, it brings man nearer to a knowledge of God. All opposites are of God, therefore man must bend to this burden; and in so doing he finds that God in his "oppositeness" has taken possession of him, incarnated himself in him. He becomes a vessel filled with divine conflict.

7:659

The light God bestrides the bridge—Man—from the day-side; God's shadow, from the night side. What will be the outcome of this fearful dilemma, which threatens to shatter the frail human vessel with unknown storms and intoxications? It may well be the revelation of the Holy Ghost out of man himself. Just as man was once revealed out of God, so, when the circle closes, God may be revealed out of man.

65: 267

A living example of the mystery drama representing the permanence as well as the transformation of life is the Mass. If we observe the congregation during this sacred rite we note all degrees of participation, from mere indifferent attendance to the profoundest emotion. The groups of men standing about near the exit, who are obviously engaged in every sort of worldly conversation, crossing themselves and genuflecting in a purely mechanical way—even they, despite their inattention, participate in the sacral action by their mere presence in this place where grace abounds. The Mass is an extramundane and extratemporal act in which Christ is sacrificed and then resurrected in the transformed substances; and this rite of his sacrificial death is not a repetition of the historical event but the original, unique, and eternal act. The experience of the Mass is therefore a participation in the transcendence of life, which overcomes all bounds of space and time. It is a moment of eternity in time.

17: 209

I wish everybody could be freed from the burden of their sins by the Church. But he to whom she cannot render this service must bend very low in the imitation of Christ in order to take the burden of his cross upon him. The ancients could get along with the Greek wisdom of the ages: "Exaggerate nothing, all good lies in right measure." But what an abyss still separates us from reason!

72: 37

What the Christian sacrament of baptism purports to do is a landmark of the utmost significance in the psychic development of mankind. Baptism endows the individual with a living soul. I do not mean that the baptismal rite

in itself does this, by a unique and magical act. I mean
that the idea of baptism lifts man out of his archaic identification with the world and transforms him into a being
who stands above it. The fact that mankind has risen to the
level of this idea is baptism in the deepest sense, for it means
the birth of the spiritual man who transcends nature.

9:136

If God is born as a man and wants to unite mankind in
the fellowship of the Holy Ghost, he must suffer the terrible torture of having to endure the world in all its reality.
This is the cross he has to bear, and he himself is a cross.
The whole world is God's suffering, and every individual
man who wants to get anywhere near his own wholeness
knows that this is the way of the cross. But the eternal
promise for him who bears his own cross is the Paraclete.

65:265

LIST OF SOURCES

List of Sources

Unless otherwise indicated, dates of first publication are given in parentheses after the titles; multiple dates indicate important revisions in both the Swiss and the Anglo-American editions. Jung's forewords, introductions, commentaries, and reviews are entered under the name of the author (or translator) of the book in question. Interviews appear under a group entry. An asterisk indicates that the source is a work later included in Volume 18 of the Collected Works, or a work omitted from the Collected Works (4A, 10A, 11, 97A, and 100A) or later included in *C. G. Jung Speaking* (39A–H). For details of the Collected Works, see the list at the end of this volume.

1. "After the Catastrophe" (1945). In CW 10: *Civilization in Transition*. 1964/1970.
2. "Aims of Psychotherapy, The" (1931). In CW 16: *The Practice of Psychotherapy*. 1954/1966.
3. *Aion* (1951). CW 9, Part II. 1959/1968.
4. "Analytical Psychology and Education" (1926/1946). In CW 17: *The Development of Personality*. 1954.
4A* ——. First English version. (Contains passages deleted in 1946 edition.) In *Contributions to Analytical Psychology*, tr. H. G. and Cary F. Baynes. London and New York, 1928.
5. "Analytical Psychology and Weltanschauung" (1928/1931). In CW 8: *The Structure and Dynamics of the Psyche*. 1960/1969.
6.* *Analytical Psychology: Its Theory and Practice: The Tavistock Lectures* (1935). London and New York, 1968. Now included in CW 18, retitled "The Tavistock Lectures."
7. "Answer to Job" (1952). In CW 11: *Psychology and Religion: West and East*. 1958/1969.

8.* "Approaching the Unconscious." In *Man and His Symbols*, ed. C. G. Jung. London and New York, 1964. This essay was written in English, and on publication had been edited and rearranged under the supervision of John Freeman. Quotations usually follow Jung's original version, revised. In CW 18 (in preparation), retitled "Symbols and the Interpretation of Dreams."

9. "Archaic Man" (1931). In CW 10: *Civilization in Transition*. 1964/1970.

10. "Archetypes of the Collective Unconscious" (1935/1954). In CW 9, Part I: *The Archetypes and the Collective Unconscious*. 1959/1968.

10A.* ——. First English version. (Contains passages deleted in 1954 edition.) In *The Integration of the Personality*, tr. Stanley M. Dell. New York, 1939; London, 1940.

11.* Basel Seminar (1934). Multigraphed for private circulation by the Psychology Club, Zurich.

12. "Basic Postulates of Analytical Psychology" (1931) In CW 8: *The Structure and Dynamics of the Psyche*. 1960/1969.

13. "Brother Klaus" (1933). In CW 11: *Psychology and Religion: West and East*. 1958/1969.

14.* Brunner, Cornelia. *Die Anima als Schicksalsproblem des Mannes* (Zurich, 1963). Studien aus dem C. G. Jung-Institut, XIV. Foreword by C. G. Jung now included in CW 18.

15.* Cahen, Roland. *L'homme à la découverte de son âme* (Geneva, 6th edn., 1962). Epilogue (1944) by C. G. Jung now included in CW 18.

16. "Concerning the Archetypes, with Special Reference to the Anima Concept" (1936/1954). In CW 9, Part I: *The Archetypes and the Collective Unconscious*. 1959/1968.

17. "Concerning Rebirth" (1940/1950). In CW 9, Part I: *The Archetypes and the Collective Unconscious.* 1959/1968.

18. "Content of the Psychoses, The" (1908). In CW 3: *The Psychogenesis of Mental Disease.* 1960.

19. "Cryptomnesia" (1905). In CW 1: *Psychiatric Studies.* 1957/1970.

20.* "Depth Psychology and Self-Knowledge" (= "Tiefenpsychologie und Selbsterkenntnis"). In *DU* (Zurich) III:9 (September 1943), 15-18. Now included in CW 18.

21. "Development of Personality, The" (1934). In CW 17: *The Development of Personality.* 1954.

22. Evans-Wentz, W.Y. *The Tibetan Book of the Dead* (London and New York, 1927/1957). [German version: *Das Tibetanische Totenbuch,* Zurich, 1935/1953.] Psychological Commentary (1935/1953) by C. G. Jung in CW 11: *Psychology and Religion: West and East.* 1958/1969.

23. ———. *The Tibetan Book of the Great Liberation* (London and New York, 1954). Psychological Commentary (written 1939) by C. G. Jung in CW 11: *Psychology and Religion: West and East.* 1958/1969.

24.* "Existe-t'il une poésie de signe freudien?" In *Journal des Poètes* (Brussels) 3:5 (11 December 1932). Now included in CW 18, titled "Is There a Freudian Type of Poetry?"

25. "Fight with the Shadow, The" (1946). In CW 10: *Civilization in Transition.* 1964/1970.

26. "Flying Saucers: A Modern Myth of Things Seen in the Skies" (1958). In CW 10: *Civilization in Transition.* 1964/1970.

27.* Fordham, Michael. *New Developments in Analytical Psychology* (London, 1957). Foreword by C. G. Jung now included in CW 18.

28. "Freud and Jung: Contrasts" (1929). In CW 4: *Freud and Psychoanalysis*. 1961.

29. "Fundamental Questions of Psychotherapy" (1951). In CW 16: *The Practice of Psychotherapy*. 1954/1966.

30. "General Aspects of Dream Psychology" (1916/1948). In CW 8: *The Structure and Dynamics of the Psyche*. 1960/1969.

31. "Gifted Child, The" (1943). In CW 17: *The Development of Personality*. 1954.

32. "Good and Evil in Analytical Psychology" (1959). In CW 10: *Civilization in Transition*. 1964/1970.

33.* Harding, M. Esther. *The Way of All Women* (London and New York, 1933). Foreword by C. G. Jung now included in CW 18.

34.* Helsdingen, R. J. van. *Beelden uit het onbewuste* (Arnheim, 1957). Foreword by C. G. Jung now included in CW 18.

35.* Heyer, Gustav Richard. *Der Organismus der Seele* (Munich, 1932). Review by C. G. Jung, *Europäische Revue* (Berlin) IX:10 (October 1933), 639, now included in CW 18.

36. "Holy Men of India, The" (1944). In CW 11: *Psychology and Religion: West and East*. 1958/1969.

37. "In Memory of Sigmund Freud" (1939). In CW 15: *The Spirit in Man, Art, and Literature*. 1966.

38. "Instinct and the Unconscious" (1919). In CW 8: *The Structure and Dynamics of the Psyche*. 1960/1969.

39. Interviews:

39A* "America Facing its Most Tragic Moment." In *New York Times*, 29 September 1912, section V, p. 2.

39B* "Art of Living, The" (1960). In Gordon Young, *Doctors Without Drugs* (London, 1962), Epilogue, pp. 133-53.

39C* "Diagnosing the Dictators." In *Hearst's International Cosmopolitan* (New York), January 1939, pp. 22, 116-119.

39D* "Face to Face: BBC Interview with John Freeman"
(1959). In Hugh Burnett, *Face to Face*, pp. 48-51
(London, 1964).

39E* "Four Filmed Interviews with Richard I. Evans"
[1957]. Edited and rearranged version in Evans, *Conversations with Carl Jung* (Princeton: Van Nostrand,
1964).

39F* "Men, Women, and God." In *Daily Mail* (London).
A:28 April 1955; B:29 April 1955.

39G* "The Postwar Psychic Problems of the Germans."
Translated from "Werden die Seelen Frieden finden?" in *Die Weltwoche* (Zurich) 13:600 (11 May
1945).

39H* "Roosevelt 'Great' in Jung's Analysis." In *New York
Times*, 4 October 1936.

40.* Jung, C. G. Foreword to *Seelenprobleme der Gegenwart* (1931). Rascher Paperback, Zurich, 1969. Now
included in CW 18.

41. Keyserling, Count Hermann. *La Révolution mondiale* (Paris, 1934). Review by C. G. Jung, *Basler
Nachrichten*, Sonntagsblatt, XXVIII:19 (13 May
1934), 78-79, in CW 10: *Civilization in Transition*.
1964/1970.

42. Kranefeldt, W. M. *Secret Ways of the Mind* (New
York, 1932; London, 1934). [Original version: *Die
Psychoanalyse*, Berlin and Leipzig, 1930.] Introduction by C. G. Jung in CW 4: *Freud and Psychoanalysis*. 1964.

43.* "Marginalia on Contemporary Events." Partly published as "Zur Umerziehung des deutschen Volkes"
("On the Re-education of the Germans") in *Basler
Nachrichten*, Nr. 486, 16 November 1946. Now included in CW 18.

44. "Marriage as a Psychological Relationship" (1925).
In CW 17: *The Development of Personality*. 1954.

45. "Meaning of Psychology for Modern Man, The"

(1933/1934). In CW 10: *Civilization in Transition.* 1964/1970.

46. "Mind and Earth" (1927/1931). In CW 10: *Civilization in Transition.* 1964/1970.

47.* Moser, Fanny. *Spuk: Irrglaube oder Wahrglaube?* (Zurich, 1950). Foreword by C. G. Jung now included in CW 18.

48. *Mysterium Coniunctionis* (1955-56). CW 14. 1963/ 1970.

49.* Neumann, Erich. *Depth Psychology and a New Ethic* (London and New York, 1969). [Original version: *Tiefenpsychologie und neue Ethik,* Zurich, 1948.] Foreword by C. G. Jung (written 1949 for the English edition) now included in CW 18.

50.* ——. *The Origins and History of Consciousness* (New York, 1954; London, 1955). [Original version: *Ursprungsgeschichte des Bewusstseins,* Zurich, 1949.] Foreword by C. G. Jung now included in CW 18.

51.* Neumann, Karl Eugen. *Die Reden Gotamo Buddhos* (Zurich, Stuttgart, and Vienna, 1956). Statement by C. G. Jung for publisher's brochure in Jung, Gesammelte Werke, 11: *Zur Psychologie westlicher und östlicher Religion,* Anhang, pp. 690-93. Zurich, 1963. Now included in CW 18.

52. "On the Nature of Dreams" (1945/1948). In CW 8: *The Structure and Dynamics of the Psyche.* 1960/ 1969.

53. "On the Nature of the Psyche" (1947/1954). In CW 8: *The Structure and Dynamics of the Psyche.* 1960/1969.

54. "On Psychic Energy" (1928). In CW 8: *The Structure and Dynamics of the Psyche.* 1960/1969.

55. "On the Relation of Analytical Psychology to Poetry" (1922). In CW 15: *The Spirit in Man, Art, and Literature.* 1966.

56. "Paracelsus" (1929). In CW 15: *The Spirit in Man, Art, and Literature*. 1966.

57. "Paracelsus the Physician" (1941). In CW 15: *The Spirit in Man, Art, and Literature*. 1966.

58. "Paracelsus as a Spiritual Phenomenon" (1942). In CW 13: *Alchemical Studies*, 1967.

59. "Phenomenology of the Spirit in Fairytales, The" (1946/1948). In CW 9, Part I: *The Archetypes and the Collective Unconscious*. 1959/1968.

60. "Philosophical Tree, The" (1945/1954). In CW 13: *Alchemical Studies*. 1967.

61. "Practical Use of Dream Analysis, The" (1934). In CW 16: *The Practice of Psychotherapy*. 1954/1966.

62. "Principles of Practical Psychotherapy" (1935). In CW 16: *The Practice of Psychotherapy*. 1954/1966.

63. "Problems of Modern Psychotherapy" (1929). In CW 16: *The Practice of Psychotherapy*. 1954/1966.

64. "Psychic Conflicts in a Child" (1910/1946). In CW 17: *The Development of Personality*. 1954.

65. "Psychological Approach to the Dogma of the Trinity, A" (1942/1948). In CW 11: *Psychology and Religion: West and East*. 1958/1969. (In the passage on p. 365, the last sentence was in the original version in *Eranos Jahrbuch 1940/41* but was omitted from the 1948 version.)

66. "Psychological Aspects of the Kore" (1941). In CW 9, Part I: *The Archetypes and the Collective Unconscious*. 1959/1968.

67. "Psychological Aspects of the Mother Archetype" (1939/1954). In CW 9, Part I: *The Archetypes and the Collective Unconscious*. 1959/1968.

68. "Psychological Foundations of Belief in Spirits, The" (1920/1948). In CW 8: *The Structure and Dynamics of the Psyche*. 1960/1969.

69. *Psychological Types* (1921). CW 6. 1970.

70. "Psychological Typology" (1936). In CW 6: *Psychological Types,* Appendix, 4.

71. "Psychological View of Conscience, A" (1958). In CW 10: *Civilization in Transition.* 1964/1970.

72. *Psychology and Alchemy* (1944). CW 12. 1953/ 1968.

73. "Psychology and Literature" (1930/1950). In CW 15: *The Spirit in Man, Art, and Literature.* 1966.

74. "Psychology and Religion" (1938/1940). In CW 11: *Psychology and Religion: West and East.* 1958/ 1969.

75. "Psychology of Eastern Meditation, The" (1943). In CW 11: *Psychology and Religion: West and East.* 1958/1969.

76. "Psychology of the Child Archetype, The" (1940). In CW 9, Part I: *The Archetypes and the Collective Unconscious.* 1959/1968.

77. "Psychology of the Transference, The" (1946). In CW 16: *The Practice of Psychotherapy.* 1954/1966.

78. "Psychotherapists or the Clergy" (1932). In CW 11: *Psychology and Religion: West and East.* 1958/1969.

79. "Psychotherapy and a Philosophy of Life" (1943). In CW 16: *The Practice of Psychotherapy.* 1954/1966.

80. "Psychotherapy Today" (1945). In CW 16: *The Practice of Psychotherapy.* 1954/1966.

81. "Real and the Surreal, The" (1933). In CW 8: *The Structure and Dynamics of the Psyche.* 1960/1969.

82. "Realities of Practical Psychotherapy, The" [1937]. In CW 16: *The Practice of Psychotherapy,* 1966 edition, Appendix.

83.* "Religion and Psychology: A Reply to Martin Buber" (1952). In Jung, Gesammelte Werke, 11: *Zur Psychologie westlicher und östlicher Religion,* Anhang, pp. 657-65. Zurich, 1963. Now included in CW 18.

84.* "Return to the Simple Life" (= "Rückkehr zum ein-fachen Leben"). In *DU* (Zurich) I:3 (May 1941), 6, 7, 56. Now included in CW 18.

85. "Role of the Unconscious, The" (1918). In CW 10: *Civilization in Transition*. 1964/1970.

86.* Schleich, K. L. *Die Wunder der Seele* (Popular edition, Berlin, 1934). Foreword by C. G. Jung now included in CW 18.

87.* Schmitz, O. A. *Märchen aus dem Unbewussten* (Munich, 1932). Foreword by C. G. Jung now included in CW 18.

88. "Sigmund Freud in His Historical Setting" (1932). In CW 15: *The Spirit in Man, Art, and Literature*. 1966.

89. "Some Crucial Points in Psychoanalysis: A Correspondence between Dr. Jung and Dr. Loÿ" (1914). In CW 4: *Freud and Psychoanalysis*. 1961.

90. "Soul and Death, The" (1934). In CW 8: *The Structure and Dynamics of the Psyche*. 1960/1969.

91. "Spirit and Life" (1926). In CW 8: *The Structure and Dynamics of the Psyche*. 1960/1969.

92. "Spirit Mercurius, The" (1943/1948). In CW 13: *Alchemical Studies*. 1967.

93. "Spiritual Problem of Modern Man, The" (1928/1931). In CW 10: *Civilization in Transition*. 1964/1970.

94. "Stages of Life, The" (1930). In CW 8: *The Structure and Dynamics of the Psyche*. 1960/1969.

95. "State of Psychotherapy Today, The" (1934). In CW 10: *Civilization in Transition*. 1964/1970.

96. "Structure of the Psyche, The" (1927/1931). In CW 8: *The Structure and Dynamics of the Psyche*. 1960/1969.

97. "Study in the Process of Individuation, A" (1934/1950). In CW 9, Part I: *The Archetypes and the Collective Unconscious*. 1959/1968.

97A.* ———. First English version. (Contains passages deleted in 1950 edition.) In *The Integration of the Personality*, tr. Stanley M. Dell. New York, 1939; London, 1940.

98. Suzuki, D. T. *An Introduction to Zen Buddhism* (London and New York, 1949). [German version: *Die grosse Befreiung: Einführung in den Zen Buddhismus*, Leipzig, 1939.] Foreword by C. G. Jung in CW 11: *Psychology and Religion: West and East.* 1958/1969.

99. "Swiss Line in the European Spectrum, The" (1928). In CW 10: *Civilization in Transition.* 1964/1970.

100. *Symbols of Transformation* (1952). CW 5. 1956/1967.

100A* ———. Original version (1912). *Wandlungen und Symbole der Libido.* Leipzig and Vienna.

101. "Theory of Psychoanalysis, The" (1913). In CW 4: *Freud and Psychoanalysis.* 1961.

102. "Transcendent Function, The" ([1916]/1957). In CW 8: *The Structure and Dynamics of the Psyche.* 1960/1969.

103. "Transformation Symbolism in the Mass" (1942/1954). In CW 11: *Psychology and Religion: West and East.* 1958/1969. (In the passage on p. 13, the last sentence was in the original version in *Eranos Jahrbuch 1940/41* but was omitted from the 1954 version.)

104. *Two Essays on Analytical Psychology.* CW 7 (1953/1966).

    A. "On the Psychology of the Unconscious" (1912/1917/1926/1943)

    B. "The Relations between the Ego and the Unconscious" (1928)

    C. Appendix I: "New Paths in Psychology" (1912 version of A). New version with variant readings in 1966 edition.

105. "Ulysses: A Monologue" (1932). In CW 15: *The Spirit in Man, Art, and Literature.* 1966.

106. "Undiscovered Self, The" (1957). In CW 10: *Civilization in Transition.* 1964/1970.

107. "Visions of Zosimos, The" (1938/1954). In CW 13: *Alchemical Studies.* 1967.

108. "What India Can Teach Us" (1939). In CW 10: *Civilization in Transition.* 1964/1970.

109. Wickes, Frances G. *Analysis der Kinderseele* (Stuttgart, 1931). [Original version: *The Inner World of Childhood*, New York, 1927.] Expanded introduction by C. G. Jung (for 1931 edition) in CW 17: *The Development of Personality.* 1954.

110.* ——. *Von der inneren Welt des Menschen* (Zurich, 1953). Foreword by C. G. Jung now included in CW 18.

111. Wilhelm, Richard, tr. *I Ching, or Book of Changes,* tr. Cary F. Baynes (London and New York, 1950/ 1967). Foreword by C. G. Jung in CW 11: *Psychology and Religion: West and East.* 1958/1969.

112. ——, tr. *The Secret of the Golden Flower* (London and New York, 1931/1962). [Original version: *Das Geheimnis der goldenen Blüte*, Munich, 1929.] Commentary by C. G. Jung in CW 13: *Alchemical Studies.* 1967.

113.* Wittels, F. *Die sexuelle Not* (Vienna and Leipzig, 1909). Review by C. G. Jung, *Jahrbuch für psychoanalytische und psychopathologische Forschungen* (Vienna and Leipzig), II (1909), 312-15, now included in CW 18.

114. "Woman in Europe" (1927). In CW 10: *Civilization in Transition.* 1964/1970.

115. "Wotan" (1936). In CW 10: *Civilization in Transition.* 1964/1970.

116. "Yoga and the West" (1936). In CW 11: *Psychology and Religion: West and East.* 1958/1969.

THE COLLECTED WORKS OF

C. G. JUNG

T HE PUBLICATION of the first complete edition, in English, of the works of C. G. Jung was undertaken by Routledge and Kegan Paul, Ltd., in England and by Bollingen Foundation in the United States. The American edition is number XX in Bollingen Series, which since 1967 has been published by Princeton University Press. The edition contains revised versions of works previously published, such as *Psychology of the Unconscious*, which is now entitled *Symbols of Transformation*; works originally written in English, such as *Psychology and Religion*; works not previously translated, such as *Aion*; and, in general, new translations of virtually all of Professor Jung's writings. Prior to his death, in 1961, the author supervised the textual revision, which in some cases is extensive. Sir Herbert Read (d. 1968), Dr. Michael Fordham, and Dr. Gerhard Adler compose the Editorial Committee; the translator is R. F. C. Hull (except for Volume 2) and William McGuire is executive editor.

The price of the volumes varies according to size; they are sold separately, and may also be obtained on standing order. Several of the volumes are extensively illustrated. Each volume contains an index and in most a bibliography; the final volumes will contain a complete bibliography of Professor Jung's writings and a general index to the entire edition.

In the following list, dates of original publication are given in parentheses (of original composition, in brackets). Multiple dates indicate revisions.

* Published 1957; 2nd edn., 1970.   † Published 1973.

* Published 1960.   † Published 1961.

‡ Published 1956; 2nd edn., 1967. (65 plates, 43 text figures.)

* Published 1971.   † Published 1953; 2nd edn., 1966.
‡ Published 1960; 2nd edn., 1969.

* Published 1959; 2nd edn., 1968. (Part I: 79 plates, with 29 in colour.)

* Published 1964; 2nd edn., 1970. (8 plates.)
† Published 1958; 2nd edn., 1969.

A Psychological Approach to the Dogma of the Trinity (1942/1948)

Transformation Symbolism in the Mass (1942/1954)

Forewords to White's "God and the Unconscious" and Werblowsky's "Lucifer and Prometheus" (1952)

Brother Klaus (1933)

Psychotherapists or the Clergy (1932)

Psychoanalysis and the Cure of Souls (1928)

Answer to Job (1952)

EASTERN RELIGION

Psychological Commentaries on "The Tibetan Book of the Great Liberation" (1939/1954) and "The Tibetan Book of the Dead" (1935/1953)

Yoga and the West (1936)

Foreword to Suzuki's "Introduction to Zen Buddhism" (1939)

The Psychology of Eastern Meditation (1943)

The Holy Men of India: Introduction to Zimmer's "Der Weg zum Selbst" (1944)

Foreword to the "I Ching" (1950)

*12. PSYCHOLOGY AND ALCHEMY (1944)

Prefatory note to the English Edition ([1951?] added 1967)

Introduction to the Religious and Psychological Problems of Alchemy

Individual Dream Symbolism in Relation to Alchemy (1936)

Religious Ideas in Alchemy (1937)

Epilogue

†13. ALCHEMICAL STUDIES

Commentary on "The Secret of the Golden Flower" (1929)

The Visions of Zosimos (1938/1954)

Paracelsus as a Spiritual Phenomenon (1942)

The Spirit Mercurius (1943/1948)

The Philosophical Tree (1945/1954)

‡14. MYSTERIUM CONIUNCTIONIS (1955-56)

AN INQUIRY INTO THE SEPARATION AND
SYNTHESIS OF PSYCHIC OPPOSITES IN ALCHEMY

The Components of the Coniunctio

The Paradoxa

The Personification of the Opposites

Rex and Regina   *(continued)*

* Published 1953; 2nd edn., completely revised, 1968. (270 illustrations.)
† Published 1968. (50 plates, 4 text figures.)
‡ Published 1963; 2nd edn., 1970. (10 plates.)

* Published 1966.
† Published 1954; 2nd edn., revised and augmented, 1966. (13 illustrations.)
‡ Published 1954.

The Development of Personality (1934)
Marriage as a Psychological Relationship (1925)

*18. THE SYMBOLIC LIFE
Miscellaneous Writings

†19. GENERAL BIBLIOGRAPHY OF C. G. JUNG'S WRITINGS

†20. GENERAL INDEX TO THE COLLECTED WORKS

See also:

C. G. JUNG: LETTERS
Selected and edited by Gerhard Adler, in collaboration with Aniela Jaffé.
Translations from the German by R.F.C. Hull.

VOL. 1: 1906–1950
VOL. 2: 1951–1961

THE FREUD/JUNG LETTERS
Edited by William McGuire, translated by
Ralph Manheim and R.F.C. Hull

C. G. JUNG SPEAKING: Interviews and Encounters
Edited by William McGuire and R.F.C. Hull

* Published 1976.
† Published 1978.

00 '03 ♣